JESUS CHRIST IN THE OLD TESTAMENT

Anthony Tyrrell Hanson

*Professor of Theology, University of Hull
and Examining Chaplain to the Archbishop of York*

WIPF & STOCK · Eugene, Oregon

Wipf and Stock Publishers
199 W 8th Ave, Suite 3
Eugene, OR 97401

Jesus Christ in the Old Testament
By Hanson, Anthony Tyrrell
Copyright©1965 SPCK
ISBN 13: 978-1-61097-352-6
Publication date 3/14/2011
Previously published by SPCK, 1965

Fratri dilecto,
in hoc opusculo perficiendo
consilio, exemplo, hortatione
socio fidelissimo.

Contents

Acknowledgements		vi
Abbreviations		viii
1.	The New Testament Interpretation of the Old Testament	1
2.	Christ in the Old Testament according to Paul	10
3.	Christ in the Old Testament according to the Epistle to the Hebrews	48
4.	Christ in the Old Testament in Stephen's Speech	83
5.	Christ in the Old Testament in the Fourth Gospel	104
6.	Christ in the Old Testament in the Catholic Epistles	127
7.	Prophetic Prayer and Dialogue in Paul	139
8.	Jesus in the Old Testament	161
Notes		179
Bibliography		195
Index of Biblical References		201
Index of Patristic References		208
Index of Authors		210

Acknowledgements

I wish to acknowledge with gratitude the help received from Mrs Martin, Librarian of the Assembly's College, Belfast, who proved so willing and helpful in procuring for me some of the books I needed. I should like to thank Professor C. K. Barrett for some acute suggestions concerning chapter 5. And lastly I must acknowledge the trouble my wife took in typing out the first draft of this work.

The scripture quotations in this book are from the *Revised Standard Version of the Old Testament*, copyrighted 1952 by the Division of Christian Education of the National Council of the Churches of Christ in the United States of America and used by permission.

Abbreviations

AT	Ancien Testament or Altes Testament
AV	Authorized Version, i.e. the King James Version of 1611
ICC	International Critical Commentary
Krit.-Exeg. Komm.	*Kritische-Exegetische Kommentar* (orig. ed. E. Maier)
LXX	The Septuagint, the Greek translation of the OT and Apocrypha
MT	Masoretic Text
NEB	*New English Bible* (NT only) of 1961
NT	New Testament
OT	Old Testament
PG	Patres Graeci in Migne's edition of the Fathers
PL	Patres Latini in the same
RSV	American *Revised Standard Version* of 1952
RV	Revised Version of 1884
S-B	*Kommentar zum neuen Testament aus Talmud und Midrasch* by Herman Strack and Paul Billerbeck (Munich 1961, rev. ed.)
TWZNT	*Theologisches Wörterbuch zum Neuen Testament*, ed. R. Kittel (Stuttgart 1954)

All quotations from the English Bible are from the American *Revised Standard Version* (copyrighted 1946 and 1952) and Apocrypha (copyrighted 1957).

All quotations from the Greek OT are from Alfred Rahlfs' edition of the LXX (Stuttgart 1935, 4th ed.).

All quotations from the Greek NT are from the British and Foreign Bible Society's Greek NT (2nd ed. of 1958).

All quotations from the Hebrew Bible are from Rudolf Kittel's edition of the *Biblia Hebraica* (Stuttgart 1949, 4th ed.).

I

The New Testament Interpretation of the Old Testament

Our debt to the Victorian commentators on the Bible is immense. Men such as J. B. Lightfoot, B. F. Westcott, and F. J. A. Hort, as well as a large number of scholars from the Church of Scotland and the Free Churches, made it possible for thinking Christians to claim the message of the New Testament as substantially their own. The access of new knowledge about the physical universe, and the rise of the disciplines of literary and historical criticism, had compelled Christians drastically to revise the traditional approach to the Bible. But these great scholars succeeded in convincing the great majority of educated Christians in the West that, despite the necessity for rejecting the traditional doctrine of the verbal inspiration of the Bible, the Christian faith could be in the twentieth century essentially the same as it was in the first.

In one sphere, however, the Victorians failed to carry through that rehabilitation of the gospel which they so courageously undertook. The New Testament writers' method of interpreting the Old Testament was something with which they never completely came to terms. Typology and allegory were concepts which were alien to the Victorian outlook. The Victorians had a matter-of-fact approach to life and a self-confidence in their own intellectual categories; consequently, when they encountered interpretations of the OT that seemed to them bizarre or farfetched, they tended to set them on one side as peripheral to the argument, or else to assume that they were not interpretations at all, but illustrations or felicitous echoes of familiar phraseology.

To take one example out of many: Romans 10 is a chapter which is thickly studded with citations from the OT. Unless we had positive evidence to the contrary, we should expect that Paul was intending to prove something by means of all these quotations, and indeed his language sounds as if he were conducting a closely knit argument. But the citations seem to us to-day to be so very far from proving anything relevant to what Paul is attempting to establish, that it would not be surprising if many scholars were to treat the quotations not as proofs, but as examples. Thus J. Agar Beet in his admirable commentary on Romans is faced with Paul's citation of Deuteronomy 30.12 in Romans 10.6:[1]

> Do not say in your hearts, "Who will ascend into heaven?" (that is, to bring Christ down).

Beet comments that here, according to Paul, Moses enunciates a principle. Beet thus avoids the suggestion that, according to Paul, Moses was speaking directly to Christ, or the even more bewildering suggestion that it might be Christ himself who uttered these words. He has removed the quotation to the sphere of general principles, where it can be regarded as no more than an illustration. Similarly a few verses later (Romans 10.18) we come upon an even more puzzling citation. Paul quotes Psalm 19.4:

> Their voice has gone out to all the earth, and their words to the end of the world.

The context would seem to suggest that Paul regards the citation as a proof that the gospel was to be preached to all the world. But anyone who reads Psalm 19 with the eyes of a modern would fail to see any connection between a Psalm concerned with the glory of God manifested in the universe and a gospel which was first proclaimed hundreds of years after the Psalm was written. Beet therefore explains the quotation thus: "Paul simply makes use of the Psalmist's words to express his own thoughts." Once more, what looks at first sight as if it was intended for a proof has been reduced to something less than an illustration, a mere verbal echo. Paul, according to Beet, is misusing the Psalm quotation much as we misuse a hackneyed quotation from *Hamlet* when we quote "the play's the thing" in order to emphasize the importance of judging a play on its own merits.

The New Testament interpretation of the Old Testament was doubtless an embarrassment to the Victorians, and this is why they tended to assume that the NT writers were using the OT much as they did themselves, as an admirable source of illustrations and happy quotations. But they did at least pay the writers of the NT the compliment of assuming that their intepretation of the OT was one which moderns could accept. The scholars of the Liberal school, which (in England) followed that of the great Victorians, felt themselves to be under no obligation to approach NT concepts with a similar sympathy. They were for the most part quite ready to admit that Paul intended his OT citations to be proofs of his argument, but they did not conceal their opinion that this merely showed how completely astray Paul was in his thinking. Hastings Rashdall, for example, in his discussion of Paul's use of the word translated "expiation" in Romans 3.25 (*hilastērion*),[2] is quite confident that Paul has derived the thought of an atoning death from 4 Maccabees 17.22, a work which Paul may have regarded as authoritative. But Rashdall is equally certain that any such idea is impossible for modern man to accept, and that Paul's argument merely indicates how completely he was enslaved to the letter of what he regarded as Scripture. A modern exponent of essentially the same view, far though he be from the Liberal school of theology in other respects, is Rudolf Bultmann. He writes thus of the whole range of NT interpretation of the OT: "The method of interpreting the OT in this way—the use of allegory, that is—is everywhere the same. It is not specifically Christian, but was taken over from Judaism, especially from its Hellenistic branch, which in its turn had taken it over from Greek Hellenism."[3] Bultmann in the same passage maintains that this approach to the OT tends to reduce the gospel to a merely intellectual, and therefore esoteric, cult. We shall have reason later on to question both Bultmann's assumptions and his conclusions on this question, but it may stand now as a characteristic method of disposing of the NT interpretation of the OT.

To many Christians, therefore, the advent of "biblical theology" brought relief as far as this problem is concerned, for it brought with it a renewed interest in typology. The Victorians had tended to suggest that typological exegesis had not played an important part in the formation of NT theology. The Liberal theologians, while admitting that typology was central to the NT understanding of the OT, had rejected it as part of the useless lumber of theological accretion that must be got rid of if we were to return to the original message of Jesus. The essence of the new "biblical theology" was the conviction that the Bible must be allowed to speak for itself. Consequently, if typology really was an integral part of the NT message, then it was worth serious consideration. When serious consideration was given to it, it proved to be a treasure house of suggestions for a deeper understanding of the Bible. New patterns were found that threw light on many passages in the NT. Writers such as Mark and Luke, who up to then had been regarded as sober, matter-of-fact authors, proved to be profound theologians whose works were full of subtle references to OT events. The relation between the NT and the OT, which at times during the dominance of the Liberal theology had seemed to be one of almost complete discontinuity, was once more established as absolutely integral. One might sum up the conclusions of the typological school by saying that according to them the NT writers found all the main patterns for God's act in Christ already existing in the OT: the clue therefore to the NT writers' interpretation of the OT lay in the recognition of the fact that they were seeking to lay bare in the OT that pattern of divine action which was fully accomplished in the new dispensation.

The typological approach to the question of OT interpretation has recently received fresh support by the much-needed distinction that has now been established between allegory and typology. Fr J. Daniélou in *Sacramentum Futuri*[4] and R. P. C. Hanson in *Allegory and Event*[5] have shown that typology as used in the

NT is quite distinct from allegory. The former is a peculiarly Jewish-Christian product, the latter owns the pedigree attributed to both typology and allegory by Bultmann in the quotation given above. What is more, there is very little allegory to be found in the NT, and what there is is peripheral and not generally used in order to prove theological conclusions. Typology, on the other hand, is regarded by both Daniélou and R. P. C. Hanson as an essential element in the NT interpretation of the OT. The establishment of this distinction means that scholars in their sympathetic approach to NT thought are rid of the haunting suspicion that there may be an element of sheer arbitrariness in the NT interpretation of the OT. Both the arbitrary fancies of the Rabbis and the arbitrary allegorizing of the Fathers have been shown to be almost entirely absent from the New Testament itself.

It may be as well at this point to mention what is perhaps the latest suggestion about NT exegesis of the OT. It has recently been claimed that the Qumran documents give us the real clue to the nature of NT exegesis. B. Lindars in *New Testament Apologetic*[6] has claimed that these documents exhibit a distinctive method of biblical exegesis. This he calls the *midrash pesher* method. It consists in explaining the Scriptures as prophesying a series of events which are contemporary with the commentator. It is well known, for instance, that this is the technique of the author of the Habakkuk Commentary. Nearly every detail in the two chapters of Habakkuk which he expounds is described as being fulfilled in some historical event or personage near the time of the author, though it is still very far from obvious what exactly that time was and which were the events to which he refers. The word *pesher* is derived from the phrase *pishro* "its meaning", which was used after quoting the text commented on, in order to introduce the contemporary explanation which the author advances. This, says Lindars, is the category into which NT exegesis of the OT should be put.

It is doubtful, however, whether all NT exegesis of the OT will fit into this category, and indeed the precise element in NT exegesis which is to be examined in this book does not fit into the *pesher* category at all. There are, of course, many passages in the NT where prophecy is claimed to have been fulfilled in events of the new dispensation. Peter, for example, in his speech at Pentecost reported in Acts 2 claims that Joel's prophecy of the pouring out of the Spirit in the last days has been fulfilled now. But this represents a fairly general correspondence: Peter does not go on to specify who are the old men, who the young men, how exactly it can be said that the moon had been turned into blood, and all the other details that one would expect the *pesher* method to supply. And when we turn to St Paul the method seems hardly to apply at all. Far from showing in detail how OT prophecies have been fulfilled in the events of Christ's life, Paul frequently perplexes us by apparently throwing Christ's activity back into the OT. He does not, for example, say in 1 Corinthians 10 that the type of the rock from which the water burst was fulfilled in Christ, nor that the meaning of Moses' activity at the crossing of the Red Sea was to point to the coming activity of Christ. Even in Romans 10, where he is more concerned with expounding actual texts from Deuteronomy and elsewhere, and less concerned with OT events, he does not appear to be saying: "These texts were fulfilled centuries later in Christ." What he seems to be saying is: "This is what Christ says."

The *midrash pesher* suggestion, therefore, will not solve all our problems. It might well be left as an accurate description of the school of exegetes typified by the clergyman whom Macaulay met in Mysore, soon after he had landed in India for the first time. This divine suggested that the number 666 in the Apocalypse could only mean Napoleon Buonaparte. Macaulay gave an answer which is probably the best by far to give to the modern disciple of the *pesher* school of exegesis. He took him on at his own game and suggested that a better candidate for the position was the Mother of Parliaments, which, with a little adjustment, could be represented as numbering 666 persons.

The main aim of this book is to examine one element in NT exegesis, and to suggest that this element rather than typology as such is the most important clue to the understanding of the NT exegesis of the OT. That element may be called the real presence of the pre-existent Christ in OT history—or, to be more accurate, the real presence of the pre-existent Jesus. "Jesus in the Old Testament" is in fact the way in which the NT writers for the most part thought of it, as we hope to show. For us to-day it seems wrong to speak of the pre-existent Jesus rather than the pre-existent Christ or the pre-existent Son. But in fact we shall find the NT writers have no hesitation in speaking of Jesus as pre-existent, though they do of course frequently speak also of both Son and Christ as the title of the pre-existent Being.

Anyone who is reasonably well acquainted with the NT will be able to name at once one passage where we read about the activity of Christ in OT history. 1 Corinthians 10.4 is well known as the passage in which Paul makes the puzzling claim "and the Rock was Christ". Perhaps a little reflection would produce a second passage where the presence of the pre-existent Son is traced in OT history, John 12.37-41, where John appears to say that Isaiah saw Jesus' glory in the Temple. Commentators have noted these two passages, of course, and have agreed for the most part that here the pre-existent Christ seems to be envisaged as present in OT events. But they have not connected the two passages in any significant fashion, still less have they suggested that this sort of thing is at all widespread in the NT. Many scholars indeed have sought to avoid the puzzling implications of these two passages by using words such as "types", "prefigurations", "prophecies", which suggest that these OT events did not really witness Christ's contemporary presence, but only pointed forward to the presence that was to be manifested in the last days.

The main argument of this book is that these two passages must be taken as meaning what in fact they say—namely, that the pre-existent Jesus was actually present at certain points in OT history, according to NT writers, and that all the consequences of this belief must be faced. Beginning from the best-known passage, 1 Corinthians 10, we attempt to show that this belief is much more widespread in the NT than is generally recognized. It is traced in several passages in Paul's Epistles, notably 2 Corinthians 3 and Romans 10, and the belief is also found to underlie a number of crucial passages in the Epistle to the Hebrews. As might be expected, the same suggestion of Jesus' real presence in OT history is found to be lying just below the surface in Stephen's Speech in Acts 7. Then, beginning from the passage in John's Gospel already referred to, this belief is traced in a number of other passages in this Gospel, and is even found to underlie the most central text of all, John 1.14. After this, the same belief is traced in a few passages in the Catholic Epistles. Some conclusions must next be drawn which would seem to throw fresh light on the estimate of Jesus' humanity held by Paul. A final chapter discusses some more general aspects of this belief.

If it can be established that the belief in the activity of the pre-existent Jesus in OT history is a deep tradition widely spread among the writers of the NT, this must make a good deal of difference to what we believe about the place that typology plays in NT exegesis. One thing is certain: if Jesus was present in any event in OT history, there can be no question of that event representing a type of Jesus. We cannot have both Christ and a type of Christ at the same place and time. If Jesus was present in the events described in 1 Corinthians 10.1–11, then Moses is not there thought of as a type of Christ, no matter how strongly we may be tempted to draw this conclusion from the phraseology of 1 Corinthians 10.2. This is not to suggest that there is no such thing as typology in the NT. On the contrary, we hope to show that there is typology, and that its genesis can actually be traced inside the NT itself. But it is argued that the normative approach of the NT writers to the OT is not that of typology but rather that of what we have called "real presence". In the event, therefore, Bultmann's rejection of the NT method of interpreting the OT may have to be judged as based on precisely the wrong reason. He rejects this method on the grounds that it moves away from the challenging presence of God in OT events towards a realm of abstract ideas. If the central argument of this book is true, it moves in precisely the opposite direction. The NT writers were extremely anxious to find the presence of Christ in OT history, challenging men to faith or unfaith.

One question is not raised in this book, and that is one which it is the great glory of Bultmann to have put in all its acuteness: is this method of exegesis true? To answer this question would require another book, and it would be a book about the doctrine of the incarnation. It must be sufficient here to say that, if we are to make a serious attempt to relate to the thought of our day the NT method of interpreting the OT, we must be prepared for a process of considerable demythologization. But this does not mean, I believe, that the NT writers do not have some vitally important truth to teach us about God's activity in OT times.

2

Christ in the Old Testament according to Paul

I CORINTHIANS 10.1–11

This is the one passage in the NT where everyone admits that we have a clear example of Christ's pre-existent activity in OT history, so it is an obviously suitable one from which to start our investigation. We begin therefore by quoting it in full:

> I want you to know, brethren, that our fathers were all under the cloud, and all passed through the sea, and all were baptized into Moses in the cloud and in the sea, and all ate the same supernatural food (*pneumatikon brōma*) and all drank the same supernatural drink (*pneumatikon poma*). For they drank from the supernatural Rock which followed them, and the Rock was Christ (ἔπινον γὰρ ἐκ πνευματικῆς ἀκολοθούσης πέτρας, ἡ δὲ πέτρα ἦν ὁ Χριστός). Nevertheless with most of them God was not pleased; for they were overthrown in the wilderness. Now these things are warnings for us (*tupoi hēmōn*), not to desire evil as they did. Do not be idolaters as some of them were; as it is written, "The people sat down to eat and drink and rose up to dance." We must not indulge in immorality as some of them did, and twenty-three thousand fell in a single day. We must not put the Lord to the test, as some of them did and were destroyed by serpents; nor grumble, as some of them did and were destroyed by the Destroyer. Now these things happened to them as a warning (*tupikōs*), but they were written down for our instruction, upon whom the end of the ages has come.

This long passage can most conveniently be considered in three parts: verses 1 and 2; verses 3 and 4; and verses 5–11.

verses 1 and 2

There is plainly a comparison here implicit between the Israelites baptized "into Moses" and Christians baptized into Christ, even though Paul does not make the second half of the comparison explicit. The OT events to which Paul is referring are described in Exodus, chapters 13 and 14. When we study these chapters in the LXX we can gain considerable light on Paul's meaning here. We notice first Exodus 13.21,22:[1]

> And God led them by day in a pillar of cloud to shew them the way and by night in a pillar of fire. The pillar of cloud did not fail by day nor the pillar of fire by night before all the people.

This is no doubt what Paul was thinking of when he describes all the people as being "under the cloud". They were under the protection of the pillar of cloud. Then Exodus, chapter 14, proceeds to tell the story of the crossing of the Red Sea. It is significant that in the LXX as we have it God is throughout chapter 14 referred to as *Kyrios* or *ho Kyrios* (Lord or the Lord), except in verses 19 and 31. But these exceptions have great significance. Verse 19 refers to "the angel of God" and verse 31 runs:

> And Israel saw the mighty act, even the things which *Kyrios* had done to the Egyptians; and the people feared the Lord, and believed in God and in his minister Moses.

In both places, therefore, where "God" is used in this chapter, it is associated with, but apparently distinguished from, another name which could easily be identified by an early Christian with Christ. In verse 19 that other name is "the angel of God" and in verse 31 it is *Kyrios*.

We can point to several other places also in this chapter where Paul would very likely find confirmation of his belief that *Kyrios* throughout referred to Christ and not to the Father. One such place is verse 19, here quoted in full:

> And the angel of God who was going before the army of the children of Israel moved away and journeyed behind them; and the

pillar of cloud moved away from their van and took up position on their rear.

Scholars would no doubt tell us that this repetition is caused by the conflation of two originally separate narratives. But Paul would suspect nothing of this; to him it would only mean one thing: "the angel of God" and "the pillar of cloud" were identical. Five verses further on he would find a further identification of the pillar of cloud with the pillar of fire. Verse 24 runs:

> And *Kyrios* looked upon the camp of the Egyptians in the pillar of fire and cloud.

And if Paul required any greater confirmation of his belief that Christ was the *Kyrios* mentioned in this chapter, he would find it in verse 30:

> And *Kyrios* rescued Israel on that day from the hand of the Egyptians.

Paul uses the word translated "rescue" here himself (*rhuomai*) of Christ's action in rescuing us (e.g. Rom. 7.24; 11.26; Col. 1.13; 1 Thess. 1.10). He would see here the statement that Christ rescued Israel on that day.

We proceed, therefore, on the assumption that Paul saw in the pillar of cloud the pre-existent Christ and that when he says all our fathers were baptized into Moses in the cloud, whatever else he means, he does not mean that Moses on that occasion was a type of Christ. After all, in the next two verses he proceeds explicitly to introduce Christ into the story of the giving of the water from the Rock. Moses, everyone knew, was present at that scene, but he could not have been a type of Christ on that occasion. There is no sense in speaking about types when the reality himself is present. C. K. Barrett in a recent book has insisted that Moses in verse 2 corresponds to Christ, though he does not use the word "type".[2] He admits, however, that the correspondence has disappeared by verse 4, as Christ himself is the source of the spiritual drink. It seems simpler not to try to explain Moses' presence as in any sense a counterpart to Christ here. When Paul says that the Israelites were baptized into Moses, he does not mean to *contrast* it with Christians being baptized into Christ, for he believed (as we have argued) that Christ was present at the crossing of the Red Sea, and that the Israelites were in some sense "in him" there ("in the cloud"). The reference to Moses can be explained by Exodus 14.31 in the LXX. They were afraid of Christ and believed in God and "in his minister Moses". Moses was present as a minister and in this respect the revelation of God in Christ at the Red Sea was inferior to the incarnation: it needed a purely human mediator. We are reminded of Galatians 3.19,20 and of Hebrews 3.1–6, where Moses is described as mediator and "minister" and contrasted with Christ. Both these passages are discussed in later chapters of this book.

We must therefore take issue with Lietzmann, who comments on this passage that in Paul's typology Moses held the same relation to old Israel in the matter of salvation as Christ held to Christians in the new dispensation.[3] We have here to challenge the entire traditional conception of Paul's "typology". So far we have not met with any "types" in this passage, explicit or implicit, but only with God, Christ, and Moses—and Moses as a minister not as a counterpart to Christ, despite the tempting similarity of the phrase "baptized into Moses" to Christian baptismal phraseology. The same claim as Lietzmann's is made by R. P. C. Hanson in an article in *Theology*.[4] He says that in 1 Corinthians 10.2 Moses is a type of Christ, on the analogy that "into Moses" = "into Christ". He goes on, however, to point out that, in the reference to the manna and the water which immediately follows, "Moses is no longer a type of Christ but—if anything—a minister of a type, since St Paul identifies the rock with Christ". This sentence betrays the difficulty of the whole argument. Why should Moses be a type in the one OT "sacrament" and not in the other? In fact, we shall penetrate nearer to the centre of Paul's thought if we drop the conception of types altogether, and think rather of Christ really present at the Red Sea as in the wilderness. This is in fact what R. P. C. Hansom does in his more recent book *Allegory and Event*.

Goudge is the commentator who comes nearest to the idea

that Paul identified Christ with the cloud, for he writes: "Probably St Paul identified Our Lord with the angel 'in whom was the name of Jehovah (Ex. 23.20,21)'."[5] But he does not take the further step of identifying the angel with the cloud. Many editors refer to Wisdom 10.15–18, which is worth quoting, though it does not seem necessary to believe that Paul was directly influenced by it:

> A holy people and blameless race wisdom delivered from a nation of oppressors.
> She entered the soul of a servant of the Lord,
> and withstood dread kings with wonders and signs.
> She gave to holy men the reward of their labours;
> she guided them along a marvellous way,
> and became a shelter to them by day,
> and a starry flame through the night.
> She brought them over the Red Sea,
> and led them through deep waters.

We notice that Wisdom "delivered" the Israelites and that she is identified with the pillar of cloud. The identity of pillar of cloud and pillar of fire is also assumed. She is also the agent of their crossing the Red Sea. On the other hand, the thought of Wisdom entering Moses' soul is not found in Paul. Nor is the idea of Wisdom rewarding the Israelites for their labour at all in accord with Paul's thought—quite the reverse in fact! Héring is not quite accurate when he says that according to the Book of Wisdom it is God who became a pillar of cloud to shelter the Israelites;[6] it is in fact Wisdom, as we have seen. In the same way Robertson and Plummer are inaccurate in saying that in Wisdom 11.4 Wisdom is described as giving water from the Rock to the Israelites.[7] A careful study of Wisdom 11.1–7 shows that Wisdom is only the subject in verse 1. In verses 2–7 God is addressed in the second person singular. Thus in verse 7

> Thou gavest them abundant water unexpectedly

refers to God and not to Wisdom. This is confirmed by the reference to God as a father in verse 10. This word could hardly apply to Wisdom. Thus the Book of Wisdom offers only a very partial parallel to 1 Corinthians 10.1–11.

We might also compare Ecclesiasticus 24.4:

> I dwelt in high places,
> and my throne was in the pillar of cloud.

W. L. Knox in *St Paul and the Church of the Gentiles*[8] suggests that this passage is a late addition to Ben Sira's book. We cannot tell therefore its chronological relationship to the Book of Wisdom. It is to be noticed, however, that there is no mention of the Exodus here, and the mention of the pillar of cloud may be purely poetical.

There are a few references in Christian writers of the second century which confirm the view that Paul saw Christ as the divine agent in the crossing of the Red Sea. For example Justin in *Dialogue* 37 applies to Christ Psalm 99 (LXX 98).7:[9]

> He spoke to them in a pillar of cloud.

In the next section Trypho says: "You think you can persuade us that this man who was crucified was with Moses and Aaron, and spoke to them in the pillar of cloud." There is a fine passage also in Melito's *Homily on the Passion* where Christ is identified with a whole series of divine appearances in the OT:

> He it was who led thee down into Egypt [Melito is addressing Israel], and guarded and nourished thee there. He it was who gave thee a guiding light in the pillar and sheltered thee in the cloud, who cut the Red Sea in two and led thee through and destroyed thy enemy. He it was who gave thee manna from heaven, who gave thee drink out of the rock, who gave thee the law on Horeb, who gave thee the land for thine inheritance, who sent forth prophets to thee, who raised up kings for thee. He it was who visited thee . . .[10]

and so on to describe the incarnation. As we shall be seeing, most of these instances of Christ's appearances in OT history can be paralleled in the NT itself, so Melito was drawing on a well-established tradition. A third example can be found in Irenaeus. In the *Proof of the Apostolic Preaching* the Son is identified with the angel in the burning bush.[11] He kept descending and ascending for the deliverance of his people in Egypt, and he freed the Israelites at the Red Sea.

verses 3 and 4

Why does Paul call the food and drink here "supernatural" (*pneumatikon*)? He refers, of course, to the manna from heaven and the water from the Rock. Once more, recourse to the text of the LXX throws light on this question. Chapter 16 of Exodus describes the giving of the manna; verses 15 and 16a run thus in the LXX:

> And the children of Israel seeing it [the manna] said one to another: "What is this?", for they did not know what it was. And Moses said to them: "This is the bread which *Kyrios* has given you to eat. This is the word (*rhēma*) which *Kyrios* has enjoined."

We know, of course, that "word" in Greek translates *dabhar* in Hebrew, and that *dabhar* can mean "thing" or "event" just as much as "word". But we are not justified in assuming that Paul realized this as we do. He would think of the manna as coming from the Lord, by which he would understand Christ, and he would see it as associated with the word of God. He would be confirmed in this interpretation by reading the other account of the giving of the manna in Deuteronomy 8.3:

> [God] fed you with manna which you did not know, nor did your fathers know, that he might bring home to you that man shall not live by bread alone, but by every word (*rhēmati*) that proceeds out of the mouth of God shall man live.

We conclude, therefore, that Paul calls the manna "supernatural food" because it was given by Christ. In other words, the Israelites in the wilderness were sustained by the Word of God in a way analogous to what is described in chapter 6 of St John's Gospel.

We need not spend long in discussing why the drink is called "supernatural". It was given by Christ, who was personally present. This much Paul says explicitly. No doubt the narrative that Paul has in mind is Exodus 17.1–7. It describes the temptation in the wilderness and the giving of the water from the Rock. In verse 2 Moses says:

> Why do you tempt *Kyrios*?

In verse 9 below Paul warns the Corinthians against tempting the Lord, and he certainly means Christ there. There can be little doubt that in Exodus 17.1-7 he takes *Kyrios* of the LXX as Christ. It may even be that a strange phrase in verse 6 confirmed him in his belief that the Rock was Christ. The LXX as we have it does not make sense, as a word seems to have dropped out.[12] One MS. supplies the word, to give the sense:

> It is I who stood on the Rock in Horeb before thou didst come.

Héring has noticed the difficulty in the LXX text here, but he says that this does not explain Paul's identifying the Rock with Christ, as in Exodus 17.6 there is no mention of the Messiah. But Paul did not need to light on a traditionally messianic passage before he could connect it with Christ. For him the use of *Kyrios* in the LXX, and the other indications we have noted, would be enough.

Commentators have almost without exception missed the point of the word *pneumatikon* ("supernatural"). Thus Robertson and Plummer would render the last phrase in verse 4 as "and the Rock represents Christ", though they qualify it by adding: "There was a real presence of Christ in the element which revived their bodies and strengthened their faith." McFadyen explains, "The manna had a spiritual value. . . . The use of the word 'spiritual' shows that Paul did not himself accept this grotesque tradition, but he appears in this passage to have adapted it."[13] So far we have indicated a tradition of exegesis that attempted to tone down the shocking realism of Paul's view of Christ in OT history. Another school tends to call in allegory and symbol as an aid. Thus Venard writes of verse 4: "Despite the formal evidence, it is not certain that he would have considered the Rock as being properly speaking the figure, or type, of Christ; and it seems more likely that we have here an allegorical development of a literary nature."[14] In fact what we have here is neither typology nor allegory; we have, according to Paul, the actual presence of Christ. Héring similarly comments: "We are in the middle of that spiritual exegesis dear to Philo and the Rabbis", thereby confounding two quite different traditions in one phrase, neither of which is really applicable to this passage. Indeed all the French commentators seem anxious to "spiritualize" this passage. Allo writes: "Paul has used the legend to be found in the Targum, but in so doing he has given it a symbolic interpretation, giving it the purely spiritual meaning of Christ, who accompanied the children of Israel to sustain them with miracles."[15] Here language is being used loosely: if a Protestant writer, discussing Christ's presence in the Eucharist, were to equate "symbolic" and "spiritual" in this way, he would soon be taken to task by the learned Dominican! "Spiritual" here can only be rightly understood in the sense of "conveying the real presence of Christ". This is not what is normally meant by "symbolic". Bonsirven writes in the same strain: "St Paul affirms the typological significance of sacred history. It was a prefiguration of Christian history, providing already an anticipation of baptism and the Eucharist and the veiled presence of Christ."[16] This is more cautious, but that word "typological" is not the right one: where Christ is present there is no room for the type of Christ, and Christ was certainly present here according to Paul. It was in a sense a "veiled" presence, though the word "indirect" might be better. Bonsirven is right here in seeing anticipations of baptism and the Eucharist, but not "types". Christ's real presence was common to both OT and NT sacraments. Daniélou seems to be off the mark when he writes: "In the statement that the pillar of light prefigures Christ (*figure le Christ*), we find a theme which goes back to Judaism itself. The Book of Wisdom sees there the figure of the divine Wisdom."[17] It is a mistake to suggest that in Paul's thought the pillar of cloud "prefigures" Christ. He believed that it was Christ in the same way that the Rock was Christ. Here is a relation of identity not of type and fulfilment.[18] R. Bultmann takes essentially the same point of view as the French scholars when he writes: "What is involved here is not a paralleling of historical persons and events, but an interpretation of OT history as a foreshadowing of what would happen in the eschatological period." Compare also his remark: "The desert generation of Israel, which once had received prototypes of the Christian sacraments, were not thereby preserved from destruction."[19] Obviously he takes *tupoi* as meaning "types" without examining the question closely.

Ellis appears to take exactly the same path: "The Old Covenant, like the New, had a food and drink in which Christ was (typically) present",[20] and he adds in a footnote that *pneumatikon* here means "in its typical or prophetic significance". He has plainly been misled by that fatal word *tupikōs* in verse 11. In fact Paul says that the Rock was Christ, not that it prefigured or prophesied Christ. K. J. Woollcombe seems to be getting nearer to the point when he says: "The events which the Fathers experienced in the Exodus directly corresponded to the events which he (Paul) and his contemporaries were experiencing, *because Christ was the prime mover in both.*"[21] Unfortunately, however, he says in the same passage that in 1 Corinthians 10.4 Paul interpreted the Rock allegorically. Whatever Paul is doing here, he is not using allegory, and, I would add, he is not using typology either. In our review of English commentators we should make an honourable exception of T. C. Edwards.[22] Of the words "the same" in verse 3 he makes the acute remark that it means "the same which we Christians eat", not "the same for all Israelites". This in itself would make the use of the word "type" inappropriate to these incidents. O. Cullmann, though he claims that the incident has a "typological significance", explains it more in terms of real presence: "Paul does not intend absolutely to identify the following Rock with Christ, as if he had assumed the appearance of the Rock. The Messiah remains a spiritual reality."[23] But he adds that Christ is all the same not to be divorced from the actual Rock then or from the eucharistic gift now. "He is the same Christ, standing over both old and new covenant in his existence both before and after the incarnation, whose faithfulness to his people then as to-day Paul has emphasized by the words 'which followed them'."

Of all the Fathers none has discussed this passage more carefully than Chrysostom. It is well worth reproducing what he says at some length:

> But, since Paul wishes to bring the types close to reality, he does not express it in typological language, but he uses the terminology belonging to reality when he is speaking of the type. The first incident is a figure of baptism; but what follows is a figure of the holy table. For as you eat the body of the Lord, so they ate the manna; and as you drink the blood, so they drank the water from the Rock. For, though the events were visible, they were ordained with a spiritual purpose, not following the order of nature but according to free grace, and they nourished not only the body but also the soul, leading it to faith. For this reason Paul added nothing about the food, for it was transfigured not only in the method of giving but in its own nature, since it was manna. But the drink required some explanation since it was only in the manner of giving it that the miraculous appeared. Thus, when he had said "They drank the same spiritual drink", he added, "for they drank of the spiritual Rock which followed them", and he put in as well "and that Rock was Christ". It was not a natural emission of water from the Rock, he says, for in that case it would have burst forth before that. But it was a different, spiritual Rock that carried out all these things—that is, Christ, who was everywhere present with them, and was the author of all the wonders; that is why Paul used the phrase "the Rock that followed them". You see Paul's wisdom, how he shows Christ to be the provider of both dispensations, and this is how he brings the type near to the reality. For, says Paul, he who provided those benefits for the Jews is the same who has prefigured this table [sc. the Eucharist at which the Homily was delivered]. The same one led them through the sea and you through baptism, and supplied manna and water to them and to you his body and blood.[24]

Chrysostom uses the language of type and reality, which had become traditional in his day. But he is quite certain that Christ was really (not typically) present to the Jews of old, and undoubtedly he has given the right explanation of why Paul explicitly connects Christ with the water and not with the manna.

Before we pass to consider Paul's use of the strange legend of the moving Rock, it would be appropriate to quote a comment on this passage by R. P. C. Hanson, because it seems to sum up the essential issues with great clarity:

> It is obvious that Paul is here elaborating his conviction that the situations which occurred and the events which took place during the critical period of the Exodus and the wilderness wanderings were being repeated in some sense in the experience of the contemporary Church, and especially in the administration of the sacraments. So far we have only "similar situation" typology; that is presumably what St Paul meant by "examples". . . . The only possible instance of allegory that I can find here is the phrase "and the Rock was Christ". . . . This would certainly be allegory if it meant "the Rock described in Exodus 17 signified or predicted Christ", as, for instance, the Fathers of the Church say that the stone referred to by Isaiah was a prophecy or figure of Christ. But it is much more likely that Paul here means that the Rock really was Christ. The word "was" ($\tilde{\eta}\nu$) is expressed in the Greek. That is to say, he believed that the Messiah was in some form present with the people, who were all the time in their ultimate significance the Messiah's people, during this critical period in the wilderness, for salvation, and for judgement, just as in 2 Corinthians 3.17 he expresses his belief that the "Lord" to whom Moses turned when he entered the tabernacle, and contact with whom caused Moses' face to shine, was the Spirit. In that case, this would not be an allegory at all, but an example of Paul's tendency to read back, so to speak, the Messiah into the Old Testament. For Paul, when Moses wrote "Rock" he meant Christ present then and there, not a figure or a forecast or symbol of Christ, except in so far as a name is a symbol.[25]

This is well said and clears the air admirably. One would only want to add "not a type of Christ", and therefore to query the usefulness of employing that word "typology" at all. A similar situation there certainly was, but not one that was necessarily foreordained to be repeated in all details. On the contrary, Paul draws out the similarity specifically in order to avoid a full repetition.

How Christ was the Rock is a question which we cannot stop to examine. It is probably as incapable of a full answer as is the precisely parallel question about the mode of Christ's presence in the Eucharist. We will merely note the surprising fact that those whose theological tradition would most dispose them to be realists about the second question are on the whole inclined to be symbolists about the first one.

The Rabbinic legend about the following Rock has given much concern to commentators. The older scholars of the last century tend to jib at attributing this grotesque midrash to Paul. Hodge expresses it most clearly when he says: "This view of the passage [sc. that Paul accepted the legend] makes the apostle responsible for a Jewish fable, and is inconsistent with his divine authority."[26] Other editors take a different view of Paul's authority, but join with Hodge in trying to repudiate the fable. More modern scholars, however, realize that we have no right to set arbitrary limits to what Paul could or could not believe. Bousset gives a very convincing account of how the legend originated:[27] it began, he says, when Numbers 21.17–19 was read continuously, and the verb "they went" in verse 18 was omitted, giving a translation like this:

> Then Israel sang this song:
> "Spring up. O well (sing to it, the well which the princes dug, which the nobles of the people delved, with the sceptre and with their staves),
> from the wilderness on to Mattanah, and from Mattanah to Nahaliel. . . ."

This gives a picture of the well springing up and following the children of Israel on their journeyings. It only remained to identify the well with the water from the Rock, and we have Paul's legend. S-B gives a good account of the legend, which has recently been supplemented by T. F. Glasson. If we put both their accounts together we get a good picture of how it may well have existed in Paul's day: "So the well, which was with Israel in the wilderness, was like a rock of the size of a $k^e bara$ (a large round vessel), and was oozing out and rising as from the mouth of this flask. The water from the rock went with them up the mountains and followed them down into the valleys; in the place where Israel stopped it stopped opposite them by the entrance to the tabernacle."[28] All authorities insist that nowhere is the Messiah identified with this Rock. But S-B quotes a Rabbinic comment on Exodus 17.6, the verse which we noted was incompletely translated in the LXX: "God said to him [Moses], Wherever thou findest the footprint of a man, there am I before thee."[29] According to S-B this means that God was in some way present in the Rock. We can see how easily such a belief could be altered by Paul into a conviction that Christ was present in the Rock.

We cannot say with certainty to what stage the legend had developed in Paul's day. It must have been fairly well known or Paul could not have mentioned it so casually. We need not believe that he would have recounted it in the absurd detail supplied by S-B and Glasson. We can, however, see why Paul used it: the manna was a continuous process, they kept on eating it all through the wilderness period. The giving of the water from the Rock was a single incident. Paul wanted a process parallel to the giving of the manna whereby the water was continuously supplied, and he found it in the legend of the following Rock.

verses 5–11

We need not spend much time on the rest of the passage, as the main issues have been clarified already. As we have seen, much misunderstanding has been caused among commentators by the two words we meet in verses 6 and 11, *tupoi* and *tupikōs*. In both instances, if you translate "types" and "typically" you end by missing the sense. If Christ at the giving of the water was a type, then he was a type of himself, which is nonsense. And if you take *tupikōs* to mean "in the form of a type", it makes the next clause unnecessary.[30] If it happened to them in the form of a type, there is no need to add that it was written for our admonition. We have the admonition already in the type. It makes much better sense to take it as "it happened as a warning example to them, and was recorded for our admonition". This point is clearly made by C. K. Barrett.[31] Besides, it is worth noting that Paul does not say that persons were *tupoi*, only events. Lietzmann, by consistently translating *tupos* as "Vorbild" and *tupikōs* as "vorbildlich", misses the sense. G. A. F. Knight tends rather to darken counsel by his comments on this passage: "This typological exegesis is in the Rabbinical manner. Yet both here and in Romans 9—11 it is the fact of Israel as an historical people which compels Paul to seek to interpret their *raison d'être*. In order to do this, Paul makes use of events that happened to, and concepts connected with, the life of Jesus. . . . What he does is to interpret God's action in the life of Israel in the light of what he knows to have been God's action so recently, from his point of view, in the life of Christ. No sooner had God brought his Son to the birth, he declares, than he baptized him 'in the cloud and in the sea'."[32] This seems to be bringing a rather strained interpretation of the OT into the exegesis of the NT. Paul nowhere suggests that the calling of Israel from Egypt was the bringing of God's Son to birth. On the contrary, he traces the birth of the people of God back to Abraham. Knight writes as if Paul were drawing a parallel between the life of Christ-in-the-Church and the life of Israel. That there is a parallel between the life of the Church and the life of Israel we must grant, and in this sense (*if* this sense) the word "typological" may be allowed. But the whole point of the parallel is that the life of Christ is common to both histories, the old and the new.

We are now left with only one point. It occurs in verse 9:

We must not put the Lord to the test, as some of them did.

The actual incident of the serpents is described in Numbers 21.4–9, but the word for "put to the test" (*peirazō*) is not used there in our version of the LXX, nor is there any word like it. It seems probable, therefore, that Paul has still got in mind Exodus 17.1–7, which, as we have suggested above, there is reason to think he did study. As we have noted, the phrase, "Why do you tempt *Kyrios*?" occurs there. Besides, if Paul did have Numbers 21.4–9 in mind, it is very strange that he makes nothing of the sign of the brazen serpent which John (and after him most of the Fathers) saw as a prophetic sign of Christ. After all the discussion that has gone before, we need hardly spend time in proving that "We must not put the Lord to the test" in verse 9 refers to Christ rather than to the Father. There is an alternative reading "Christ" which has considerable support.[33] We may guess that this is either the original reading or a correct early interpretation. Robertson and Plummer with indomitable confidence suggest that Jehovah, not Christ, is intended here, and quote Hort on 1 Peter 2.3 to the effect that *Kyrios* in the OT never means Christ in the NT: "No such identification can be clearly made out in the NT." One would have thought that a consideration of John 12.41 would have been enough to cast doubts on the absolute accuracy of this statement. Certainly if there is any force whatever in the evidence brought forward in this book, Hort's claim can no longer stand.

2 CORINTHIANS 3.7–18

The task of fully interpreting Paul's mind in this obscure chapter 10 of 1 Corinthians has been laborious and detailed; but it will have proved worth while if it has served to establish the fact that Paul undoubtedly conceived of Christ as personally present in OT history, and to cast a serious doubt on the validity of the word "typology" as commonly applied to Paul's interpretation of the OT. We must now pass on to a passage where his meaning is even more obscure, but one which has received less detailed attention from commentators. It is 2 Corinthians 3, the passage about the glory that shone on Moses' face. It will be sufficient, however, if we only reproduce 2 Corinthians 3.7–18:

> Now if the dispensation of death, carved in letters of stone, came with such splendour that the Israelites could not look at Moses' face because of its brightness, fading (*tēn katargoumenēn*) as this was, why should not the dispensation of the Spirit be attended with greater splendor? For if there was splendor in the dispensation of condemnation, the dispensation of righteousness must far exceed it in splendor. Indeed, in this case, what once had splendor has come to have no splendor at all, because of the splendor that surpasses it. For

C

if what faded away (*to katargoumenon*) came with splendor, what is permanent must have much more splendor. Since we have such a hope, we are very bold, not like Moses, who put a veil over his face so that the Israelites might not see the end of the fading splendor (τὸ τέλος τοῦ καταργουμένου). But their minds were hardened; for to this day, when they read the old covenant, that same veil remains unlifted, because only through Christ is it taken away (*katargeitai*). Yes, to this day, whenever Moses is read a veil lies over their minds; but when a man turns to the Lord the veil is removed. Now the Lord is the Spirit, and where the Spirit of the Lord is, there is freedom. And we all, with unveiled face, beholding the glory of the Lord, are being changed into his likeness from one degree of glory to another; for this comes from the Lord who is the Spirit.

Not surprisingly, scholars have found this passage difficult to interpret. A number of questions arise at once: why, according to Paul, did Moses not want the Israelites to see "the end of the fading splendor"? What is the subject of "turns to the Lord" in verse 16 (there is no word in the Greek corresponding to "a man" in the English)? Is there a typological scheme in Paul's mind, and if so, of whom is Moses the type? Perhaps we shall come nearest to understanding Paul's mind if we do what has been done in the previous discussion, and turn back to the LXX of the OT passage on which this chapter is based, reading as far as possible with Paul's eyes. The passage in question is certainly Exodus 34.27–35, which describes what happened when Moses came down from the mountain with the two (renewed) tables of the Law in his hands. It will be sufficient if we actually quote verses 29–35, though the whole passage is certainly in Paul's mind:

> And when Moses came down from the mountain then the two tables were in the hand of Moses. And as he came down from the mountain he did not know that the appearance of the flesh of his face had been transfigured while he had been speaking with him [sc. the Lord]. And Aaron and all the elders of Israel saw Moses and the appearance of the flesh of his face was transfigured; and they feared to approach him. And Moses called them, and Aaron and all the rulers of the assembly turned towards him and Moses spoke to them. And after that all the children of Israel came to him, and he instructed them in

all the things which *Kyrios* had spoken to him on the Mount Sinai. And when he had ceased speaking to them he put a veil on his face. But whenever Moses went in before *Kyrios* to speak to him, the veil was removed until he came out again, and he used to come out and tell all the children of Israel whatever *Kyrios* had instructed him. And the children of Israel saw Moses' face that it was transfigured, and Moses put a veil on his face until he went in to converse with him.

In view of our conclusions about 1 Corinthians, chapter 10, it does not seem unreasonable to suggest that Paul would read in this passage the narrative of the converse which Moses held with the pre-existent Christ in the tabernacle, and indeed he would probably draw the conclusion that it was Christ who had appeared to Moses on Mount Sinai and delivered the Law to him. At least if we approach 2 Corinthians 3 with this idea in mind, we may well find that some of the difficulties of the passage are resolved.

It is important at the outset to notice a point which seems to have escaped the notice of all commentators: there is no mention, either in 2 Corinthians 3 or in Exodus 34, of the glory on Moses' face fading. The word translated by the RSV in verses 7, 11, and 13 of 2 Corinthians 3 as "fading" is *katargeisthai*, which means "to be annulled" or "rendered ineffective". It is a favourite word of Paul's; he uses it twenty-five times in his extant works, always in the sense indicated here, and sometimes of the old dispensation being annulled by the new (cf. 1 Cor. 13.8; Eph. 2.15). It never carries any suggestion of fading away. For that meaning some quite different word would be required, perhaps *aphanismos* ("vanish away") as in Hebrews 8.13. The RSV is very unhappy in its rendering of this verb in 2 Corinthians 3, for in the fourth place where it occurs in this chapter it gives the translation "taken away", which, as we shall see, is quite inappropriate. Once we realize that there was never any question of the glory on Moses' face fading, we can approach afresh the question that has caused so much concern to commentators: why did Moses not want the children of Israel to see "the end of that which was being annulled"—to give what is a more accurate translation?

Whatever reason we assign, it was not because he was afraid that the Israelites might discover that his glory had faded away. Thus Paul can at once be acquitted of giving us a picture of Moses in which the great leader is trying to save his face, or even attempting to deceive the Israelites (as both Plummer and Strachan suggest[34]). Exodus never suggests that the glory faded at all, and Paul says that it was "rendered ineffective or abolished".

We may therefore ask again: What is "the end of that which was being annulled"? The solution, I believe, has already been suggested by R. P. C. Hanson in his brief commentary on 2 Corinthians.[35] He points out that the answer really lies in Romans 10.4:

> For Christ is the end of the law ($\tau\acute{\epsilon}\lambda o\varsigma\ \gamma\grave{\alpha}\rho\ \nu\acute{o}\mu o\nu\ X\rho\iota\sigma\tau\acute{o}\varsigma$), that everyone who has faith may be justified.

It is very likely that "end", *telos*, in Romans 10.4 means "fulfilment" rather than "termination", for Paul did not believe that the Law had come to an end, in the sense of disappearing altogether. We may therefore take "the end of that which is being annulled" in 2 Corinthians 3.13 as "the fulfilment of the order which was being superseded", i.e. Christ, who was this fulfilment. C. K. Barrett in *From First Adam to Last* (pp. 51–2) reaches a very similar conclusion. He writes of "that which is being annulled" as follows: "What this is, is not made clear; the gender shows that it is not simply the glory . . . that is being referred to." Later he well compares Romans 7.2, where the same verb qualifies "Law". He is not, however, completely free of the idea that according to Paul the glory faded, and he nowhere suggests that Moses talked with Christ in the tabernacle. The fact of the matter is, however, that in Paul's view Moses' motive in putting the veil on his face was to prevent the children of Israel seeing Christ. We are not justified in suggesting that, if Moses had not put the veil on, the Israelites would have witnessed the fading of the glory from Moses' face. The glory was the glory of the Law, and it would have remained until the Messiah came in the flesh. No, what Moses wished to avoid was the children of Israel recognizing from the glory on his face that he had been talking to Christ. That reflected glory of the pre-existent Christ was indeed to come to its fulfilment and be replaced by the glory of the incarnate Word, but, till that happened, the glory of the Law was the glory of Christ. If it be suggested that Paul never could suggest that the glory of Christ (even pre-existent) could be abolished, it may be answered that, on any other interpretation, it is the glory of God, who had spoken face to face with Moses on Sinai, that was to be abolished or superseded. So that, however we understand this chapter, Paul is saying that the divine glory manifested in the old dispensation is superseded.

We are still left with the question: Why did Moses not wish the Israelites to see Christ? But here we can suggest a likely solution.[36] Paul says in verse 14 "But their minds were hardened". This reminds us of Romans 11.7 and 11.25, where he says "but the rest were hardened" and "a hardening has come upon part of Israel". This hardening or blinding process is according to God's will (cf. Mark 4.12; John 12.39,40). We must imagine, therefore, that Moses, who had talked with Christ and knew his will, was aware of the divinely intended hardening and deliberately hid the glory of Christ reflected on his own face, in order that the Israelites should not recognize the pre-existent Christ. Even though this glory was inferior and impermanent, being the glory of the as yet not incarnate Christ, and therefore not direct or eternal, it was nevertheless the glory of Christ himself, and could have been a means by which the Jews might have recognized Christ. Paul always maintains that the Law can be a means of knowing Christ, as we shall see when we investigate Romans 10.

That same veil remains unlifted among the Jews to this day, because only through Christ is it taken away.[37] But just as the word which we have rendered "annulled" cannot mean "faded away", so neither can it mean "taken away" as RSV translates it in verse 14. Both Paul and the LXX supply us with the right word for that meaning: it is the word used in 2 Corinthians 3.16, and correctly translated by the RSV there as "removed" (*perihaireitai*). It is also found in the LXX of Exodus 34.34. It is astonishing that the RSV should give what is in fact the wrong translation for *katargeisthai* four times in the course of eight verses! In verse 14, as throughout the chapter, it means "abolished, annulled, superseded". If this seems a strange word to use of a veil, it is because Paul is already thinking of the veil in a metaphorical sense. It is the veil on the hearts of the Jews in his day, the hardening (cf. Ephesians 2.15). Paul's thought thus leads smoothly on to verse 17, where he reminds his readers that the Lord of whom the Exodus passage is speaking is the Spirit. He is not doing here what several commentators have suggested, identifying the Lord who spoke to Moses in the tabernacle with the third Person of the Trinity. He has already throughout this chapter assumed that the *Kyrios* of Exodus 34 is the second Person of the Trinity (to use language which is of course an anachronism in Paul's day). What he is doing is reminding his readers that the Lord (Christ) whom Moses saw, and to whom the Jew can turn to-day, is the Spirit and is therefore the giver of freedom. This does seem to involve an identification of what we would call the second and third Persons of the Trinity. But this is not so serious for Paul as for us, as in his day the Church had not yet even begun to work out in serious theological terms the implications of its doctrine of God in Christ, rich though it was in dynamic and significant titles and intuitions. Last of all comes verse 18, where Paul applies his argument to all Christians, not just to the ministers his colleagues or to the converted Jew. We can now all behold[38] the glory of Christ openly and partake of that glory. It does seem absolutely necessary to take *Kyrios* throughout this chapter as meaning Christ. Otherwise Paul's argument must fall to the ground: if *Kyrios* when used of the Presence who appeared to Moses in the tabernacle means God the Father, there is no middle term of comparison.

S-B provides an interesting light on this: the Targum on the passage from Exodus 34 uses the phrase "the rays of the glory of the Sh^{e}kinah of Adonai" to describe the light that shone on Moses' face.[39] Now there can be little doubt that Paul identified the *Sh^{e}kinah* with Christ implicitly, as John does explicitly in

John 1.14. Indeed the identification becomes almost explicit in 2 Corinthians 4.6, only a few verses beyond this passage, where Paul speaks of

> the light of the knowledge of the glory of God in the face of Jesus Christ.

Paul may well have argued in some such way as this:
Moses saw the *Sh^ekinah*;
But Christ is the *Sh^ekinah*:
Therefore Moses saw Christ.

By contrast S-B quotes another Rabbinic passage as saying that all the time Moses was writing down the Law, he was so humble that he did not lift up his eyes to behold the *Sh^ekinah* and that this is why he did not know that his face shone.[40] Here is a remarkable contrast with the "confidence" of the Christian.

The commentator who comes nearest to the interpretation outlined above is Hodge. He writes of verse 16: "By 'Lord' here, as the context shows, we are to understand Christ. He is the Lord whom Moses saw face to face on Mount Sinai, and to whom the Jews and all others must turn if they are to enjoy the light of salvation." The literalist is thus sometimes in a better position to understand the mind of Paul than the critical scholar. But he does not seem to apply this insight throughout the passage, for he objects to taking *telos* in verse 13 as Christ, on the grounds that Moses veiling his face would not prevent the Israelites from seeing Christ. But it would, if Moses had been speaking to Christ in the tabernacle and the glory of the pre-existent Christ was still visible on his face.

Windisch rightly points out that in the original Exodus passage the purpose of Moses' veiling his face was to spare the Israelite the strain of enduring the unveiled rays of the divine glory, and he thinks that Paul has imported two new ideas into the incident:[41]

1. It was a manœuvre by Moses in order to preserve appearances, but God used it in accordance with a higher purpose connected with the obduracy of the Jews.

2. The fading of the glory on Moses' face was a symbol of the temporary nature of the Mosaic dispensation.

As we have suggested, this is unnecessarily elaborate. There is no need to attribute to Moses an anxiety to preserve appearances. Moses, according to Paul, knew that he was speaking to Christ on Mount Sinai and in the tabernacle, and he knew that this dispensation, though ordained by Christ, was temporary. But it was necessary to hide from the Jews the fact that the legal dispensation would be superseded by the new dispensation ushered in by the incarnation, and this meant hiding the glory of Christ reflected in his face, because that glory, though temporary, did reveal Christ. Now that the Messiah is come in the flesh such veiling is no longer necessary. Similarly Lietzmann says that the disappearance of the glory is not even hinted at in the text of Exodus, but is imported by Paul to show the inferiority of the legal dispensation. We have argued that Moses' motive was rather to hide the *telos* than to hide the disappearance, which was, after all, only destined to take place centuries later. Christ could in some sense be seen immediately in Moses' face.

We turn now to those scholars who would interpret this passage in terms of typology. R. P. C. Hanson in *Allegory and Event* (p. 80 n) maintains that in this passage we have what he calls "similar situation" typology. He writes: "Just as the people of Israel could have seen God's light reflected in Moses' face but for the veil, so Christians to-day, possessing the Spirit, see God's light reflected in Christ." But this is not in fact the comparison that Paul makes here: we see Christ as Moses did. Paul reflects Christ as Moses did not, because Moses put a veil on his face. In any case, in verse 16 what Paul must mean is: "The Lord in that passage in Exodus is the Spirit." Consequently he cannot mean Christians have what Moses had not. Apparently, according to Paul, the Law dispensation came from Christ (who is the Spirit) quite as much as the dispensation of the new covenant. But the Law dispensation was not intended for salvation: it was intended for judgement ("the dispensation of condemnation", ἡ διακονία τῆς κατακρίσεως, 2 Cor. 3.9), and the dispensation of the Spirit was deliberately withheld (with the connivance of Moses) till the fullness of time. Far from Moses being a type of Christ, there is no typology proper here at all, but simply the presence of Christ under both dispensations.

Jeremias also uses the language of typology. He says that Paul here deals expressly with Moses as a type. He stands for two things at the same time: the office bearer of the old covenant who exercises a ministry of death (ἡ διακονία τοῦ θανάτου, 2 Cor. 3.7), and a symbol of the veil that lies on the hearts of the Jews. He writes: "Paul therefore applies the typology of Moses differently from the early Church, in as much as he sees in Moses the representative of the office bearer and of the community of the old covenant, with whom conversely the office bearer and community of the new covenant are in contrast."[42] There is much truth in this, but one must ask: Is there any justification for employing the language of typology here? If Moses is a type of anyone here, he is a type of Paul. What is gained in clarity by saying that Moses is a type of Paul? We can quite truly say that Moses is a representative of the old dispensation, but there is nothing very original in that. Paul nowhere suggests that Moses' behaviour was intended to predict or foreshadow the behaviour of the ministers of the new covenant. Rather the reverse in fact, since Moses hid Christ, while Paul declares him. In fact we find that there is no more typology here than there is when Paul says in Romans 5.14 that Adam is a "type of the one who was to come". There is a certain resemblance, but it is not the resemblance of prophet to prophesied, nor is it a resemblance of what the Fathers called the type to the fulfilment. We may justly conclude, therefore, that to use the language of typology is to create darkness rather than light.

We must therefore take issue with Munck when he says that in this passage Paul is comparing himself to Moses and deciding that he is superior.[43] This is to miss the point: Paul is the last man to concern himself about his superiority to others. In any case there is no real comparison here: Moses, according to Paul, had his own special part to play. Knowing Christ face to face (although the pre-existent, not the incarnate, Christ), he had to conceal him in order to carry out God's design which involved the obduracy of the Jews. Paul's task was different, bold and open declaration of Christ incarnate. But Paul nowhere suggests that Moses as such was inferior to himself, only that the dispensation that Christ gave him to administer was inferior. The same misleading emphasis is to be found in W. D. Davies. He quotes Strachan with approval: "Here Paul, as a minister of Christ, assumes that he himself is no less distinguished a person than Moses."[44] Not "distinguished" but "privileged", and the same could be said of every Christian, as is plain from 3.18: "We all, with unveiled face..."

The idea that it was Christ who uttered the Law to Moses on Sinai, and who spoke to him in the tabernacle, is certainly to be found in the Fathers. We have already noticed it in Melito (see page 15): "He it was... who gave thee the law on Horeb." Irenaeus certainly believed this: for example in *Adversus Haereses* he writes as follows: "And the Word indeed spoke to Moses, appearing in his sight 'as a man speaks to his friend' (Ex. 33.11). But Moses desired to see clearly him who spoke with him."[45] Irenaeus then quotes Exodus 33.21: "Behold there is a place by me where you will stand on the Rock", and he says that this desire of Moses was only fulfilled at the Transfiguration. We need not go into Irenaeus' discussion of the mode of Christ's presence in the OT. It is sufficient to note that he undoubtedly believed the *Kyrios* of this passage from Exodus 33 to be Christ.

Tertullian actually discusses 2 Corinthians 3.4-18, and insists that it was Christ whom Moses saw in the tabernacle and whose glory Moses hid from the Israelites: "If the Messiah belonging to the Creator who was proclaimed by Moses had not yet come, what interest had Paul in anything that was veiled by Moses?",[46] i.e. what does it matter to Paul what Moses hid, if he did not hide Christ? It is a fair argument, and surely demonstrates that Tertullian understood Paul's mind here better than many a modern editor has.

To sum up our interpretation of this controversial passage

briefly: in verse 11 *to katargoumenon*, wrongly translated in the RSV as "what faded away", is the Law, which Christ delivered to Moses. The phrase "what is permanent" refers to the dispensation of grace. The difference between "the written code" and "the Spirit" in verse 6 is not a difference between a Law given by God and grace coming through Christ; it is a difference between Law given by Christ, but indirectly through Moses, and grace coming directly through Christ incarnate. The old covenant was given by Christ and points forward to him. If Moses had not put a veil on his face, the Israelites in the wilderness would have seen the glory of Christ in his face. If it were not for the veil on their hearts to-day, the Jews would see Christ when the Law is read to them. Just as Moses put on a veil when speaking to the people, so when he is read to the people to-day there is a veil on their hearts. But when Moses turned back to the tabernacle to speak to Christ the veil was removed. So when a Jew turns to Christ to-day the veil is removed from his heart. And in this new dispensation of grace all Christians stand where Moses stood and can see Christ openly.

Romans 10
The last passage which we expound at length as evidence of the activity of the pre-existent Christ in OT times according to Paul's belief constitutes virtually the whole of Romans 10. It is therefore too long to quote *in extenso*, but we will be quoting many verses from it. It is the chapter which represents perhaps the core of Paul's argument about the transition from old Israel to the Christian Church, and it is full of deliberate citations of the OT. The aim of our treatment in this chapter is to show that Paul's meaning is clarified if we assume Christ is speaking in most of the OT quotations, and that the rest either refer to, or are directly addressed to, Christ.

This chapter of Romans is one which has given most scope to those scholars to whom we referred in chapter 1, who cannot bring themselves to believe that Paul really used all these OT quotations as proofs of his argument, and who therefore bring forward all sorts of explanations aimed at representing the quotations as illustrations or even as mere decorations. This is what Sanday and Headlam do when faced with Romans 10.5-8:

> Moses writes that the man who practises the righteousness which is based on the law shall live by it. But the righteousness based on faith says, Do not say in your heart, "Who shall ascend into heaven?" (that is, to bring Christ down) or "Who will descend into the abyss?" (that is, to bring Christ up from the dead). But what does it say? The word is near you, on your lips and in your heart (that is, the word of faith which we preach).

They write as follows of the words "the righteousness based on faith says": "It is noticeable that Paul does not introduce these words on the authority of Scripture . . . nor of Moses . . . but merely as a declaration of righteousness in its own nature."[47] This seems totally unjustified: if the previous verse may be allowed to be Moses' description of legal righteousness, it seems absurd to deny that this is an equally authoritative description of righteousness through Christ. Indeed the formula of introduction, far from conveying less authority, probably hints at a greater authority than Moses. "The righteousness based on faith", when represented as speaking, probably meant to Paul nothing less than Christ himself speaking in the words of Deuteronomy. This is how Deuteronomy 30.11-14 runs:

> For this commandment which I command you this day is not too hard for you, neither is it far off. It is not in heaven, that you should say "Who will go up for us to heaven and bring it to us, that we may hear it and do it?" Neither is it beyond the sea, that you should say, "Who will go over the sea for us, and bring it to us, that we may hear it and do it?" But the word is very near you; it is in your mouth and in your heart, so that you can do it.

It is not far-fetched to suggest that Paul would see this as an utterance of Christ through Moses to the children of Israel in the wilderness. He who had given them the Law through Moses is also telling them of the dispensation of faith which is ultimately to supersede it. Compare Romans 6.13-19, where Paul first speaks of Christians yielding their members to God as instruments of righteousness, and then later writes: "so now yield your members to righteousness for sanctification". Righteousness seems to stand for God. Moreover only a few verses earlier than the passage in chapter 10 which we are examining, Paul has written (10.3,4):

> For being ignorant of the righteousness that comes from God and seeking to establish their own, they did not submit to God's righteousness. For Christ is the end of the law . . . etc.

The word for "submit" is most appropriately used of obeying a person, and "submitting to righteousness" here no doubt means obeying Christ. Compare also 1 Corinthians 1.30, where Paul says that Christ is made our righteousness.

Sanday and Headlam, however, continue explaining away Paul's scriptural proofs as scriptural allusions or illustrations throughout this chapter. Thus, for example, they explain the citation of Psalm 19.4 in verse 18 in the following terms: "Paul wishes to express a well-known fact in suitable terms." Nygren in exactly the same way writes: "So widely has the word been proclaimed that when Paul wants to state the fact he can do so in the words of Psalm 19."[48] L. Venard describes in the same way the citation of Isaiah 52.7 in 10.15 as "a simple adaptation of a biblical text without any idea of a scriptural proof".[49] It is indeed surprising that Paul should have gone to all this trouble to quote texts from the OT, some of which would at first sight seem to have very little connection with his argument, if he intended to use them only as convenient methods of expressing what he intended to say, much as Victorian and Edwardian divines used to quote Tennyson from the pulpit by way of illustration and adornment to their discourse. One suspects that these commentators fight shy of the idea that these might have been intended as proof texts by Paul, because they are bewildered by the conclusion that must follow if this is the case, namely that Paul's way of understanding the OT was extremely different from that which the rise of biblical criticism has compelled us to adopt to-day.

We proceed then to expound this chapter on the assumption

that Paul meant his OT citations to prove his argument, and not merely to illustrate it. As a sort of title to his theme comes verse 4:

> For Christ is the end of the law, that every one who has faith may be justified.

Paul then quotes Moses' summary of legal righteousness from Leviticus 18.5. Paul has already treated of this text in Galatians 3.12, where, as we have maintained elsewhere,[50] it is most certainly a proof text, for it helps to show that Christ did not live by legal righteousness but by faith. We take the phrase "But the righteousness based on faith says" as an indirect way of expressing "But Christ says", and we suggest that Paul looked on this word from Deuteronomy as originally uttered by Christ. Paul inserts in the passage we have quoted from Deuteronomy 30 two glosses: "that is, to bring Christ down", and "that is, to bring Christ up from the dead". The point is that the Christian does not need to attempt to save himself: incarnation and resurrection are to be God's work. Kirk is therefore completely off the track when he accuses Paul here of "drastic and unwarrantable allegorising".[51] Far from using allegory, Paul is not even using typology. He simply sees Christ speaking to Israel in this OT passage. Lietzmann relevantly points out that Paul has substituted the personified "Righteousness" for the original phrase in Deuteronomy "this commandment".[52] This gains greater significance if we assume that according to Paul Christ originally gave the commandment and was himself the "Righteousness" speaking here.

Then verse 8 explains the meaning of Deuteronomy 30.14: "The word is near you, on your lips and in your heart". Paul explains it as "the word of faith which we preach". This is the same as the "preaching of Christ" in verse 17 (the two phrases are more closely parallel in the Greek: τὸ ῥῆμα τῆς πίστεως and διὰ ῥήματος Χριστοῦ). Here then we seem to have an utterance of Christ in OT times. How far the words were believed by Paul to be applicable only to the future, it is very difficult to say. C. H. Dodd *à propos* 10.6 remarks: "All through we are left in some doubt whether Paul means that in the time of the prophets the

Gospel was declared to the Jews and rejected by all but the 'Remnant', or whether the prophets foretold the preaching of the Gospel, which was actually carried out by the apostles of Christ. Paul, we may suppose, would have said that both these were true."[53] This is a wise conclusion, but one might add that the real presence of Christ in the chosen people of old would suggest that the gospel of faith was in some sense apprehensible to Israel of old. We have already observed in our discussion of 2 Corinthians 3 that in Paul's view Moses must have known all about Christ. This must surely be our conclusion about this Deuteronomy passage also. In his article already quoted from *Theology* R. P. C. Hanson takes just this view: "Paul clearly thinks of Moses as speaking about the word of faith in Christ, as in some sense 'a minister of the word'." This latter conclusion does not necessarily follow, since, as we shall see, Paul can quite easily write "Moses says" when he means "Christ says through Moses".

In verses 12 and 13 we may take it as a matter of course that "Lord" refers to Christ, not to the Father. This is accepted by most editors, though not by J. A. Beet. Dodd remarks of verse 12: "Wherever the term *Kyrios*, Lord, is applied to Jehovah in the OT, Paul seems to hold that it points forward to the coming revelation of God in the Lord Jesus Christ." This is at once too sweeping and too tame. Paul as he read his LXX did not always identify *Kyrios* with Christ. To take two examples at random, in Romans 9.28 and 11.3 occur quotations containing the word *Kyrios* where we have no reason to believe that Paul thought of it as meaning Christ. Again, in Paul's view, *Kyrios* where it meant Christ did not point forward to him. It indicated that Christ was present in OT times. Jülicher has an alternative explanation:[54] he suggests that Paul took the view that any exegesis which could illuminate God's salvation in Christ was justified. But this is unjust to Paul; he was not trying to fit the OT to Christ; he genuinely believed that he found Christ there.

So far what we have found in chapter 10 of Romans is Christ foretelling his incarnation and resurrection (verses 6 and 7), proclaiming the message of faith in himself as a present Saviour (verse 8), and announcing the universal salvation through his name that is to be available at the end time (verses 11-13). Now in verses 14-21 Paul seems to suggest that Israel had the opportunity all along of hearing Christ and believing in him. It is still possible, of course, that all the OT citations here are thought of as only being fulfilled in the end time. Only in the end time, for instance, did the Gentiles come to acknowledge Christ, and this is the point of the citation of Isaiah 65.1 in verse 20, as Paul makes clear by contrasting in the next verse what was said to Israel. But even so, the prophets who uttered these words knew their meaning, and must be regarded as being in the same situation as Moses in 2 Corinthians 3: they knew Christ and they knew what was to happen to him in the end time. And one cannot help feeling that it was at least theoretically possible, according to Paul, for all Israel to have known what the prophets knew. The prophets, after all, did not put a veil on their faces, even though there was a veil on the hearts of the Israelites who heard their words.

In verse 15, then, Paul quotes Isaiah 52.7 in order to prove that in Isaiah's time there were those who preached the gospel. It is clear that by the words "those who preach good news" Paul understands the preaching of the gospel, because he refers to it in verse 16 as "the gospel". He follows this reference in verse 16 by another citation of Isaiah:

Lord, who has believed what he has heard from us?

The words "what he has heard" represent only two words in Greek: τῇ ἀκοῇ literally "the hearing", and in verse 17 this is explicitly identified with "the preaching of Christ". But here also the RSV is slightly ambiguous, for the Greek is *rhēmatos Christou*, literally "the word of Christ", which might mean just a word uttered by Christ as well as the gospel about Christ. The simplest way of understanding Paul's citation of Isaiah 53.1 is to take it as uttered by the prophet to Christ. Isaiah has been proclaiming the gospel and no one has believed him. "Lord" is of course Christ here, and here then is a clear example of Christ and prophet conversing in OT times according to Paul. It is very interesting, however, that Justin interprets this sentence as uttered by the Son to the Father.[55] This is not an interpretation which we can dismiss at once. It would give full significance to "the word of Christ" in the next verse. The fact that Paul introduces the quotation with the words "for Isaiah says" does not necessarily imply that Paul thought them to be Isaiah's words and not Christ's. Justin, for example, introduces the citation himself with the words: "When he [sc. Christ] says through Isaiah"; and we shall be seeing in connection with verses 19–21 below that these verses must be attributed to Christ even though Paul formally assigns them to Moses and Isaiah respectively. On the whole, however, there is not sufficient evidence to justify us in saying that Paul believed the Son was addressing the Father in Isaiah 53.1. It is simpler to look on it as the prophet addressing Christ. It is interesting to note that Jülicher considers that, according to Paul, the prophet is addressing Christ in Isaiah 52.7.

Paul, as we have seen, has quoted Isaiah 52.7 in one verse and 53.1 in the next. In between these verses in the OT lies a passage which he must have read carefully, and which he must have regarded as providing a full proclamation of the gospel. It is studded with sentences which to his mind could apply to Christ and no one else. Thus the second half of Isaiah 52.7 in the LXX runs:

> For I will make known thy salvation saying,
> "Sion, thy God shall reign."

And again

> v. 10: And *Kyrios* will reveal his holy arm before all the nations, and all the ends of the earth shall see the salvation from God.
> v. 13: Behold my servant shall understand, and shall be exalted and greatly glorified.
> v. 15b: ... because those to whom no proclamation concerning him came shall see,
> and those who did not hear shall understand.

Incidentally, a consideration of this passage should serve to show how rash it is to conclude that Paul did not think of Jesus as the Servant of Isaiah 52—3. Indeed, only the assumption that Paul read his OT in isolated *Testimonia* could lead to such a conclusion. In fact, all the evidence goes to show that Paul studied the Scriptures for himself; he did not need the early Church to predigest them and present them to him in tabloid form.

Now follows proof of what the passage just discussed (Isa. 52.7—53.1) has clearly indicated, that the gospel is to be preached to all the world. The proof is to our minds bizarre in the extreme, so much so that, as we have seen, many editors have tried to explain it away as a mere adaptation of familiar words taken right out of their context. This we cannot accept, for the reasons we have given above. We must therefore ask ourselves the question which we accused the commentators of a former generation of evading: Why did Paul think that a citation of Psalm 19.4 proved that the gospel was to be preached throughout the world?

> Their voice has gone out to all the earth,
> and their words to the end of the world.

We must look at Psalm 19 in the LXX (where it is Psalm 18). It begins with the title *eis to telos*. This is literally "unto the end", and is the LXX translators' rendering of a Hebrew phrase which may mean "to the choirmaster" (*sic* RSV) or else "for propitiation" (*sic* Mowinckel). It is a Psalm which is much more concerned with the Law, and only fourteen verses above Paul has described Christ as the *telos* of the Law. We have no reason to believe that Paul was any better informed about the real meaning of this Psalm title than were the translators of the LXX (or, for that matter, than are modern scholars, who are reduced to guesswork). It is not therefore absurd to suggest that Paul would see a deep meaning in this title: it is a Psalm that is concerned with the end time, or with the end of the Law, which is Christ. At any rate in verse 4 Paul sees the theme of Isaiah 52—53, the proclamation of the gospel to the world. Then in verse 5 comes a reference to a bridegroom:[56]

> which comes forth like a bridegroom leaving his chamber.

Perhaps Paul would here see a reference to Christ's coming into the world. We know Jesus did compare himself to a bridegroom

(Mark 2.19 sq.; cf. John 3.29), and Paul uses the metaphor (though not the word) in 2 Corinthians 11.2. (Cf. also Eph. 5. 22–33; Rev. 19.7–9; 21.2.) Then in verse 7 Paul would read in the LXX:

> The witness of *Kyrios* is faithful, making wise little children (*nēpia*).

This would speak to Paul of the gospel, in which God's faithfulness is fulfilled and his strange wisdom displayed (cf. 1 Cor. 1.6, 9, 18 sq.; 2 Cor. 1.18–22). We might even cite verse 9:

> the ordinances of *Kyrios* are true,
> justified all together.

This is the LXX's clumsy translation of the Hebrew, which is better rendered by the RSV:

> the ordinances of the Lord are true and righteous altogether.

But the LXX translation might indicate to Paul the strange righteousness of Christ.

Further confirmation of this suggestion about Paul's understanding of Psalm 19 comes from the early Fathers, some of whom take Psalm 19 in a christological sense. In *Dialogue* 42.1 and *Apology* I.40[57] Justin takes this Psalm as a prophecy of the apostolic preaching. Compare also *Dialogue* 64, where he implies that the glory of God which the heavens declare is Christ. Why should this not also have been in Paul's mind? As we have seen for him *doxa* (glory) = *Sh^{e}kinah* = Christ, as we have suggested à propos 2 Corinthians 3. In none of these references from Justin can we be sure that Justin is influenced by Paul; it may be part of his tradition to find Christ active in the OT. But even if he is inspired only by Paul's interpretation, it shows at least that Justin took Paul literally; he accepted these OT texts as proofs not just as illustrations.

We could also refer to Tertullian, *Adversus Marcionem* IV.11.7 in confirmation of this interpretation of the Psalm. What he writes is this:

> I find my Christ even in the name of "bridegroom", about whom the Psalm says: "He is like a bridegroom coming forth from his chamber."

In view of this, we must reject Bonsirven's suggestion that the problem created by Paul's quotation of Psalm 19 can be solved by that blessed word "typology". He writes as follows: "We reach the extreme limits of typology when we apply the universal hymn of creation (Ps. 19.5) to the apostolic preaching spreading throughout the whole world."[58] However Paul interpreted Psalm 19, he did not interpret it typologically. In it he found Christ, not a type of Christ.

Paul now turns to a possible objection that might be raised: "Granted that God was going to make the gospel of Jesus Christ known to all the world, but did Israel have any means of knowing this? Did God warn them about this?" Paul proceeds to prove that they were warned by quoting Deuteronomy 32.22. We must reproduce verses 18-21 from the LXX:

> Thou hast left God who begat thee
> and hast forgotten God who nourished thee.
> And *Kyrios* saw and was jealous,
> and was provoked because of the rage of his sons and daughters.[59]
> And he said, I will turn my face from them,
> and will show what will be their fate in the last times (*ep' eschatōn*);
> For they are a perverse generation,
> sons in whom there is no faith.
> They have made me jealous with a no-god,
> they have provoked me with their idols.
> So I shall make them jealous with a no-people,
> by means of a people without understanding will I provoke them.

If we assume that Paul envisaged Christ as speaking in verses 19-21, we will find much that would seem significant to him. Verse 18b "and hast forgotten God who nourished thee" would seem to him to be a reference to Christ's feeding of the people in the wilderness with manna, which we have traced in 1 Corinthians 10. The provocation of *Kyrios* referred to in verse 19 fits in very well with 1 Corinthians 10.9: "We must not put the Lord to the test". Indeed Deuteronomy 32.21 is actually quoted in 1 Corinthians 10.22: "Shall we provoke the Lord to jealousy?" In both these passages in 1 Corinthians 10 the Lord to whom Paul refers is undoubtedly Christ, so it is hard to resist the conclusion that his second reference to the same passage in Romans 10.19 should also be referred to Christ. Next, in Deuteronomy 32.20b Paul would find a reference to the last days, the days of the Messiah: "I will show what will be their fate in the last times". Indeed the reference to the conversion of the Gentiles, which is what Paul actually cites this whole passage in order to prove, shows what this last verse meant to Paul. The last two lines of verse 20 in the Deuteronomy passage actually remind us of an utterance of Jesus himself: "O faithless generation" (Mark 9.19). The version of this logion in the First Gospel (Matt. 17.17) makes the cross-reference even clearer: "O faithless and perverse generation." It looks very much as if this passage from Deuteronomy may have been considered a messianic one in the early Church. For Paul, there can be very little doubt, the phrase "sons in whom there is no faith" could refer to faith in Christ and nothing else. It seems inevitable, therefore, to conclude that in Paul's view it was possible to have faith in Christ in Moses' day.

It is worth noticing that Paul introduces this quotation with the words: "First Moses says." But most of the passage to which he refers is certainly a divine utterance, of God's if not of Christ's, in particular the line which he actually quotes. This shows that the attribution of an utterance to Moses, or David, or Isaiah does not inhibit Paul from regarding the utterance as God's or Christ's. As E. E. Ellis well remarks: " 'The Scripture says', 'God says', and 'Isaiah says' are for Paul only different ways of expressing the same thing."[60]

In Romans 10.20,21 Paul ends by quoting two verses from Isaiah which we must translate in full from the LXX:

I have revealed myself to those who did not seek me,
I have been found by those who did not enquire for me;
I have said, Here am I, to a nation that did not call upon my name;
I have stretched out my hands all the day long to a disobedient and
    contradictory people,
who have not gone in the right way, but after their own sins.

In its context in Isaiah this is a declaration that God has always been ready to reveal himself to Israel, always eagerly sought their return; but they have not sought him and have ignored his advances. Paul does here as he does in Romans 9.25,26, and as the author of 1 Peter does in 1 Peter 2.10, he interprets a passage originally referring to Israel as referring to the Gentiles—or, to be more exact, to the mixed Jewish-Gentile Church. It seems quite plain that in Romans 10 Paul takes the first three lines of this quotation as uttered by Christ of the Gentiles, and the last two lines as uttered by Christ of the unbelieving Jews. It must be Christ who speaks, not God the Father, for in the days of the Messiah the Jews did not cease to believe in God the Father; it was Christ in whom they failed to believe. Indeed one might conjecture, though the evidence does not permit a definite conclusion, that Paul saw the words "I have stretched out my hands all day long" as a specific reference to the Cross. This is how the Epistle of Barnabas understands Isaiah 65.2.[61] We must give considerable weight to this testimony, whether we take it as inspired by Romans 10.21, or as a piece of original exegesis.

To sum up the conclusions we have drawn from Paul's OT citations in Romans 10: according to Paul, Christ spoke in OT times to Moses, to David, and to Isaiah, proclaiming a gospel of faith in himself, and commissioning them to preach this faith, and foretelling his incarnation, cross, resurrection, and the accession of the Gentiles. Faith and unbelief in Christ, acceptance or rejection of the gospel of faith in Christ, these must all have been in some sense possible in OT times as well as in the new dispensation. All these citations are designed to prove, not only that Israel for the most part had unjustifiably rejected their Messiah under Pontius Pilate, but even more that this rejection has been taking place in OT times as well, and that Israel could have recognized Christ at certain points in OT history, and even that certain individuals did recognize him.

Strange as this interpretation of the OT may seem to us, it is not really fair to characterize it as arbitrary or eclectic, as some scholars have done. It is emphatically not Rabbinic: Paul does not play with texts from the OT (at least in his references to Christ) as the Rabbis do, making puns and putting together sentences from different parts of Scripture that have no integral connection. Once grant Paul his one great assumption, that Christ spoke and acted in OT times, and his interpretation becomes homogeneous and comprehensible. This is not the place to ask whether his interpretation is the right one, or to to inquire how he acquired this method of interpretation. But he should be defended from the charge of arbitrary interpretation. In his tradition of exegesis he was neither a solitary pioneer nor an irrational crank. We may add for good measure that, as far as the passages we have considered in this work so far are concerned, he was not a typologist either.

3

Christ in the Old Testament according to the Epistle to the Hebrews

Apparently no one has ever suggested that the thought of the pre-existent Christ active in OT history is to be found in the Epistle to the Hebrews. But it is the main contention of this chapter that this belief is implied in the OT exposition of the author to the Hebrews, and that it occurs not just once but throughout the Epistle. Indeed, relative to the size of his work, the author to the Hebrews shows more evidence of this belief than any other writer in the NT.

Hebrews 3.1–6

> Therefore, holy brethren, who share in a heavenly call, consider Jesus, the apostle and high priest of our confession. He was faithful to him who appointed him, just as Moses also was faithful in God's house [Greek "his house"]. Yet Jesus has been counted worthy of as much more glory than Moses as the builder of a house has more honor than the house. (For every house is built by some one, but the builder of all things is God.) Now Moses was faithful in all God's house as a servant, to testify to the things that were to be spoken later, but Christ was faithful over God's house [Greek "his house"] as a son. And we are his house if we hold fast our confidence and pride in our hope.

As many commentators have realized, for a full understanding of this passage we must turn back to Numbers 12.1–15, the incident to which this passage refers. Here surely there can be no question of the author relying on isolated *Testimonia* for his OT citations:

Numbers 12.1-15 by itself makes a very strange *testimonium* to Christ. We must assume that the author read the whole passage in Numbers. It will be sufficient for our purpose if we translate from the LXX Numbers 12.4-8. The situation is that Aaron and Miriam have challenged Moses' action in marrying an Ethiopian wife. They exclaim: "Has the Lord indeed spoken only through Moses? Has he not spoken through us also?" The Lord hears this, and the narrative proceeds as follows:

> And *Kyrios* immediately said to Moses and Miriam and Aaron: "Come out, you three, into the tent of testimony." And *Kyrios* came down in the pillar of cloud and stood at the door of the tent of testimony, and Aaron and Miriam were called and both went forth. And he said to them: "Hear my words: if there shall be a prophet of yours to *Kyrios*, I shall make myself known to him in a vision, and in a dream I shall speak to him. Not so is my minister Moses; he is faithful in all my house. Face to face shall I speak to him, openly and not by oracles, and he has seen the glory of *Kyrios* (καὶ τὴν δόξαν Κυρίου εἶδεν). And why were you not afraid to speak against my minister Moses?"

Let us suppose for a moment that the author to the Hebrews was inclined to trace the presence of the pre-existent Christ in OT history; we can see at once how clearly he would recognize that presence here. God is called *Kyrios* throughout (except once where Moses addresses him as *ho Theos* in prayer). His presence is manifested in the pillar of cloud, which we have shown reason to believe was understood by Paul to have been a manifestation of the pre-existent Christ. Above all, Moses is to see *Kyrios* face to face, openly. The Greek is *en eidei*, in his real form. The temptation to apply these words to Christ rather than to the ineffable Father would have been very strong for the author with his Philonic background. The conclusion that he did so apply it is made even more likely by the words: "and he has seen the glory of *Kyrios*". Exactly these words are used by the author of the Fourth Gospel to describe Isaiah's vision of the glory of the Lord in the Temple; see John 12.41: "he saw his glory". And we remember Paul's identification of Christ with the glory or

Sh*e*kinah of God. Incidentally, this citation of Numbers 12.7 must put a question mark against W. L. Knox's assertion that, according to Paul, Moses only saw dimly (δι' αἰνιγμάτων). Commenting on 1 Corinthians 13.12, he writes: "Here, like the prophets, he (man) had only glimpses of God seen as in a mirror through riddles; naturally Moses' vision was no better."[1] In Numbers 12.8 we have the explicit denial of this. God will speak with Moses ἐν εἴδει καὶ οὐ δι' αἰνιγμάτων, literally "in real form, not in riddles". Moses therefore saw the Lord face to face.

We proceed therefore to read Hebrews 3.1–6 on the assumption that it was Christ whom Moses saw face to face in the tabernacle, and who spoke to him there. When we do so, many of the obscurities in this passage vanish. In verse 2, as many editors acknowledge, "him who appointed him" (τῷ ποιήσαντι αὐτόν) cannot mean "him who made him", for it seems wildly unlikely in view of the whole of chapter 1 of the Epistle that the author regarded Christ as a created being. We must take the verb in the sense of "appointed". We notice also that Christ's faithfulness is emphasized here, and we may legitimately ask: In what was this faithfulness manifested? It was shown at least in Christ's life and ministry. But we must bear in mind the possibility that his faithfulness was also shown in the pre-incarnate activity of the Messiah in the house of Israel.

Christ was faithful to God, as was Moses in his house. Whose house? The RSV, followed by most editors, assumes that it is God's house, but of course the Greek does not require this meaning. That is undoubtedly the sense of Numbers 12.7. But we cannot assume that this is how our author understood Numbers 12. On the contrary, it seems more likely in the context of Hebrews 3.2 that "in his house" means "in Christ's house". The word "his" would more naturally refer to the subject of the last "him", which is certainly Christ, "that appointed him". It would be difficult grammar to skip over "him" and refer it to "him who appointed". If "his house" in verse 2 is referred to God and not to Christ, then we must assume that our author has two houses in mind, the house of Israel in the OT (God's house), and the spiritual house of the NT, the Christian Church (Christ's house). But can we legitimately introduce into this passage the idea of two houses? Despite the fact that the majority of scholars have done so, it seems a most precarious conclusion. It would mean in verses 5 and 6 interpreting "in all his house" of God's house, and "over his house" as Christ's house. The RSV has obscured this point by translating in verse 5 the Greek καὶ Μωϋσῆς μὲν πιστὸς ἐν ὅλῳ τῷ οἴκῳ αὐτοῦ ὡς θεράπων as "Now Moses was faithful in all God's house as a servant" without explaining as it does elsewhere that the word "God" is not in the Greek. When we move on to verse 3, we at once find confirmation of the suggestion that "his house" in verse 2 is Christ's house. Christ is worthy of greater honour just as he who constructed the house is worthy of greater honour than the house itself. It seems impossible to refer "the builder of a house" here to anyone except Christ. The analogy demands it. In verse 5 Moses' position as a servant in the house is contrasted with Christ's. Now, if in verse 3 Christ is thought of only as the builder of a new house, the Church, and not of the whole house of Israel, then we have the strange comparison: Christ is greater than Moses inasmuch as the builder of one house is more important than another house (old Israel, with which alone Moses can be connected). We seem thus to be reduced to two alternatives:

(*a*) "the builder" in verse 3 is Christ, and there is only one house, the Jewish-Christian Church continuous from Moses to the epoch in which the author is writing.

(*b*) "the builder" is God the Father. This is a desperate alternative, since, as we have seen, it cuts right across the analogy. But it is adopted by Westcott,[2] who suggests that Christ's superiority is implied in the fact that he is the Son of God. But in that case surely the author to the Hebrews would have written: "in as much as the son of the builder has more glory than the house"— a doubtful analogy in any case.

Windisch has got nearer to the true sense of this passage:[3] he insists that "the builder" in verse 3 is Christ, and that "house" throughout refers to the Israel-Christian Church looked on as one continuous entity. Verse 4 will thus become something of a parenthesis, but a parenthesis the point of which we can see. The author has just implied that it was Christ who built the house of Israel, but he is anxious not to suggest that this excludes God the Father; on the contrary, God is the author of the whole dispensation. He acts through Christ throughout, just as he acts through Christ in the great act of reconciliation on the Cross in 2 Corinthians 5.18–21. We can see therefore why our author uses the slightly unusual word *kataskeuazein* for "build" here, instead of *oikodomein* or even *ktizein*. He is thinking of that spiritual house Israel old and new, and this community was not created *ex nihilo* or built up brick by brick. It was "fashioned", which is exactly what *kataskeuazein* means.[4]

Thus in verses 5 and 6 the contrast is between Moses as a minister in the house of Christ ("God's house" of the RSV being treated as a misinterpretation), and Christ as the Son in his own house. The natural reminder follows that we are that house as the true heirs of Israel.[5] One problem however remains: What is the meaning of "to testify to the things that were to be spoken later"? Windisch (followed by Moffat[6]) very acutely points out that in the Numbers passage the tabernacle is called "the tent of testimony", and that this may well have been in our author's mind when he wrote this phrase. The tent was the place where the Lord (understood here by our author as Christ) spoke to Moses face to face. Moses could therefore witness that he had seen Christ, and his witness would be confirmed in the days to come when the gospel about Christ would be preached openly. We are reminded of our discussion on 2 Corinthians 3. Most editors agree that this phrase refers to the last days. This interpretation is confirmed by 2.3:

> (such a great salvation) was declared at first by the Lord, and it was attested to us by those who heard him.

The meaning, therefore, of the phrase in verse 5 is that Moses' faithfulness to Christ during the desert sojourn was a witness pointing forward to the time when the true apostolic testimony to Christ should be given. Peake, however, suggests that the words refer to the legislation that was to follow on Sinai.[7] But we must remember that by this point in Numbers a great deal of legislation had already been given. Also, the impression we gain from Numbers 12 is that this incident took place after the theodicy on Sinai was over. Michel has still another explanation of this phrase:[8] it signifies the witness to what Moses was later to say about Christ. But in fact in the text of the Pentateuch, as we have it, there are very few passages that could be construed as messianic even by the most fervent early Christian. One can only think of Deuteronomy 18.15 (which is not quoted by our author, though it is cited as a messianic proof-text in Acts 7.37), and also various passages in the two Songs at the end of Deuteronomy. It seems, therefore, much more likely that our author had in mind the end time.

The Epistle of Barnabas has an interesting reference to Numbers 12, which may well be consciously based on Hebrews 3.1–6.[9] Barnabas 14.1 runs as follows:

> But let us see the covenant which he swore to the fathers to give to the people, whether he did give it. Yes, he gave it, but they were not worthy to receive it because of their sin. For the prophet says: "And Moses was abiding in the mountain of Sinai forty days and forty nights, in order to take the covenant of *Kyrios* to the people." And he received from *Kyrios* the two tables written with the finger of *Kyrios'* hand, in the Spirit. And *Kyrios* said to Moses: "Moses, Moses, go down quickly, for thy people whom thou didst lead out of the land of Egypt has broken the Law." And Moses realized that they had again made for themselves molten images; and he cast the tables of the covenant of *Kyrios* out of his hands and they were smashed. Now Moses received the covenant as a minister, but they did not prove worthy. But how did we receive it? Notice: Moses received it as a minister, but *Kyrios* himself gave it to us as to the people of the heritage. He waited for our sake. And he was manifested in order that they might fill up the measure of their sins, and that we might receive the covenant of Lord Jesus through him who inherited it.

We find here the belief that the first covenant, broken by Moses in his anger at the golden calf, was the true spiritual covenant, the new covenant, which Jesus ultimately brought. The second covenant was the legal one, given because of the hardness of Jewish hearts. Some scholars have traced a similar belief in Acts 7.38,39 (a passage which we discuss later on). It is clear that according to the author of the Epistle of Barnabas it was Christ who gave both covenants. He gives no hint whatever that between the *Kyrios* which he quotes from the LXX and the words "*Kyrios* himself gave it to us [Christians]" a change of subject has occurred. We notice also that he points a contrast between the way Israel received the true spiritual covenant and the way Christians received it. Israel received it indirectly, through Moses; we might describe it in the words of Paul in Galatians 3.19 "by the hand of a mediator". But the Lord himself gave it to us Christians. This contrast between Christ giving the Law in the OT indirectly and his giving it himself directly to us in the incarnation is one which we shall meet in Hebrews. We have hinted at its existence in 1 Corinthians 10.2 (the fathers were baptized into Moses), and we shall find it more clearly in the passage in Galatians just mentioned, and also in Stephen's Speech in Acts 7. What is more, the author of the Epistle of Barnabas has glossed the text of the LXX for us in order to bring out clearly its christological meaning. He inserts in Exodus 24.18 the words: "in order to take the covenant of *Kyrios* to the people". Where the LXX text says that the tables were written with the finger of God, the author of Barnabas has written "the finger of *Kyrios*' hand". In Exodus 31.18 he adds the explanatory phrase "of the covenant of *Kyrios*" to the words "the tables", and in addition says that the tables of the first covenant were written "in the Spirit". All these changes and additions seem to be made in order to bring out clearly that the first tables contained Christ's covenant. Finally, he remarks of Jesus "he waited for our sake", and this implies that it was Christ who gave the Law on Sinai, and carries with it the rider that it was Christ with whom Moses conversed on Sinai. The emphasis on Moses as the minister in this passage would appear to indicate that it was Christ also with whom Moses spoke in the tabernacle. The fact that the Epistle of Barnabas, like the Epistle to the

Hebrews, shows traces of Alexandrian influence makes it a weighty witness when we seek to understand Hebrews' method of interpreting the OT.

Much later, Tertullian can be cited as another witness to the view that it was Christ with whom Moses spoke in the tabernacle. In *Adversus Marcionem* IV.22.15 he quotes Numbers 12.6 and comments as follows:

> And if there shall be a prophet among you, I shall make myself known to him in a vision, and in a vision shall I speak to him; not as I do to Moses. Face to face shall I speak to him, in real form (that is, in the form of a man which he was to assume), not in an oracle.

Tertullian, of course, interprets this passage as a prophecy of the Transfiguration, but the point to notice for our present purpose is that he assumes the identity of the Presence who spoke to Moses with the pre-existent Christ.

As we have observed, no modern commentator has suggested that in Hebrews 3.1–6 Moses is understood to have been the minister and interlocutor of Christ. Hollmann has an acute discussion of the passage.[10] Like Windisch, he recognizes that Christ is the builder in verse 3, and he writes that Christ is "founder of the OT theocracy as a pre-existent Being". He adds: "Moses could only hint at that which would one day be made known through the Son", but he does not seem to realize that, according to this passage, Moses saw Christ. T. Robinson approaches Hollmann's position when he writes: "Seen *sub specie aeternitatis* even Moses derived his position and his authority from his relation to, and from his appointment by, the eternal Christ."[11] But one cannot help suspecting that the Latin phrase covers a certain vagueness about what exactly the author to the Hebrews believed about Moses' relation to Christ. Spicq supposes that we have in this passage a contrast between the authority of the Church and the authority of old Israel. He writes: "The Church being superior to Israel, its founder has more glory than the chief of the Hebrew people."[12] But our author does not say, "Christ is superior to

Moses because the builder of the new house is superior to the builder of the old", which is what Spicq's interpretation presupposes. Bonsirven[13] and Bultmann[14] both assume that here Moses is a type of Christ. This is quite impossible if Christ is conceived as actually speaking to Moses. As we have had occasion to remark before, Christ and his type cannot both be present at the same time.

Sverre Aalen, in an article called " 'Reign' and 'House' in the Kingdom of God",[15] has recently argued that Hebrews 3.1–6 is as much influenced by the account of God's promise to David narrated in 1 Chronicles 17 as by the Numbers passage. The same view is defended by Canon Synge.[16] Dr Aalen points out that the Targum on 1 Chronicles 17.10 "the Lord will build you a house" has inserted the word "sure" before "house", thus showing that it means a dynasty not a building. In 1 Chronicles 17.12 Solomon (described as David's offspring) is to build God's house, and in the next verse Solomon is described as God's son. Aalen would therefore derive the epithet "faithful" in Hebrews 3.2 not from Numbers 12, but from the Targum on 1 Chronicles 17.10, and he maintains that it is because of the reference to the son building the house in the 1 Chronicles passage that in Hebrews 3.1–6 both the Father and the Son are described as building the house of Israel. He concludes: "In this way we also find the explanation of the curious idea that both Christ and God are the builder of the house, verses 3 and 4. Both could be read in the OT text... The motif of the faithful Son who is the builder of God's house and is in God's house is exactly what we find in Targum 2 Samuel 7.12–14."

Dr Aalen presumably means to imply that the author of Hebrews saw in 2 Samuel 7 (and in its parallel 1 Chronicles 17) a messianic prophecy, whereby it was possible to envisage both God and the Messiah as builders of the house of Israel. We note that this is not incompatible with the interpretation of Hebrews 3.1–6 which we have suggested, i.e. that the inspiration is Numbers 12.1–15, and Dr Aalen himself admits a reference to the Numbers passage. Moreover, his interpretation does assume that the author has only one house in mind throughout, as we have argued. But even so it seems rather gratuitous to seek the explanation for the word "faithful" in a Targum which applies the word not to Moses or to the Messiah, but to the house, especially when we have a specific passage in Numbers where the word is explicitly applied to Moses. We do not know whether the author of Hebrews was acquainted with the Targums, or with whatever was the predecessor of the Targums in his day. All the evidence goes to show that he read his OT in Greek and not in Hebrew. Again, whatever else Hebrews 3.1-6 is trying to say, it *is* trying to say something about Moses, and there is no reference to Moses in either 2 Samuel 7 or 1 Chronicles 17. It seems to me much more likely that our author is thinking only of Numbers 12, and that the reference to the Father as being the ultimate founder (in verse 4) is motivated by a desire not to seem to be excluding God just because Christ is represented as the true founder of Israel of old.

To sum up our interpretation of this passage: our author finds Christ referred to in Numbers 12 where the LXX reads *Kyrios*; he concludes that Moses was faithful in all Christ's house (old Israel), and that he saw Christ face to face. Christ's faithfulness therefore deserves more honour that that of Moses, because it was Christ who actually built the house of Israel by calling Jacob's descendants into covenant with himself on Sinai, whereas Moses merely served within the house. It is, of course, God who is ultimately behind this calling, but God acts through Christ in OT times as well as under the new dispensation. Moses' faithfulness to the Christ with whom he spoke in the tabernacle is a witness pointing forward to the time when that same Christ should speak the words of salvation in the flesh, and be himself proclaimed by those who had seen him in the flesh. But it is Christ's faithfulness as Son over his own house that we Christians are to imitate now that the old house of Israel has become the spiritual house made of living stones, the Christian Church. This is therefore one of the places where the belief that Christ appeared among the children of Israel in OT times is integral to the author's argument.

Hebrews 4.1–9

Ideally the theme of "Christ in the OT according to Hebrews" would take the form of a running commentary on the text of the entire Epistle. The argument, at least from 1.1 to 4.13, is so closely knit, and the leading ideas recur so frequently, that it is very difficult to isolate one passage. This is specially true of the section we are now to examine. The citation of Psalm 95 harks back to its citation in chapter 3; the emphasis on the urgency of the crisis is taken up again in 4.10–13. It would be very awkward, however, to treat the whole of chapters 3 and 4 as our next passage, and the core of the argument with which we are concerned is to be found in 4.1–9.

Before we actually quote any verses at length, we might well observe the remarkable resemblance of theme between these chapters and 1 Corinthians 10.1–13. In both Paul and Hebrews the example of disobedient Israel in the desert is quoted as a warning to Christians prone to disobedience and grumbling. In both the example is quoted as a warning, in the hope that the same situation will *not* develop in the Christian Church. In both it is made clear that ancient Israel did know Christ and could have received his grace. In both (as I hope to show) Christ is envisaged as actually present and active in the history of the OT people. What the significance of this is for our understanding of the earliest Christian catechesis, we have not space here to consider. But it seems most likely that we have here a favourite element in that catechesis.

In 4.2 we have a surprising inversion of what we would expect: we would quite understand if the author had said that the Israelites of old had heard the gospel, just as we have. In fact he says that we too have heard the gospel, just as they had. It is almost as if he had to prove that Christians really had heard the gospel, whereas no one would dispute that the Israelites of old had heard it. Chapter 4.1,2 runs thus:

> Therefore, while the promise of entering his rest remains, let us fear lest any of you be judged to have failed to reach it. For good news came to us (καὶ γάρ ἐσμεν εὐηγγελισμένοι) just as to them; but the

message which they heard (ὁ λόγος τῆς ἀκοῆς) did not benefit them, because it did not meet with faith in the hearers.

The RSV by translating "good news came to them" rather blunts the point here. It was not just any good news that Christians and ancient Israelites had in common, it was the gospel, the knowledge of Christ. This is made certain by the phrase "the message which they heard" in verse 2. This phrase occurs elsewhere in the NT exactly in this form only in 1 Thessalonians 2.13, where the context makes it absolutely plain that it means the preaching of the gospel. But in other places also "hearing" (Greek *akoē* translated by RSV "which they heard") indicates the gospel. Thus in Romans 10.16,17 Paul writes:

> But they have not all heeded the gospel: for Isaiah says: "Lord, who has believed what he has heard (*tē akoē*) from us?" So faith comes from what is heard (*ex akoēs*), and what is heard comes by the preaching of Christ.

We have maintained in our last chapter (p. 40 above) that Paul in the Romans passage envisages Isaiah as actually preaching a gospel about Christ which demands the response of faith. For *akoē* compare also Galatians 3.2, where the RSV translates ἐξ ἀκοῆς πίστεως as "by hearing with faith", and the context shows that it must mean hearing the gospel. Even more relevant is John 12.38 (a passage which we examine in chapter 5 below). There Isaiah 53.1 is quoted and the evangelist goes on to say quite explicitly that Isaiah's report was based on his having actually seen Christ.

We must therefore conclude that, according to the author to the Hebrews, the Israelites of old had heard the gospel of Christ and could have responded to it with faith, though in fact most of them failed to do so. The question must arise: When was this? In Hebrews 3.1–6 we have seen Moses acting as Christ's minister, but when could the Israelites have heard about Christ? I think the only conclusion can be that the author thought of Christ as uttering most of Psalm 95 on which he lays so much emphasis in this passage. Probably the reference to God's voice led him in this direction: "Today, when you hear his voice . . .". The quotation is in 3.7 attributed to the Holy Spirit, but we must bear in mind that the verb changes from third person to first person in 3.9, and also that our author could have had no difficulty in imagining Christ speaking through the Holy Spirit, as he spoke through Moses or David or Isaiah. We shall be seeking to show later on in this chapter that in 12.26 the author interprets the voice of God on Sinai as an utterance of Christ. Again, the introduction of Christ's name in 3.14 with nothing but "for" as a link suggests that the author has had in mind Christ as the object of faith throughout the whole passage. I would go so far as to say that this applies even to the phrase "the living God" in verse 12. We observe how Psalm 95 is introduced again in 3.15 without any indication that we are now to think of faith in God rather than in Christ. Indeed grammatical consistency would require that "his voice" in verse 15 should refer to "Christ" in verse 14; and if so "was he provoked" in verse 17 must refer to Christ also. There is nothing whatever surprising in the thought of Christ as the speaker in Psalm 95, since in 10.5 sq. our author attributes Psalm 40.6–8 to the Son, in the course of which the Son addresses the Father, explaining the meaning of his offering of himself. We do not suggest, of course, that the author thinks of the pre-existent Christ as having uttered Psalm 95 on Sinai. He carefully respects historical order as he knew it in this regard, and would certainly recognize Psalm 95 as having been first uttered in the time of David. What we do suggest is that the Psalm is regarded by him as an explanation on the part of the pre-existent Christ of what happened on Sinai. In the course of the Psalm Christ tells us that the voice that was heard on Sinai was his.

Then in 4.6,7 occurs another reference to the gospel of Christ in the OT:

> Since therefore it remains for some to enter it, and those who formerly received the good news (οἱ πρότερον εὐαγγελισθέντες) failed to enter because of disobedience, again he sets a certain day, "Today", saying through David so long afterward, in the words already quoted:

"Today, when you hear his voice, do not harden your hearts." For if Joshua ('Ιησοῦς) had given them rest, God would not speak later of another day.

The argument of course is that the word "Today" in Psalm 95 must refer to some time other than the desert period, since the Psalm was uttered in David's day long after Israel had left the desert. If so, the author argues, the promise about the rest must apply to some other period also: that period is the present era, in which Christ offers his people a sabbath rest. This carries the same implication as does 4.2: the Israelites of old had an opportunity of hearing Christ, of hearing his voice on Sinai.

One other remarkable conclusion must be drawn: 'Ιησοῦς in verse 8 may very well be intended to mean quite literally Jesus, and not Joshua! Thus Peake's comment acquires an ironic flavour: "The substitution of 'Joshua' by the Revisers [sc. of 1884] for the Greek form of his name 'Jesus' in the AV removes a serious difficulty for English readers." This is not the first time that pre-critical commentators have shown themselves nearer to NT thought. Moffatt proves equally misleading when he writes: "'Ιησοῦς is never applied by him [sc. the author] to Christ before the incarnation." We would challenge this in 3.2, as our exposition has shown, and when we come to examine 12.24-7 we shall show reason to conclude that Jesus is represented as having spoken on Sinai. Indeed, the very title of this book is something of a challenge to Moffatt's theory. To this we may add the remarkable fact (whose significance must be considered later on) that Paul seems to have no hesitation in applying the name Jesus to the pre-existent Christ. See 2 Corinthians 8.9. The same can probably be said of the author of the Fourth Gospel (cf. John 12.36-41). Daniélou does in fact see a sort of pun in the name 'Ιησοῦς in 4.8, for he claims that there is an implicit contrast between Joshua who did not give the rest and Jesus who did.[17] But this explanation involves an abrupt and unheralded change of subject. This comes out clearly in both RSV and NEB, both of which insert "God" as the subject of "would not speak" in verse 8. There is, of course, no justification for this in the text. The RSV inserts a marginal note explaining that the Greek has "he" not "God". The NEB does not even take this precaution.

We can find a certain amount of support in the Fathers for taking 'Ιησοῦς in Hebrews 4.8 as Jesus rather than Joshua. The Epistle of Barnabas, for example, claims that Moses in giving the name 'Ιησοῦς to his successor was deliberately prophesying Christ.[18] Similarly, Justin in *Dialogue* 24.2 writes:

> Jesus Christ circumcises all who wish it, as was proclaimed earlier on, with stone knives.

He then proceeds to draw an allegorical meaning from the stone knives. The reference seems to be to Joshua 5.3 in the LXX.

> And Joshua ('Ιησοῦς) made sharp stone knives, and he circumcised the children of Israel.

This does not necessarily imply that in Justin's view it was Jesus who circumcised the children of Israel. It is more likely perhaps that he would regard Joshua's action as a type of the coming spiritual circumcision to be administered by Jesus, though he does not actually call it a type here. We can trace the same tendency in *Dialogue* 75.1,-2, where Justin quotes Exodus 23.20,21.

> Behold, I send an angel before you to guard you on the way and to bring you to the place which I have prepared. Give heed to him and hearken to his voice, do not rebel against him, for he will not pardon your transgressions, for my name is in him.[19]

Justin points out that the person who actually led them into Canaan was called 'Ιησοῦς; therefore God told the Israelites beforehand that their Saviour was to be called Jesus. Similar treatment is given to the name of Joshua in Irenaeus, Tertullian, and Eusebius.[20]

If the Latin translation, in which alone a large part of Origen's work is preserved, is to be trusted, Origen seems to have come extraordinarily close to identifying Joshua with Jesus. In his *Homilies on Exodus* XI.5 he reaches the point where Joshua is first named (Ex. 17.9), and he comments as follows:

Therefore let us observe what instructions Moses gave when war was imminent. It says: "He said to Jesus, Choose for yourself men and go out and fight with Amalek tomorrow." Up to this point nowhere has there occurred a mention of the name of the blessed man Jesus. Here first the brilliance of this name shone forth. Here first did Moses call Jesus and say to him: "Choose for yourself men." Moses calls Jesus, the Law calls Christ, that he may choose for himself men of power from among the people. Moses could not choose, but it is only Jesus who could choose men of power, Jesus who said, You have not chosen me, but I have chosen you. For he himself, the leader of the elect, himself the chief among men of power, it is he who fights with Amalek. For it is he who enters into the house of the strong man and plunders his goods.[21]

Here Joshua is not actually called a type of Christ: the historical figure of Joshua has disappeared altogether and has been replaced by Christ. It is, however, possible that this is only allegory; Origen certainly allegorizes the meaning of Amalek here. But it may be that Origen imagines Christ as appearing *in persona Joshuae*, or else Exodus 17.9 represents Moses as addressing Christ and not Joshua, according to Origen. It is, we may conjecture, quite possible, therefore, that in Hebrews 4.8 the author thinks that the Scriptures are really referring to Jesus when they appear to be referring to Joshua.

Most editors dislike the suggestion that the Israelites could have known Christ or the gospel in OT times. Thus, Bruce maintains that what the Israelites heard was not the gospel but simply what the Psalmist uttered when he said "Today".[22] This seems to contain a double confusion: it *was* the gospel, for the language used about it shows it to be such; and the Israelites of the desert period could not have heard the Psalmist, for the author carefully distinguishes David's utterances as occurring much later.[23] Windisch comes nearer to the right understanding of our author's meaning when he says that the gospel in the OT is something fulfilled in Christ, not something quite different from the NT gospel. But he does not realize that the OT gospel was not something that merely pointed to Christ in the future. Christ, according to Hebrews, was present in OT times as object of faith. Michel makes the illuminating point that in the LXX *euaggelizesthai* ("to preach the gospel") is frequently found in connection with "salvation". This helps to explain why our author can so easily read the gospel into the OT. Spicq has an interesting note on "the message which they heard" (ὁ λόγος τῆς ἀκοῆς) in 4.2. He says it is a literal translation of a Rabbinic phrase, and in the Rabbis it means traditional teaching, or indeed tradition.[24] Spicq does not claim that it means "traditional teaching" here, but he seems to suggest that "good news came to us" refers to the promise of a rest: "The significance of the Hebraism is concerned with the meaning of the word, with the content of the promise rather than with its expression." It is quite true that what Christ is understood as uttering is a promise, the promise of rest. But the gospel (*euaggelion*) must be about Christ, and the argument demands that, if Israel of old had met the gospel with faith, they would have received the promise. This means that it was Christ who uttered the promise originally.

Finally, as with 1 Corinthians 10.1-13, we must point out that this is not strictly speaking an example of typology at all. Quite apart from the fact that there is not a word that could possibly convey the idea of a type in the whole passage, the essence of typology is that there should be in the OT passage types or figures which point forward to Christ or to Christian ordinances. This is not what we find here: according to the author to the Hebrews, Christ was present in OT times and could have been accepted by the faith of the Israelites in the desert. Christ cannot be his own type. Nor can we call the Israelites of old the type of the Christian Church, except in a very vague and general sense. They are our fathers, the representatives in the desert of the one continuous body of which we are the modern representatives. They are at most warning examples to us, and their admonitory value lies in the hope that we will not reproduce their behaviour. What makes the two situations similar is Christ and the Church. But this is not typology as ordinarily understood. The nearest that our author comes to the language of typology in this passage is in his

ACCORDING TO THE EPISTLE TO THE HEBREWS

use of Jesus in 4.8 in a context where it is very likely to be understood as Joshua. But our author might well have argued that the identity of names pointed not to Joshua as a type of Christ, but to Christ himself as present with Israel in the dispossession of the nations of Canaan.

Hebrews 7: The Figure of Melchisedech

Before we consider the question raised by this chapter, it may be well to review the order of divine events, the *heilsgeschichte* according to the author to the Hebrews. This will have some bearing on the chapter. According to our author, the order of events was as follows:

1. Melchisedech appears to Abraham and blesses him. Abraham gives tithes to Melchisedech.
2. The Law is given and the Levitical priesthood is established in the time of Aaron (7.11). These priests receive tithes from Israel.
3. Christ is proclaimed High Priest in the time of David.

It is only this third point that may appear novel, but this is in fact what our author maintains. Four references in the Epistle make this clear:

(*a*) 5.5–10: Christ becomes a high priest (he was not so by nature); God who proclaimed him high priest addressed him ("appointed by him who said to him, etc.", 5.5), and Christ is described in 5.10 as "designated by God a high priest". The aorist participle *prosagoreutheis* indicates that he was on one specific occasion designated by God as high priest.[25]

(*b*) 7.11: "What further need would there have been for another priest to arise . . .?" This implies that at least the proclamation of Christ's priesthood took place after the establishment of the Levitical priesthood in Aaron's time. The only other time we can imagine is in David's reign, when the proclamation was made in Psalm 110.

(*c*) In 7.18 we read "a former commandment is set aside". This likewise implies that the Law came first in time and the proclamation of Christ as high priest came later.

(*d*) In 7.28 we find:

the word of the oath which came later than the law.

This surely removes all doubt. The oath which proclaimed the highpriesthood of Christ was an event which came later than the Law.

We can now ask the question with which we are concerned in this part of our study: according to the author to the Hebrews, Who was Melchisedech? What exactly was his status? Where does he come in the scale of being? In 7.3 remarkably exalted language is used about him:

He is without father or mother or genealogy, and has neither beginning of days nor end of life, but resembling the Son of God (ἀφωμοιωμένος δὲ τῷ Υἱῷ τοῦ Θεοῦ) he continues a priest for ever.

Westcott quotes Bengel: "Non dicitur Filius Dei assimilatur Melchisedecho, sed contra; nam Filius Dei est antiquior et antitypus"; and Theodoret: "Melchisedech is a type of Christ, and Christ is the truth of the type." Of Bengel's comment we may say that one who is described as having no beginning of days can hardly be reckoned as less ancient than Christ; and if the author had wanted to call Christ an antitype of Melchisedech he could have done so. He does in fact use the word in 9.24 (translated by RSV "a copy"), but he applies it to the earthly tabernacle, which he believed belonged to an order less real and less permanent than that to which Melchisedech belongs. He could not possibly have used this word of Melchisedech.

Naturally, editors have accepted very readily Theodoret's word for Melchisedech, "type". It is used by Nairne, Wickham, and Boylan.[26] But this word is just as inappropriate as a description of what the author believed about Melchisedech. He uses the word "type" himself only once, in 8.5 in a citation of Exodus 25.40, where it means the archetypal tabernacle, the higher reality of which the tabernacle made by Moses was a copy. But Theodoret and those who follow him would use "type" to designate Melchisedech as the inferior copy of whom Christ is the truth. When the author uses the language of typology he prefers *parabolē*. Other scholars who treat Melchisedech as a type without much further consideration are Venard (op. cit., p. 50), who speaks of allegory and typology in this context as if they were identical; Bonsirven, who calls Melchisedech "a preliminary sketch of Christ";[27] and Lampe and Woollcombe (op. cit., p. 34), who assume without argument that Melchisedech is a type of Christ. Bonsirven is also quoted by van der Ploeg as saying: "A sort of confusion seems to have arisen between Christ and the priest whose successor he is: is it not in the same sense that certain of the Fathers see in Melchisedech, described as he is here, not a man at all, but the Son of God?"[28] The confusion to which Bonsirven refers is significant for our argument, but may it not be that the confusion exists in Bonsirven's own mind? The author of Hebrews, we suggest, did not confuse Melchisedech and Christ: he identified them.

With this attempt to put Melchisedech into the category of OT type, we can also dismiss a whole range of similar words used by editors. Nairne (op. cit., p. 112) speaks of "shadow and substance" as applying to Melchisedech and Christ respectively. But this actual analogy is used by our author in 10.1, where the Law is called the shadow and Christ's dispensation the "true form". In chapter 7, however, it is made quite clear that Melchisedech belongs to the "true form" order of reality, and not to the shadow order, which his priesthood replaces. The same objection applies to Wm. Manson's phrase "a symbol of the heavenly priesthood of Christ",[29] and also to Otto Michel's words "a copy (*abbild*) of the Son of God". Spicq follows exactly the same line, describing Melchisedech as "a figure prophetic of Christ" and "a shadow and a sign". These phrases would apply admirably to the Levitical priesthood and the legal dispensation, but not to Melchisedech, who belongs unmistakably to the higher order of reality. G. Hollmann comes nearer the truth when he emphasizes very much the close resemblance between Melchisedech and Jesus, pointing out that all that is said about Melchisedech in 7.1-3 is also characteristic of the heavenly Logos. But he adds that the author does not think of Melchisedech as continuing for ever, and that he is best understood as "the never ceasing image of a priest".

This brings us face to face with another approach to the figure of Melchisedech which is to be found, the attempt to dissolve him into myth. Nairne suggests that the description of Melchisedech "is a matter of interpretation and not of prosaic fact" (op. cit., p. 344). In the same way Windisch says that for the author Melchisedech has no independent significance of his own; and Spicq comments: "The resemblance applies to the portrait in the Bible and not to the historical figure." Michel is able to show that there was much Jewish legend about Melchisedech and no lack of gnostic speculation. Philo identifies him with the Logos, and according to Héring he was identified by some Rabbis with the archangel Michael.[30] S-B tell us that he was identified with a son of Shem the son of Noah in order to maintain a line of priesthood from Adam.[31] In the same vein is what Hippolytus tells us about an Ebionite Christian called Theodotus, who claimed that Melchisedech was "the very greatest power, and was actually greater than Christ, and that Christ existed in his image".[32] M. Simon gives details of a work by Pseudo-Athanasius, probably written about A.D. 400, in which Melchisedech is represented as meeting Abraham first on Mount Tabor.[33] God is represented as saying of Melchisedech, "I love him as I love my only begotten Son". Simon remarks of this work: "Christianity is not only prefigured in the OT; it is there with the full reality of its institutions and rites." We may claim that this is to some extent true of Hebrews also. But any suggestion that Melchisedech was not considered to be an historical figure by our author is unfair. In particular it is surprising to find a scholar like Spicq making a distinction between the historical figure and the figure in the Bible. No such distinction could possibly have occurred to our author. Indeed the historicity of Melchisedech is essential to his argument. Like all the writers of the NT, the author of Hebrews accepted the OT narrative as historical fact. He was as far as could be imagined from dissolving it into myth.

It is time that we elaborated another solution to the problem: I suggest that, according to our author's own belief, Melchisedech *was* the pre-existent Christ. The unsatisfactory nature of any other explanation of our author's interpretation of Melchisedech is the most cogent argument in favour of this view, but other evidence can be cited. We have already noted how exalted must be the status of one who is without beginning of days or end of life. The phrase "without father or mother" ($\dot{\alpha}\pi\acute{\alpha}\tau\omega\rho$, $\dot{\alpha}\mu\acute{\eta}\tau\omega\rho$) suggests the attributes of deity. Windisch points out that these words are often used of deities in Greek literature, and quotes Pollux (*Onomastikon* III.26) as applying the epithet "without mother" to Athene and "without father" to Hephaistos. In this connection it is worth while considering Nairne's suggestion that "without genealogy" may be an echo of the LXX of Isaiah 53.8 "Who shall recount his generation?" (op. cit., p. 344). Nairne uses this to show that Melchisedech was a type of Christ, but it is much more effective as an argument that Melchisedech *was* Christ.

It might perhaps seem that the phrase "resembling the Son of God" in 7.3 tells against this suggestion. If Melchisedech was the Son of God, why is he described as resembling the Son of God? But the phrase does not necessarily rule out identity. For example, the fourth figure in the fiery furnace in Daniel 3.25 is described as "like a son of the gods". In Theodotion's version this phrase is translated "the appearance of the fourth is like (*homoia*) a son of God". No doubt this fourth figure is intended by the author of Daniel actually to be a son of the gods, i.e. an angel. Another interesting parallel occurs in Philippians 2.7:

being born in the likeness (*en homoiōmati*) of men.

No doubt Paul means that Christ really was man.

Then there is the evidence of 7.8:

Here tithes are received by mortal men; there by one of whom it is testified that he lives.

To what does "there" refer? The argument would seem to run like this:

> In the case of Levi it is mortal men who receive tithes: but in the case of Melchisedech he who receives tithes is described as living.

This will mean that "there" refers to the figure of Melchisedech in Genesis, not to Christ explicitly. But if so, the identification of Christ with Melchisedech is definitely implied here, because our author applies to Christ the only passage in the OT where the eternal priesthood is referred to, Psalm 110. We might express the argument thus:

> Melchisedech is superior to Abraham, because he blessed Abraham (7.7).
> Melchisedech is also superior to Levi, because Levi's line of priests is mortal, but Melchisedech lives for ever (7.8).
> But we only know that Melchisedech lives for ever because of Psalm 110.4, where God promises Christ an eternal priesthood.
> Therefore Melchisedech is identical with Christ.

No commentator has actually made this identification, though some of them come very near to it. Windisch describes Melchisedech as "the appearance of a divine being", and uses the phrases "Doppelgänger Jesu" and "Vorgänger Jesu". Michel points out that Ambrose and Jerome thought of Melchisedech as an angel, and Epiphanius tells us that in his day some Christian scholars actually identified Melchisedech with the Son, though he does not share their view.[34] Michel also aptly compares John 8.52,53, where the Jews are shocked at the suggestion that Christ can be greater than Abraham. The author to the Hebrews undoubtedly maintains that Melchisedech is greater than Abraham. Who then can he be but Christ?

J. van der Ploeg (op. cit., p. 214) advances an argument to prove that Melchisedech was envisaged by the author of Hebrews as a being of flesh and blood. It runs as follows: The author knew that the angels had a beginning; he says in 5.1 that every high priest taken from among men is intended for men. He could not have intended to exalt Melchisedech above men and angels and put him on a level with Christ. Therefore, all this exalted language is not intended to impugn Melchisedech's humanity. But this argument can very easily be turned: it proves far more simply and effectively that the author of Hebrews actually identifies Melchisedech with Christ.

The question may very well be asked: If the author believed that Melchisedech was the pre-existent Christ, why did he not say so? I suggest that it was because he did not quite have the courage to do so. It was too strong meat for his hearers. He hints in 5.11 that he would like to say a lot about Melchisedech, and that it would take a good deal of explanation. He would perhaps prefer his readers to draw for themselves the conclusion that he was aiming at. Compare what W. L. Knox says in a similar context about Paul's treatment of Christ in 1 Corinthians 10: "Paul slipped into an expression of the thought which preoccupied his mind without remembering at the moment that his readers, who had only received milk and not meat, might be unable to follow him in his speculations."[35]

One difficulty about the author's time-sequence remains. We have already argued that, according to our author, Christ was not proclaimed as high priest till the time of David, when Psalms 2 and 110 were uttered. If this is so, how can we claim that Christ appeared in the person of Melchisedech in the time of Abraham? Is this not anticipating his actual appointment in the time of David? We may answer that the author does not emphasize the appointment as such, but rather the proclamation of Christ as high priest, so much so that M. Rissi can argue for "designated" (*prosagoreutheis*) in 5.10 meaning "proclaimed" not "appointed" (see n. 25 on p. 184 below). Indeed the words the author uses to describe the event to which Psalm 110 refers do not suggest a new appointment which did not previously exist. In 5.5, 6.20, and 7.22 he uses *genesthai*, which simply means "become". In 5.10 the verb used means "be addressed as", and in 7.11 *anistasthai* means "arise". The only place he uses a word that could mean "appoint" is 7.28 (*kathistēsin*), where it is no doubt used because it first applies to the priesthood appointed by the Law. It seems likely, therefore, that in the view of the author Christ was indeed already made a high priest when he appeared to Abraham in the person of Melchisedech, but that his appointment was only proclaimed in the time of David, and his priesthood was only fulfilled and made operative in the incarnation; cf. "being made perfect" in 5.9. Some confirmation of this view may be found in Acts 7.46–50, where Stephen is recounting the history of the people of God in OT times. He brings his narrative as far as the building of the Temple by Solomon, and then breaks off, saying that God does not dwell in man-made temples. Much emphasis is rightly laid to-day on the connection between Acts 7 and Hebrews. We can say with some confidence that, if the author shared the same tradition as is represented in Stephen's speech, it would be very appropriate for him to hold that at the moment when the tabernacle (where he believed Christ spoke to the Fathers) gave way to the Temple, Christ was declared high priest in the heavenly temple (referred to in Acts 7.44), and that therefore the earthly Temple was precisely then rendered unnecessary.

In short, we maintain that, according to the private opinion of the author of the Epistle to the Hebrews, Christ appeared to Abraham in the person of Melchisedech, thereby indicating the superiority of the coming messianic priesthood to the coming Levitical priesthood; and that the eternal priesthood of Christ was formally proclaimed by God through Psalms 2 and 110 by the mouth of David; and finally that the incarnation was the process by which this priesthood actually came into operation.[36]

Hebrews 11.24-8

The point of this passage is: What exactly does "abuse suffered for the Christ" mean? The context is as follows:

> By faith Moses, when he was grown up, refused to be called the son of Pharaoh's daughter, choosing rather to share ill-treatment with

the people of God (συνκακουχεῖσθαι τῷ λαῷ τοῦ Θεοῦ) than to enjoy the fleeting pleasures of sin. He considered abuse suffered for the Christ (τὸν ὀνειδισμὸν τοῦ Χριστοῦ) greater wealth than the treasures of Egypt, for he looked to the reward. By faith he left Egypt, not being afraid of the anger of the king; for he endured as seeing him who is invisible.

The difficulty lies of course in explaining how Moses could have shared the reproach of Christ centuries before Christ came. Practically all editors either explain the phrase away or fall back on a vague form of typology. Thus Westcott: "In this wider sense the people of Israel was 'an anointed one', a 'Christ', even as Christians are 'Christs'." So also Nairne, Moffatt (modified), Spicq, and Michel. Windisch, Héring, and van der Ploeg (op. cit., p. 225) prefer to interpret it prophetically. We may let this last scholar speak for the others: "Moses in choosing the reproach, chose what was in fact to become later the reproach of Christ", and he adds that Moses chose Christ's reproach even without knowing it. This is quite opposed to what we have found so far in Hebrews about the author's view of OT characters. It is much more likely that, according to the author, Moses knew all about Christ. This is certainly St Paul's view.

Wm. Manson seems to come nearer to our author's mind when he writes: "The Christ, the pre-incarnate Son of God, was actually, though invisibly, an agent and participant in the redemption effected for Israel at the Exodus, and Moses by his decision of faith was sharing in the Saviour's passion." Similarly, Hollmann allows it to be quite natural for the author to believe that Christ, whom he thought of as an eternal spiritual Being, could have been revealed long before his revelation in the flesh.

We can, however, be much more specific than this. The first thing to be done is to find the exact reference of "by faith he left Egypt" in 11.27. This must refer to Moses' flight after killing the Egyptian, and not to his leading the Israelites out from Egypt, because the next event related is the inauguration of the Passover, which took place before Moses led them out. Admittedly our author says that Moses did *not* fear the wrath of the king, whereas

Exodus 2.6 implies that he did, but the most favourable interpretation of Moses' actions would naturally appeal to our author. Obviously he was prepared to accept Israel's traditional heroes as figures above criticism, as we can guess from his references to Samson, Jephthah, etc. We also know that he did not hesitate to reproduce legendary accretions to the scriptural text (cf. his reference to Moses' refusal to be called a son of Pharoah's daughter, of which there is no hint in Exodus 2.9,10).

Verse 27a, then, refers to Moses' flight from Egypt, and by verse 28 he is back in Egypt organizing the Passover. What lies in between will in all likelihood refer to the incident of the burning bush. What is more, we can probably find in that incident the explanation of that puzzling phrase in verse 26 "abuse suffered for the Christ". This is the LXX account of the burning bush in Exodus 3.7,8:

> I have surely seen the oppression of my people in Egypt (τὴν κάκωσιν τοῦ λαοῦ μου) and I have heard their cry from their task-masters, for I know their anguish. And I have come down to rescue them from the hand of the Egyptians and to lead them out of that land.

The very phrase "the oppression of my people" seems to be echoed in Hebrews 11.25 "to share ill-treatment with the people of God" (συνκακουχεῖσθαι τῷ λαῷ τοῦ Θεοῦ). If our author believed that it was Christ who appeared to Moses in the burning bush it would be perfectly natural for him to refer to the act of Moses in joining his people at this time as "sharing ill-treatment with the people of God" and encountering "abuse suffered for Christ". Christ had said that he had come down to be in the midst of his persecuted people. We shall be meeting evidence later to show how frequently the Fathers identify the angel in the burning bush with Christ.

More than this, in the very next chapter we shall be tracing exactly this belief in Stephen's speech in Acts 7. For the moment, however, it will be sufficient to point out the close parallel between the passage we are now considering in Hebrews and Acts 7.27–34. Like our author, Stephen also gives a brief history of Moses' life, and we find the same events mentioned in the same order. In Acts 7.27-9 we have an account of the Israelite's threat when Moses intervenes in his quarrel and Moses' retirement to Midian; as in Hebrews 11.27, the reference to Moses being afraid is omitted. Then in Acts 7.30-4 comes the account of the angel in the burning bush. Our next chapter will attempt to show that here Stephen is hinting at an appearance of Christ in the bush. We thus find a very exact correspondence between the two narratives. That in Hebrews is more compressed, but it can be interpreted in the light of Acts 7. Once again we seem to be faced with the conclusion that the belief in Christ's activity in OT history is no personal idiosyncrasy of Paul's, but was an element in the earliest tradition of Christian exegesis of the OT. The beautiful phrase "as seeing him who is invisible" must then be understood to refer to the incident of the burning bush. It will have a slightly different nuance from the sense in which it is usually taken. It does not mean "seeing the invisible God by faith", but "he had been granted through the visible Christ a sight of the invisible Father".[37]

Hebrews 12.22-7

We end our study of Hebrews with a famous but obscure passage. As one finds so often in this Epistle, this section is not easy to break up into smaller pieces, since the author's argument is closely knit. It will be sufficient to reproduce six verses here, but the whole passage from 12.12 onward is relevant:

> But you have come to Mount Zion, and to the city of the living God, the heavenly Jerusalem, and to innumerable angels in festal gathering, and to the assembly of the first-born who are enrolled in heaven, and to a judge who is God of all, and to the spirits of just men made perfect, and to Jesus, the mediator of a new covenant, and to the sprinkled blood that speaks more graciously than the blood of Abel. See that you do not refuse him who is speaking (μὴ παιραιτήσησθε τὸν λαλοῦντα). For if they did not escape when they refused him who warned them on earth (τὸν χρηματίζοντα), much less shall we escape if we reject him who warns from heaven (τὸν ἀπ' οὐρανῶν

ἀποστρεφόμενοι). His voice (οὗ ἡ φωνή) then shook the earth; but now he has promised. "Yet once more I will shake not only the earth, but also the heaven." This phrase, "Yet once more", indicates the removal of what is shaken, as of what has been made, in order that what cannot be shaken may remain.

The author has been comparing the old dispensation with the new, contrasting the spiritual and eternal nature of the new with the material and temporary nature of the old. Then he says:

See that you do not refuse him who is speaking.

Who is "him who is speaking"? It would seem reasonable to refer it to the same person as is implied by the phrase "the sprinkled blood that speaks" (the Greek verb *lalein* is the same in each case). The phrase in verse 24 refers of course to Christ, and this is how Westcott takes it. At any rate "him who is speaking" in verse 25 must refer to the same person as "him who warns from heaven" in the same verse. The argument must be:

Do not refuse him who speaks:
in OT times those who refused did not escape punishment;
much less will we if we refuse (one who speaks) from heaven.

But from this it follows that verse 26 must also refer to Christ:

whose voice then shook the earth, but now he has promised saying...

Then follows a quotation from Haggai 2.6. This in turn requires that the OT incident referred to in verse 25 be also attributed to Christ (or rather Jesus, to follow our author's nomenclature here). Most commentators however insist that "him who warned them on earth" in verse 25 indicates Moses, and that there is an implied contrast between Moses uttering an oracle on earth and Christ speaking from heaven. This is accepted by Windisch, Moffatt, T. Robinson, and Wm. Manson (op. cit., p. 159). Moffatt writes: "It is repeatedly said (Ex. 20.22; Deut. 4.36) that God spoke to the people at Sinai 'out of heaven', so that to take 'him who warned them on earth' as God would be out of keeping with 'on earth' ... He deliberately writes 'him who warned them' of Moses, keeping 'him who is speaking' as usual for God." But this exegesis encounters great difficulties: the Greek word for "him who warned" in verse 25 is *chrēmatizein*. It is not infrequent in the NT and is never used there of a human being uttering an oracle. Our author himself uses it twice of a man receiving an oracle from God, Moses in 8.5, and Noah in 11.7. It is never used in the LXX of Moses uttering an oracle, though it is twice used in this sense of Jeremiah (Jer. 33.2 (LXX); 36.23 (LXX)). Moffat quotes one passage in Josephus where it is used of Moses uttering an oracle.

Again, if we look at the passages in the Pentateuch which must have been in our author's mind as he wrote these verses, we do not find that the Israelites ever refused Moses when he uttered an oracle. On the contrary, they begged that God should not speak to them, and asked for Moses instead. Our author himself is well aware of this, as can be seen from verse 19 of this chapter.[38] It would also be strange if in verse 26 the divine voice should be described as shaking the earth, when all the time the reference is not to God's utterance, but to that of Moses. In fact, if we look at the passage from Deuteronomy that lies behind these verses, we find that it is God who gives the oracle, not Moses. Deuteronomy 5.23,24 runs thus in the LXX:

> And it came to pass, when you heard the voice from the midst of the fire, . . . that you said, "Behold *Kyrios* our God has shewn us his glory and we have heard his voice from the midst of the fire. In that day we learned that God can speak to man and that man can survive."

There follows a passage in which the people implore God to speak to them no longer, as they cannot endure it. They ask that Moses should speak to them instead. We gain the same impression from Exodus 20.18–21.

It is very interesting to note the exposition of this passage given by Estius, who for the acuteness of his observation and the breadth of his learning may well be taken to represent the best of pre-critical scholarship.[39] He sees clearly that "him who warned" in verse 25 cannot apply to Moses, because it was not Moses whom the Israelites refused. He likewise rejects the other solution favoured by modern scholars, that it refers to God the Father, for that would give a most unlikely contrast between God speaking on earth and Christ speaking from heaven. We may add that it would in fact remove any contrast at all, because, as we have shown, "him who warned" must be identified with "his voice" in verse 26, and this in its turn with "him who warns from heaven" in verse 25. Such an exegesis would therefore remove all reference to Christ from this passage, which makes it still more improbable. Estius concludes in fact "him who warned" in verse 25 must refer to an angel, and he suggests the Archangel Michael as the most likely solution. He adds that some commentators in his day did refer "him who warned" to Christ, though he does not accept this solution himself. It is most interesting that Estius has no hesitation in referring the words "His voice" in verse 26 to Christ, and he goes as far as to maintain that Christ did shake the earth at the giving of the Law on Sinai, though he actually spoke by the mouth of an angel.[40]

Spicq interprets this passage in terms of God the Father throughout. He insists that "him who is speaking" in verse 25 is God the Father, and he connects it, not with "the blood that speaks" of verse 24, but with "God spoke of old" and "he has spoken to us by a Son" in 1.1,2. Consistently with this, he maintains "him who warned" is God, and so also is "him who warns from heaven". The suggestion that "him who warned" in verse 25 indicates Christ he dismisses as "altogether inadmissible". He sees the contrast as consisting in God speaking on earth of a temporary order on the one hand, and God speaking from heaven of an eternal order on the other. We have already pointed out the improbability that there is no mention of Christ at all in this passage. But there is still another objection to Spicq's interpretation: he claims that "him who is speaking" in verse 25 refers to 1.1,2. But in that passage we are specifically told that in the new dispensation God has spoken in a Son. On Spicq's own assumption, therefore, "him who warns from heaven" in verse 25 must refer to God speaking to us in the Son, since all are agreed that this phrase refers to the new dispensation. But this is exactly the point of my exposition: unless we are ready to admit that in both old and new dispensations it was Christ (or God-in-Christ) who spoke, we are left with the contrast, rightly repudiated by Estius, between God the Father speaking from earth and God the Son from heaven. Even this interpretation is very difficult to maintain when we carefully weigh the implication of his "voice" in verse 26 and "whose words made the hearers entreat that no further messages be spoken to them" in verse 19.[41]

We conclude therefore that it is Christ who is envisaged by our author as speaking the warning oracle on Mount Sinai, and Christ whose voice was so terrible that the Israelites asked Moses to be their mediator, and Christ whose voice then shook the earth. The contrast is not between Moses delivering an oracle on earth and Christ speaking from heaven; it is between Christ delivering an oracle on earth (Mount Sinai) about a temporary dispensation ushered in by the Law, and Christ speaking in Haggai from heaven about an eternal dispensation that has now been revealed and can be enjoyed by Christians. This carries the implication that Christ's voice can be heard in Haggai's prophecy. When we examine that prophecy we see how easily our author could take it as an utterance of Christ—or should we not rather say, of Jesus? We note first that this oracle is addressed thus (Hag. 2.2,3 LXX):

> Speak now to Zorobabel the son of Salathiel, and to Jesus the son of Iosadek the high priest, and to all those who are left of the people.

Bizarre as it may seem to us, we may not rule out the possibility that the author of Hebrews could in some way understand this as a reference to Jesus, great high priest of the new order. We do not know how he would explain Zorobabel the son of Salathiel, but Hebrews 7.2 may give us a hint. Then we read in Haggai 2.5 as follows in the LXX:

> And my Spirit presides in your midst. Take courage, because thus says *Kyrios* almighty, "Once more will I shake the heaven and the

earth and the sea and the dry land. And I will shake at the same time all the Gentiles, and the desired things of all the Gentiles shall come, and I will fill this house with glory", says *Kyrios* almighty.

The reference to the Lord's Spirit presiding in the midst would seem to our author to be fulfilled in the Spirit-filled Church of his day. The accession of the Gentiles would seem completely in harmony in a messianic prophecy,[42] and the filling of the house with glory would certainly be understood as a description of Christ's glory filling the Church. It is most unlikely therefore that our author thinks of anyone but Christ (or rather Jesus) as the source of the utterance which he quotes in verse 26. But if Christ uttered Haggai 2.6, he must have spoken on Sinai, or else 12.26 has no meaning.

By far the most satisfactory interpretation of Hebrews 12.22-7, then, is to assume that Christ is thought of as the speaker all through. Christ uttered the voice that shook the earth on Sinai-Horeb, and Christ has through the prophet Haggai promised to shake the whole universe once again, an event which perhaps the author believed had already begun. But it is relevant to cite a few passages from the Fathers in which the interpretation suggested here is adumbrated, that is, the identification of the voice on Sinai with Christ's, and the approximation of the high priest Joshua with Jesus Christ. We may, however, take this opportunity of questioning the explanation of this passage to be found in Lampe and Woollcombe's *Essays in Typology*. On page 67 the reference to Mount Sinai in Hebrews 12.18 is described as "historical typology". This surely is not an adequate description. Christ spoke on Mount Sinai; he also speaks to us in the new dispensation (through a prophet). This is parallelism certainly, but Christ is common to both situations. What then is left to be a type under the old dispensation?

We have already noticed a passage in the Epistle of Barnabas in which Christ is cited as the author of the Decalogue (see p. 53 above). But we might quote another place in which the author of the Epistle attributes one of the commandments of the Mosaic Law directly to Christ. It occurs in 7.3:

When the commandment was written, "Whoever will not observe the fast shall surely be put to death", *Kyrios* prescribed it because he himself was to offer the vessel of his spirit as a sacrifice for our sins.

This is taken absolutely for granted, with no hint that anything strange is being suggested. Again, we could refer to Melito's Homily, already quoted on page 15 above, where the phrase occurs

He [sc. Christ] it was who gave thee the Law on Horeb.

Compare also Theophilus of Antioch, *Ad Autolycum* 22, where Christ is described as the voice (*phōnē*) of God.[43] A good example may also be found in Irenaeus, *Adv. Haereses* V.22.1:

... the Word of God, who in the Law indeed cries, "Hear, O Israel, the Lord thy God is one God", and "Thou shalt love the Lord thy God with all thy mind."

This must be the personal Word and not just a word, because the relative is "qui" not "quod". A final instance can be found in Hippolytus, *Refutatio Omnium Haeresium*, IX.33.10–11:

A law was prescribed full of solemnity and righteousness. And all these things does the Word of God direct, the first born of the Father, the light-giving voice (*phōnē*) that was before the morning star.

Here both the theodicy on Sinai and the Son as the Father's Voice are brought together.

We can also find a parallel for the association of Christ with the high priest Joshua in Justin Martyr. In *Dialogue* 115.3–4 he describes this Joshua as a type of Christ. He is careful not to deny the historical existence of the high priest Joshua, but he maintains that Joshua's vindication before Satan, described in Zechariah 3.1–5, is a prophecy of Christ. The angel who stands by the side of the high priest in this passage is not exactly identified with Christ, but is described as

the power of God sent to us through Jesus Christ.

This looks like an identification of the angel with the Spirit, a remarkable feature at that period.

Tertullian provides us with an illustration of the same theme. His words could be taken as an actual identification of Jesus the high priest of Zechariah's time with Jesus Christ, but probably he means no more than a foreshadowing. The words occur in *Adv. Marcionem* III.7.6:

> Thus also in Zachariah in the person of Jesus the true high priest of the Father is described (indeed the very mystery of his name is included), with his double set of clothes to indicate his two advents. First he is clothed in filthy garments, that is, in the indignity of suffering, mortal flesh, when the devil also opposes him, that is the author of Judas' treachery (I might add also the tempter who came after the baptism). Then he is stripped of his former filthy clothes, and adorned with the chasuble, mitre, and clean tiara, that is with the glory and honour of his second coming.

The Fathers therefore give us by no means negligible evidence that Joshua the high priest was a figure who might well seem to an early Christian to possess a christological significance.[44]

The Epistle to the Hebrews has provided in one sense the richest mine of references to Christ's activity in OT history that we are likely to find in the NT. But the ore has not been on the surface. The doctrine was certainly not one which would be freely communicated to catechumens. It was strong meat, only suitable for mature Christians. The author does not let his treasure appear above ground, as Paul does once (1 Cor. 10.4) and John once (John 12.41). Now we turn to a single chapter, Acts 7, where there is also no overt reference. But the doctrine of Christ's activity in the OT is so constantly to be found beneath the surface throughout Stephen's speech, that it demands a whole chapter in which to trace the evidence for the existence of this doctrine.

4

Christ in the Old Testament in Stephen's Speech

"It is quite possible . . . that the author of the Speech, like the author of the Epistle [sc. to the Hebrews], envisages Christ as present with the people of Israel in the critical moments of their history under the old dispensation. This may be the reason for the mention of the angel who appeared to Moses 'in a flame of fire in a bush' . . . who is also described as 'the voice of the Lord' . . . It may also account for 'the angel who spoke to him (Moses) in Mount Sinai', when Moses was 'in the Church in the wilderness'." This suggestion of R. P. C. Hanson's is not worked out in detail and no evidence is given.[1] The aim of this chapter is to supply that detail, and to show that evidence can be brought which makes it extremely likely that Professor Hanson has in fact hit on one of the leading themes which lie behind Stephen's extremely obscure speech as given in Acts 7. In order to clarify the argument we will divide the material to be covered into four sections.

Acts 7.2

> The God of glory (ὁ Θεὸς τῆς δόξης) appeared to our father Abraham when he was in Mesopotamia, before he lived in Haran, and said to him, "Depart from your land . . . etc."

The phrase "the God of glory" is a strange one. It reminds us of two other phrases, "the king of glory" of Psalm 24, and "the Lord of glory" of 1 Corinthians 2.8. We shall be arguing in chapter 7 that both these phrases were applied to Christ by Paul at least. But for an exact parallel to the phrase in Acts 7.2 we must turn to the LXX of Psalm 29.3 (LXX 28.3), where we meet the phrase

the God of glory has thundered.

Indeed, the whole Psalm demands our attention, for it would have certain definitely christological features as read by an early Christian. The verse in which the phrase we are concerned with occurs runs like this in the LXX:

The voice of *Kyrios* (φωνὴ κυρίου) upon the waters,
the God of glory (ὁ Θεὸς τῆς δόξης) has thundered,
Kyrios upon many waters.

The voice of the Lord appears again in Stephen's speech, especially in 7.31, where, as we shall be seeking to demonstrate, it is identified with the angel of the Lord. In our last chapter we have been observing that Christ is identified with the voice of the Lord in Hebrews 12.24–7, and by implication in chapters 3 and 4 of Hebrews, where "Today if you will hear my voice" must mean Christ's voice. It seems a reasonable conjecture therefore that Stephen[2] intended the phrase "the God of glory" as a veiled allusion to the pre-existent Christ. This would mean that in his view the pre-existent Christ was the subject of whom the Psalmist speaks in Psalm 29.

When we read on in this Psalm, we find confirmation of this view. Verses 5b–8a run as follows in the LXX:

And *Kyrios* shall smash the cedars of Libanus,
and he breaks them like the calf of Libanus,[3]
and the Beloved like a son of the unicorns.
The voice of *Kyrios* who breaks through a flame of fire,
the voice of *Kyrios* who shakes the wilderness.

In two places the Greek has misunderstood, or misread, the Hebrew. Only the second place really concerns us. The translator of the LXX has misread "and Sirion" in the Hebrew as "and

Jeshurun".[4] Jeshurun is the "pet name" which God uses for Israel. It occurs four times in the OT (Deut. 32.15; 33.5,26; Isa. 44.2), and is always translated by "the Beloved" in the LXX *ho ēgapēmenos*. Thus the LXX has introduced into Psalm 29 a reference to "the Beloved" that is absent from the Hebrew text. In view of such passages as Ephesians 1.6 where this word is used as a title of Christ, we may be quite sure that Stephen would see in Psalm 29 a direct reference to the Messiah. Similarly, he would see in the verse about God dividing the flames of fire a reference to the theophany in the burning bush, a topic in which he shows considerable interest later on in the speech. Finally, we may note that, if our exposition of Hebrews 12.24-7 is right, the author of Hebrews believed that it was Christ who shook the earth at the theodicy on Sinai. Stephen might very well see a reference to the same event in the line from Psalm 29 about the Lord shaking the wilderness. Thus in allusive, ambiguous style Stephen at the very beginning of his speech makes a reference to "the God of glory" which to Greek-speaking Christians who could study their Bibles meant that the topic of his OT exposition was in fact none other than the pre-existent Christ.

Both Bruce and Preuschen see a reference to Psalm 29, but neither connects it with Christ.[5] Wendt goes so far as to compare I Corinthians 2.8.[6] C. S. C. Williams suggests that Stephen emphasizes the appearance in Mesopotamia before the move to Haran because he wishes to show that what was promised was not so much a land as a salvation.[7] This would fit in well with our contention that it was Christ, according to Stephen, who appeared to Abraham.

Many passages from the Fathers could be quoted to show that they thought of Christ as speaking to, or appearing to, Abraham. What is not common is the belief that it was Christ who actually called Abraham out of Mesopotamia. We can, however, refer to Melito's *Homily on the Passion*, 87. He is upbraiding Israel for selling Christ, and he rhetorically asks the Jews of his day

At what price did you value the fact that you were created by him?
At what price did you value his calling of the patriarchs?

This must imply that Christ called Abraham as well as the other patriarchs. The passage is immediately followed by a reference to the sojourn in Egypt, so the Greek, which has simply "the fathers", must indicate the patriarchs, and not the fathers in the wilderness.

We might also quote Irenaeus:

> Abraham also, therefore, knowing through the Word the Father who made the heaven and the earth, confessed him to be God; and, being taught by a symbol that the Son of God would become man among men, and that by his coming his own seed would be as the stars of the sky, he longed to see that day, so that he too might embrace Christ, and, seeing him through the spirit of prophecy, he rejoiced.[8]

It is not quite clear what passages in Genesis Irenaeus has in mind here; it might be Genesis 12.1–9, or else chapter 15. In either case the call of Abraham by the Word is implied, for in 15.7 God identifies himself as he who brought Abraham up out of Chaldaea. At any rate, it is difficult to avoid the conclusion that, according to Irenaeus, it was the Word who called Abraham in the first place.

Acts 7.30–5

We now pass to the history of Moses, and we find in the narrative of the burning bush a hint that it was Christ who appeared to Moses. We must reproduce all six verses:

> Now when forty years had passed, an angel appeared to him in the wilderness of Mount Sinai, in a flame of fire in a bush. When Moses saw it, he wondered at the sight; and as he drew near to look, the voice of the Lord (φωνὴ κυρίου) came, "I am the God of your fathers, the God of Abraham, and of Isaac, and of Jacob." And Moses trembled, and did not dare to look. And the Lord said to him, "Take off the shoes from your feet, for the place where you are standing is holy ground. I have surely seen the ill-treatment of my people that are in Egypt and heard their groaning, and I have come down to deliver them. And now come, I will send you to Egypt." This Moses whom they refused, saying, "Who made you a ruler and a

judge?" God sent as both ruler and deliverer (ἄρχοντα καὶ λυτρωτήν) by the hand of the angel that appeared to him in the bush.

Stephen here follows the LXX account as we have it in Exodus 3.1–10 fairly accurately, but two points stand out. First, he introduces the phrase "the voice of the Lord came" in verse 31 which is not in the original. We may be permitted to conjecture that this is an allusion to Psalm 29, and implies that the Voice of the Lord was in fact the Beloved of the LXX of Psalm 29. Of course this is not on the surface, but it is there for anyone who reads it with the eyes of an early Christian. Secondly, Stephen undoubtedly distinguishes between God and the angel. This is clear from verse 35, where God sends Moses by the hand of the angel. This distinction is not made in the text of Exodus, where first the angel is seen in the bush (3.2), then the Lord speaks from the bush (3.4), promising to be with Moses himself (3.12). There is no further reference to the angel in the passage. Obviously it was originally only a method of avoiding an anthropomorphism. But Stephen reads into it a deeper significance, and thinks of the angel as leading out Moses and the Israelites from Egypt, no doubt identifying this angel with the pillar of cloud, as Paul does according to our understanding of 1 Corinthians 10. It is very likely also that Stephen identified Christ with the angel in whom is God's name of Exodus 23.20,21. We shall be seeing presently that the angel is referred to again in Acts 7.44, again in a context where he does not appear in the text of Exodus. The only meaning that Stephen can have intended to convey is that the angel is the Son.

Many commentators have pointed out that in 7.35 Moses is pointing forward to Christ. He is depicted as the "ruler and deliverer". Foakes-Jackson and Kirsopp Lake well compare Luke 24.21: "But we had hoped that he was the one to redeem Israel."[9] Wendt comments, "The angel represents Jahveh and the voice is the voice of God." This is no doubt true as far as the Exodus narrative is concerned in itself, but Stephen read a deeper significance into it. S-B records various speculations of the Rabbis as to which of the angels performed this office: Michael, Gabriel, and an obscure angel called Zagzagel have all been suggested. It is just possible that Stephen may have known of such conjectures, but for him, we may be sure, the figure who appeared to Moses had inherited a more excellent name than they.

That it was Christ who appeared to Moses in the burning bush is a common theme among the Fathers. There are at least two references in Justin. *Apology* I.62 runs:

> When Moses was looking after the sheep of his maternal uncle in the land of Arabia, our Christ in the shape of fire from a bush talked with him, and said, "Loose thy sandals and come near and listen." He, loosing them and approaching, heard that he must go down to Egypt and lead out from there the people of Israel; and he received mighty strength from Christ, who spoke to him in the form of fire.

This is very specific, and the fact that Justin could put it into an Apology intended for non-Christians shows how convinced he was about it, and how much he took it for granted. Compare also *Dialogue* 59.

The same identification will be found in Irenaeus *Adv. Haereses* IV.9.1–2 and in *Proofs of the Apostolic Preaching* 46. Chrysostom, who is no fanatic for finding Christ in the OT, is perfectly clear on this point. In his *Commentary on Acts*, à propos 7.30–3 he writes:

> He calls the Son of God an angel as one who is also man . . . not only does he shew here that the angel who appeared to Moses was the Angel of Great Counsel,[10] but he also shews how great was the compassion that God manifests through this appearance. . . . There is no Temple as yet, so the place is holy by the appearance and activity of Christ. This is much more wonderful than the place in the holy of holies.[11]

Compare also Eusebius *Eccl. Hist.* 1.ii.9 and Jerome's *Commentary* on Galatians, in Galatians 3.19.[12] Martin Werner in *The Formation of Christian Dogma*, p. 124, sees that the angel of Acts 7.30 sq. is identified with Christ, but he does not study the chapter in detail.[13] Some implications of it would hardly square with his theory of the origin of Christian doctrine.

Acts 7.44

Next in order comes Acts 7.38, but that verse is best taken with 7.53, so we go straight to Acts 7.44, as it lends itself to fairly succinct treatment.

> Our fathers had the tent of witness in the wilderness, even as he who spoke to Moses (ὁ λαλῶν τῷ Μωυσῇ) directed him to make it, according to the pattern (*kata ton tupon*) that he had seen.

Here we have a mysterious, indirect reference to the speaker on the mount as "he who spoke to Moses". It reminds us of the use of "him who is speaking" in Hebrews 12.25. It is very significant that Foakes-Jackson and H. J. Cadbury, who have no inkling that Christ is referred to here, ask the question: Is it also an angel? Stephen is not openly identifying Christ with the angel of the bush, or with "he who spoke" in verse 44, but he is hinting at it. This would suggest that the speech was originally intended for Jews, as it appears in its context in Acts, and not for Jewish Christians. R. P. C. Hanson, in his article in *Theology* of April 1947 already referred to, maintains that according to Stephen's argument here God was to have no permanent dwelling place until the coming of the Word. One could take this further and express it thus: God always dwelt in the Word, and Moses saw and heard the Word on Mount Sinai and therefore realized that God would never dwell in a house made with hands.

There is no need to adduce patristic parallels to the thought of Christ speaking to Moses on Sinai or in the tabernacle. We have already pointed to some in our examination of 2 Corinthians 3. But we can point to a very remarkable parallel in Hebrews. In Hebrews 8.3–7 the author is discussing the Levitical priesthood and showing its inferiority to Christ's. He says of human priests in 8.5:

> They serve a copy and shadow (*hupodeigmati kai skia*) of the heavenly sanctuary; for when Moses was about to erect the tent, he was instructed by God, saying, "See that you make everything according to the pattern which was shown you on the mountain" (κατὰ τὸν τύπον τὸν δειχθέντα σοι ἐν τῷ ὄρει).

90   JESUS CHRIST IN THE OLD TESTAMENT

Scholars have often pointed out that this OT citation forms one of many links connecting Stephen's speech with the Epistle to the Hebrews. But it is more than this: it seems quite possible that in both places it is Christ who is represented as instructing Moses about the model of the tabernacle.

In the context of Hebrews Christ is the most probable subject for "saying" (*phēsin*). We are told in verse 2 that the tent in heaven was pitched by the Lord and not by man. This is a quotation from Numbers 24.6, Balaam's Song, which apparently relates a vision enjoyed by Balaam. The account of the vision opens with these words:

> The vision of Balaam the son of Beor,
> the oracle of the man whose eye is opened,
> the oracle of him who hears the words of God,
> who sees the vision of the Almighty.

In the last line the LXX has

> who has seen the vision of God.

This verse would alert an early Christian to expect a reference to Christ. This occurs in the LXX (not the Hebrew) of Numbers 24.6. Balaam is praising the beauty of the tents of Israel, and verse 6c runs:

> like the tents which *Kyrios* pitched.[14]

Immediately there follows a reference which the later Church certainly took as messianic. We translate the LXX:

> there shall come a man out of his seed,
> and he shall rule over many nations.

We may therefore confidently suggest that "the Lord" in Hebrews 8.2 is the pre-existent Christ, who showed the pattern of the tabernacle to Moses on the sacred mount. The same conclusion will follow in Acts 7.44.

No doubt this conception of the heavenly temple was an inheritance from Alexandrian Judaism. We find essentially this idea in the Book of Wisdom. Solomon is represented as speaking thus of the earthly Temple which he built in Wisdom 9.8:

Thou hast given command to build a temple on thy holy mountain, and an altar in the city of thy habitation, a copy of the holy tent (μίμημα σκηνῆς ἁγίας) which thou didst prepare from the beginning.

Both the author of Hebrews and Stephen, however, have departed from the Alexandrian tradition markedly in introducing the idea of the pre-existent Messiah as the author of this heavenly tabernacle.

Acts 7.38,53; Galatians 3.19,20; Hebrews 2.2,3

We begin by reproducing verses 38 and 53 of Acts 7:

v. 38: This is he who was in the congregation in the wilderness (ἐν τῇ ἐκκλησίᾳ ἐν τῇ ἐρημῷ,) with the angel who spoke to him (τοῦ ἀγγέλου τοῦ λαλοῦντος αὐτῷ) at Mount Sinai, and with our fathers; and he received living oracles (*logia zōnta*) to give to us.

v. 53: you who received the law as delivered by angels (εἰς διαταγὰς ἀγγέλων) and did not keep it.

For the sake of convenience we print two other passages from the NT here which we shall find relevant to these two verses from Stephen's speech. The first is Galatians 3.19,20:

Why then the law? It was added because of transgressions, till the offspring should come to whom the promise had been made; and it was ordained by angels though an intermediary (διαταγεὶς δι' ἀγγέλων ἐν χειρὶ μεσίτου). Now an intermediary implies more than one; but God is one.

The third passage is Hebrews 2.2,3:

For if the message declared by angels (ὁ δι' ἀγγέλων λαληθεὶς λόγος) was valid, and every transgression or disobedience received a just retribution, how shall we escape if we neglect such a great salvation? It was declared at first by the Lord (ἥτις ἀρχὴν λαβοῦσα λαλεῖσθαι διὰ τοῦ κυρίου), and it was attested to us by those who heard him.

In Acts 7.38 we have the angel of the bush mentioned again, this time in connection, it seems, with the giving of the Law. Preuschen, followed by Wendt, well points out that the phrase "the day of the assembly" (ἡμέρα τῆς ἐκκλησίας) 'means the day on which the Law was given in Deuteronomy 4.10; 9.10; 18.16. The mention of the angel in connection with the giving of the Law is Stephen's own addition. There is no mention of an angel in Deuteronomy, chapters 9 and 10, which describe the occasions on which the tablets of the Law were given to Moses; nor do we find any mention of an angel in the parallel account in Exodus 19. Rendall is therefore misleading when he writes: "Moses communed with the angel of God's presence in the face of the congregation, as recorded in Exodus 33.8-11."[15] There is in fact no mention of an angel in that passage, and the LXX does not import an angel into Exodus 33.14, where it might have relieved the anthropomorphism of "my face". When we move on to Acts 7.53, with its striking phrase "delivered by angels", we find that angels have been brought in again. Commentators have not been slow to adduce evidence for the presence of angels at the giving of the Law in the traditions of late Judaism and the Rabbis. Bruce quotes Josephus to the effect that the finest and holiest part of the legislation was conveyed to Israel by angels from God,[16] and he has noted the relevance of Exodus 33.14, though it is only fair to add that the passage is less suggestive of a divine hypostasis in the LXX. In the next chapter we shall be suggesting that John saw the presence of the Word in this passage, so it would not be surprising if Stephen did also. In Jubilees 1.27, 2.1 an angel is represented as talking with Moses on Sinai. Similarly, in Jubilees 49 and 50 an angel instructs Moses about Passover regulations and about how to observe the Sabbath. But an angel is not represented as actually delivering the Law.[17] S-B likewise (in loc. Gal. 3.19) gives many references to the presence of angels on Sinai at the theodicy; they come as God's retinue, or to honour Israel. In some traditions they actually deliver the Law to Israel and expound its provisions; for example, Rabbi Johanan (fl. A.D. 279), in giving a fantastic exegesis of the Song of Songs, describes an angel as dictating every clause to the Israelites. It is significant in view of our conclusions below that S-B thinks the whole midrash is based on Deuteronomy 33.

Bonsirven describes the angels as transmitting the divine words to Israel,[18] being ready to punish them if they refused, and kissing them on the mouth and crowning them when they accepted the Law.

We have still to consider the strange phrase in Acts 7.38

and he received living oracles to give to us.[19]

W. L. Knox suggests that Stephen believed the first set of tables presented to Moses contained the perfect Law, while the second set, which Moses did not smash but gave to Israel, contained the imperfect and temporary Law later abrogated by Christ's coming in the flesh.[20] We have already noticed this theory in the Epistle of Barnabas, combined with the belief that it was Christ who gave the Law. There is support for the theory put forward by Knox in Rabbinic tradition. S-B (in loc. 2 Cor. 3) says that, according to this tradition "he who fashioned the second table was not God but Moses... the recipient of this table was also the the man who constructed it". We may suggest that what we have in Acts is in fact this theory as we find it modified in the Epistle of Barnabas: the first set of tables was given directly by the pre-existent Christ. The commands were therefore directly from the lips of Christ. With this would go the implication that the first tables held the gospel, or at least the dispensation of grace and faith which Paul claims was known to Moses from his intercourse with Christ. The first table was smashed because Israel was not ready for it. We have surely essentially the same idea in the saying of Jesus himself recorded in Mark 10.5:

For your hardness of heart he [sc. Moses] wrote you this commandment.

It was not God's original intention. But we shall have more to say about these "living oracles" presently.

Before going on to look at the background to this passage in the OT, we must take issue with W. L. Knox about his interpretation of it. He writes as follows (op. cit., p. 55, n. 33): "But he (Stephen) adds to this the idea that the original law, which was thus rejected, was not merely a version of that subsequently given, but a better law ('living oracles' which are the original law 'delivered by angels'). Owing to the rejection of this original law . . . the children of Israel lost the opportunity, which they then had, of being made like angels." This is to equate the "living oracles" with the Law delivered by angels. But this will hardly stand. The Jews broke the Law given by angels (Acts 7.53), but on Knox's own assumption they never received the living oracles. Moses smashed the tables which contained them before he could deliver them to Israel. It is much more likely, therefore, that the living oracles mean the direct oracles of Christ which Moses was privileged to hear. The content of these utterances was probably the gospel as far as it could be apprehended before the incarnation (Heb. 4.2). The presence of the angels with the Law that was actually delivered is a sign of indirectness. Just because it was delivered through angels, it was not a living Law.

Stephen speaks about an angel on Sinai, whom we have good reason to believe he identified with Christ, and later about the services of angels on the same occasion. We must keep the angel of the bush, "he who spoke", "the voice of the Lord", distinct in our minds from the angels of verse 53, for, as we shall find, they are very far from being identical. Both S-B and the authors of *The Beginnings of Christianity* point back to Deuteronomy 33 as the source of speculations about angels at Mount Sinai; when we examine this chapter we find that in all likelihood it is also the source of Stephen's christological speculations. Deuteronomy 33.2-5 runs as follows in the LXX:

> *Kyrios* came to us from Sinai and appeared to us from Seir,
> and hastened from the mountain Pharan with the myriads of Kades;
> on his right are his angels with him.
> And he spared his people,
> and all his sanctified ones under thy hands;
> and these are under thee,
> and he received from his words a law, which Moses commanded us,
> an inheritance for the congregations of Jacob.
> And there shall be in the Beloved (ἐν τῷ ἠγαπημένῳ) a Ruler

as the rulers of the peoples are gathered together
in company with the tribes of Israel

At several places the LXX represents the Hebrew very badly and the Hebrew itself is not always clear.²¹ But it is the LXX translation with which we are concerned, and we are fully justified in asking: what would this passage in the LXX have meant to Stephen? In the first place, he would certainly have seen a reference to angels accompanying the giving of the Law here, as did both the Targums and the Rabbis. As we have seen (n. 21), the LXX has actually emphasized the presence of angels here more than the Hebrew. He would see a clear distinction between the pre-existent Christ and the angels. The latter are under Christ, he is superior to them (cf. Heb. 1.6, a quotation from the LXX of Deut. 32.43). The reference in this passage to "the Beloved" (in Hebrew of course "Jeshurun" referring to Israel) would infallibly speak to Stephen of the pre-existent Christ. Indeed, the words as they stand in the LXX may even have suggested to him that Moses only rules in Christ (cf. the Israelites being baptized "into Moses" but also in Christ in 1 Cor. 10.4); and it is just possible that this accounts for the words "ruler and deliverer" which are applied to Moses in Acts 7.35. If so, it would be inaccurate to describe Moses as a type of Christ in that verse. He is one who holds his office in the power and authority of Christ—very much the conception we have already met in Hebrews 3.1–6. Stephen would therefore identify the angel of whom he speaks in 7.38 with the *Kyrios* of Deuteronomy 33.2. Thus we have a clear distinction in Stephen's mind between the angel whom he identifies with the pre-existent Christ, and who was the author of the Law, and the angels who accompanied the theodicy.

We now take up again the problem of the "living oracles". The actual phrase may have been suggested by Deuteronomy 32.47, as the authors of *The Beginnings of Christianity* suggest:

> For this word is not empty for you, but it is your very life (*hē zōē humōn*).

This would certainly speak to Stephen of Christ. Even more

likely, in my opinion, is the suggestion that "oracles" comes from Balaam's formula in Numbers 24.4,16. Balaam is described as one who "hears the words (LXX *logia*) of God". We have already traced a connection between Hebrews 8.5 and Balaam's prophecies, and it is extremely likely that Stephen also would regard them as messianic. It is worth noting that in biblical usage *logia* is by no means confined to the precepts of the Law. In Romans 3.2; Hebrews 5.12; and 1 Peter 4.11 the word certainly cannot be restricted to the Law. In the LXX of Deuteronomy 33.9 it is used of Levi as the keeper of the divine oracles. Isaiah uses it four times, mostly of God's word to the prophet. It is, therefore, a perfectly adequate word to describe the living utterances of Christ as contrasted with the dead precepts of the Law.[22]

We can now approach the strange phrase in Acts 7.53 with some hope of seeing it in its right perspective:

> you who received the law as delivered by angels and did not keep it.

Editors have inevitably compared Galatians 3.19, and most of them have concluded that Stephen's attitude to the angelic mediation of the Law is different from Paul's: Stephen uses the presence of angels to enhance the sanctity of the Law, Paul to demonstrate its inferior and indirect character. Thus the authors of *The Beginnings of Christianity*, C. S. C. Williams, and C. K. Barrett (*From First Adam to Last*, p. 61). What we have observed, however, about Stephen's belief in the presence of Christ on Sinai must give us pause before we accept this conclusion. Stephen might mean that, seeing the Jews failed to keep a Law given them by indirect methods (and therefore inferior), it is not surprising that they killed him who spoke living words directly to Moses. Compare the suggestion of the author of Hebrews that the Israelites were culpable in refusing to hear Christ and asking to hear Moses instead. If our reference to Deuteronomy 33 is correct, then Stephen would look on these angels as assistants rather than chief actors. We suggest, therefore, that the train of thought in Stephen's mind is something like this: You could have heard the direct utterances of Christ which Moses heard, but you were unworthy of them. Instead of that, you were given an inferior Law conveyed to you not directly by Christ, but by the mediation of angels. Even this Law you failed to keep. It is not surprising therefore that when the Christ came in the most direct way of all, in the flesh, you failed to recognize him and put him to death.

We quote Chrysostom as a clear example of one of the Fathers who adopts this interpretation:

> Some people say he means the Law was ordained by angels. But this is not so. Where do we find angels ordaining the Law? But the Law which he describes as ordained is that which was entrusted to Moses by the Angel who appeared to him in the bush. For was he not man?[23]

Thus we do not have to suppose that by his mention of angels Stephen was glorifying the Law. On the contrary, what he seems to mean is that even the unsatisfactory alternative which Israel chose was not properly observed by them. His argument is therefore closely in line with Paul's in Galatians 3.19,20. Here certainly the introduction of angels indicates inferiority. The Law is inferior to the promise because it is indirect: both Moses and angels had a hand in delivering it. It is contrasted with the promise, which is direct from faith to faith. There is in Galatians no clear indication that Christ is thought of as the author of the Law on Sinai. But we have already seen in Paul the belief that Christ was present in the wilderness with Israel, and spoke to Moses in the tabernacle, and indeed was therefore in some sense the author of the old dispensation as well as of the new. If our interpretation of 2 Corinthians 3 is correct, Paul must have thought of Christ as the author of that Law of which he was also the fulfilment. A great many of the Fathers fall to the temptation of taking the word for "intermediary" (*mesitēs*) in Galatians 3.19 as indicating Christ, not Moses. Fascinated by the fact that the word is used of Christ in 1 Timothy 2.5, and that it is applied to him three times in Hebrews (8.6; 9.15; 12.24), they unhesitatingly make the identification here. Chrysostom may speak for the rest:

He either calls the priests angels, or else says that the angels themselves assisted at the giving of the Law. And he says that Christ is there the mediator, shewing that he pre-existed and himself gave the Law.[24]

We must, however, resist this temptation: the mediator is Moses. The word is actually used of him by the Rabbis.[25] Lietzmann expresses the nature of the Law's inferiority somewhat differently.[26] He says that the Law does not proceed from one personality (God), but from a multiplicity (of angels), and therefore is not absolutely divine. But the contrast seems to be between the promise made directly by God to Abraham and fulfilled directly in Christ on the one hand, and on the other hand the Law, which only reached Israel by several stages, borne by angels to Moses, communicated by Moses to Israel. Schlier has his own peculiar theory about this passage:[27] he quotes various gnostic speculations about the angels, and suggests that, according to Paul, the Law was actually produced by evil angels. "The angels", he writes, "are somehow thought of by Paul as the authors of the Law." He would take verse 20 to mean: God is one, whereas a mediator implies a plurality of gods, i.e. angels. All such speculation about the sources of Paul's thought is made somewhat doubtful by a comparison with Acts 7. The association of angels with the giving of the Law stems from Deuteronomy 33, and had already by Paul's time produced speculations among the Rabbis, some of which were probably known to Paul. But the point of the contrast here is between direct grace and indirect Law, and the angels are brought in to underline the indirectness, not to suggest that the Law was not from God. Martin Werner elaborates the same theory of the connection between the imposition of the Law and the rule of evil angels.[28] But his theory encounters the same difficulties as that of Schlier. He actually describes the service of the Law as "servitude under the dominion of angelic powers", and later cites Colossians 2.8-18 as embodying the same idea. Here surely he has confused two meanings of the word "service", which are valid for German (*Dienst*) and English, but not for the word used in Colossians, which is *thrēskeia*. *Thrēskeia* can mean either "worship" or "superstition", but not "servitude". See K. L. Schmidt in TWZNT, where the meaning of "servitude" is nowhere mentioned.

It is not surprising that Bultmann, with his penchant for finding gnostic myths in the NT, should write as follows: "Especially significant is the fact that in the polemic of Galatians 3.19 Paul can take up the gnostic myth of the giving of the Law by angels in order to prove that the Law of Moses is not attributable to God himself."[29] All three assertions contained in this sentence are open to question, that the presence of angels on Sinai stems from a gnostic myth, that it was angels who were the authors of the Law and not God, and that Paul does not attribute a divine origin to the Law. He seems to have taken Schlier's speculations (or others like them) as proved facts. Here is no gnostic myth, but a Rabbinic speculation or midrash based on Deuteronomy 33. Paul does not represent the Law as given by angels: they only carried it down or delivered it. According to Paul it was given by God, or, even more probably, by Christ, as Stephen and the author of Hebrews definitely imply.

This leaves us with Hebrews 2.2,3 to fit into the picture. We have already suggested that according to Hebrews 12.22–7 it was Christ who spoke on Sinai. The author of Hebrews, consequently, cannot mean that it was the angels who originated the Law on Sinai. We must take it in the same sense as Acts 7.53, that is, the angels accompanied the theodicy, and perhaps actually handed the tables over to Moses. But the author of the Law was Christ. The point of the comparison, then, is the same as Stephen's: if the Law, inferior because indirect, carried such penalties, surely we, who know of a salvation spoken of directly by the Lord Christ himself, must be even more culpable than the Israelites of old if we neglect that salvation. We may even trace a closer connection with Acts 7: according to Stephen, the Israelites might have received living oracles directly from Christ himself. Instead of that they had to put up with a legal code, originally from Christ indeed, but mediated to them by angels, who may even be thought of as having uttered the detailed precepts of the Law to Moses. In just the same way in the Epistle to the Hebrews we have the contrast between the direct voice of Christ on Sinai, which the Israelites were not willing to listen to, and the precepts of the Law, which were actually uttered to Moses and so conveyed to the Israelites, a doubly indirect process. This in turn brings Hebrews in line with Galatians 3.19, where the doubly indirect process (a mediator—Moses—and the angels) is underlined. But if this is the meaning of Hebrews 2.2,3, we must be prepared for something corresponding to the "living oracles" of Acts 7.38, and this is in fact what we find, as we shall presently see.

Windisch gives an apt illustration from *The Apocalypse of Moses*, where the archangel Michael instructs Moses to take the tables from the hand of the Lord. Michel maintains that here the author of Hebrews differs from Paul in Galatians. Paul uses angelic mediation to disparage the Law, Hebrews to enhance it. Once again, we must maintain that this is a superficial conclusion: the angelic mediation here in Hebrews is a sign of indirectness. The more our author disparages the Law here the stronger is his argument. It is not in his interest to enhance the dignity of the Law at this point, for his readers could reply: "Naturally so tremendous an event as the theodicy on Sinai carried dreadful penalties; our doubt concerns the urgency and importance of the salvation in Christ of which you speak." If, on the other hand, our author is really saying, "Even the old dispensation, with its second-hand relation to God, carried dreadful penalties, much more will the directly revealed new dispensation involve you in penalties if you ignore it", then his argument is effective and appropriate.

But, if we accept the interpretation of Hebrews 2.2,3 which we advance here, we must be prepared for a slightly startling explanation of the phrase "It was declared at first by the Lord". All commentators without exception explain this as a reference to Jesus preaching the gospel first in the days of his flesh. Thus Windisch writes: "Salvation begins with the preaching of Jesus", and Michel compares Mark 16.20. This last quotation is only valuable as an interpretation of Hebrews 2.2,3, as it may very well be influenced by it. Others very naturally compare Hebrews 1.1,2 "God . . . has spoken to us by a Son". It is difficult to get rid of a feeling of incongruity when we find the author of Hebrews apparently telling us that the salvation was first heard of when it was preached by Jesus in Galilee. It is very unlike anything else we meet in the Epistle, or indeed in any other Epistle in the NT. It strangely recalls the "liberal" notion, so popular fifty years ago, that the original Christianity was the religion of Jesus, not the religion about Jesus. Perhaps we should look at this passage again in the hope of finding an explanation more in line with the author's general outlook.

We have observed that the author of Hebrews thought of Christ as speaking on Sinai to Israel (12.22–7) and in the tabernacle to Moses (chapters 3 and 4). The Law he regards as something inferior and ineffective compared with the new dispensation revealed in Christ. It was indirectly delivered, but Christ's voice could have been heard directly, had the Israelites not refused it. May it not be, then, that the salvation spoken by the Lord of which he writes in 2.3 means the prophecies of the coming age, the promises of the great salvation to be effected by the incarnation, death, and resurrection of Christ? As we have seen throughout our study of Hebrews, the author understands Christ as frequently speaking through prophets and Psalmists, and even in the person of the ineffable *Adōnai* of the Pentateuch. The same conclusion holds for Paul and Stephen. I suggest, therefore, that the correct Targum on Hebrews 2.2,3 runs like this:

Even the legislation on Sinai carried terrible penalties for its neglect; but that came indirectly from Christ, being mediated by angels, who are subordinate to Christ. How much greater penalties, then, must attach to neglect of the new dispensation? This dispensation was directly prophesied by the Lord Christ, through prophets, Psalmists, and others, and has been attested to us, and fulfilled in our time, by those very prophets, and by those who recognized the fulfilment of prophecy in our days.

This would give the word "attest" (*bebaioun*) both the meanings which it bears in Scripture, "attest" and "fulfil". It would also mean that the "signs", "wonders", and "various miracles", as well as the "gifts of the Holy Spirit" referred to in verse 4, are to be thought of as spread out all along the history of revelation from Abraham to the author's own time. Quite apart from the question of whether or not the author thought of Christ as speaking on Sinai, this explanation seems far more in accordance with his general view of the scriptural revelation than is the traditional account of this passage.

We have left to the very end one question about Stephen's speech that should not be ignored: Does Stephen find types of Christ in OT history, in particular in Joseph and Moses? This view was effectively presented by Rackham,[30] it is supported by Lampe and Woollcombe,[31] and is accepted by both C. S. C. Williams and R. P. C. Hanson. It would certainly seem to have much to be said for it, as far as Moses is concerned at any rate. Joseph is a much more doubtful case, as not very much emphasis is laid on his rejection by his brothers. The two verses in which Stephen comes nearest to depicting Moses as a type of Christ are Acts 7.25 and 7.35. Acts 7.25 runs:

> He supposed that his brethren understood that God was giving them deliverance by his hand, but they did not understand.

The other verse is one which we have already examined. The rejected Moses is described as "both ruler and deliverer". It would be absurd to deny that there is a parallel with Christ here, but is "Moses as a type of Christ" the right description? According to Stephen, Christ was present with Moses, so it is meaningless to say that Moses himself is a type of Christ. It would be a different matter if any word remotely resembling "type", such as *parabolē* or even *skia* ("shadow") were used. As it is, it seems more satisfactory to say that in both these places Christ is thought of as acting through Moses. In 7.25 "God was giving them deliverance" could quite easily refer to the pre-existent Christ, since, if our argument is valid, the very first phrase in Stephen's speech, "the God of glory", is meant to indicate Christ. In 7.25 Stephen says explicitly that God brought deliverance (*sōtēria*) through Moses. We have already suggested that in 7.35 Stephen would find in Deuteronomy 33.5a the statement that Moses was ruling "in Christ". Here, therefore, we do not find Moses depicted as a type of Christ, but rather Christ acting as ruler and redeemer through Moses. Thus, once again a passage in the NT that seemed at first sight to provide an admirable example of typology has proved instead to witness to the presence of Christ himself in OT history.

5

Christ in the Old Testament in the Fourth Gospel

By the very nature of his work, a Gospel not an Epistle, John's allusions to Christ's activity in OT history are more likely to be indirect and obscure than those which we find in Paul's Letters or in the Epistle to the Hebrews. In this respect he is more in the position of Stephen, who is preaching Christ (however allusively) to unbelievers, and who therefore must not be too explicit about matters which would be better appreciated by mature Christians. As we shall see, most of John's allusions to Christ's activity in OT history are obscure, hints rather than statements, unseen assumptions rather than explicit assertions. We begin, however, with the one passage where John comes out into the open on this subject, even though the passage is to be found in the middle of the Gospel. After that, having shown that John undoubtedly believes the Lord to have appeared in OT times, we can go through the rest of the Gospel in order, prepared to find other allusions where such an assumption illuminates the meaning of the text.

John 12.37–41

> Though he had done so many signs before them, yet they did not believe in him; it was that the word spoken by the prophet Isaiah might be fulfilled: "Lord, who has believed our report, and to whom has the arm of the Lord been revealed?" Therefore they could not believe. For Isaiah again said, "He has blinded their eyes and hardened their heart lest they should see with their eyes and perceive with their heart, and turn for me to heal them." Isaiah said this because he saw his glory (ὅτι εἶδεν τὴν δόξαν αὐτοῦ) and spoke of him.

John begins with a reference to Isaiah 53.1; we have already examined the appearance of this quotation in Romans 10.16, and suggested that there Paul envisages the prophet as directly addressing Christ (see p. 40). We are not here dealing with isolated *Testimonia*, and we must assume that John had studied the whole passage in Isaiah. Indeed, we find that only three verses earlier in the Isaiah passage the following sentence occurs:

> Behold my servant will understand and will be lifted up and will be greatly glorified.

John certainly takes this as a reference to Christ. C. H. Dodd actually suggests that the connection in the Fourth Gospel between Jesus being "lifted up" and being "glorified" goes back to this text in the LXX.[1]

It is therefore quite clear that, when John goes on in verse 41 to say "he saw his glory", he means that, when Isaiah had his vision of the Lord of Hosts in the Temple as described in Isaiah chapter six, it was the pre-existent Word whom he saw. It is really remarkable that all the English commentators can apparently accept this fact without in any degree perceiving its implications for John's understanding of the OT. Thus Bernard writes quite simply: "The evangelist, in affirming that he spoke of the glory of Christ, identifies Christ with the Yahveh of Israel. It was a later Christian thought that the Logos was the agent of the OT theophanies and it may be that John seems to suggest this."[2] Temple in the same strain writes that Christ is "thus identified with Jehovah; and this is correct, for Jehovah is God revealed, and God revealed is the Logos, Word, self-utterance of God; and the Logos is Jesus Christ".[3] The remarkable thing is that these two scholars can so calmly assume that the pre-existent Christ is identified with the *Adōnai* of the OT. If Christ is wholly identified with *Adōnai*, then we know nothing about the Father at all, and we are in danger of ultimately arriving at the Arian Christ, the inferior deity, suitable for representing at the human level the supreme God, who is himself ineffable and unknowable.

Hoskyns and Davey, on the other hand, attempt to evade the

scandal:[4] "To the Evangelist this vision of the prophet was not a naked vision of God (1.18), but a vision of the future glory of Jesus the Messiah (cf. 8.56)." Their cross-reference to 1.18 is very significant, though they do not draw out its implications. But they are not justified in using the phrase "future glory"; neither in 12.41 nor in 8.56 is it said that Isaiah or Abraham "foresaw" Christ. In each case John says quite simply that they saw his glory or his day. Bultmann follows exactly the same line. He writes: "Both things coincide for the evangelist: what Isaiah then beheld in the Temple was the future glory of Jesus which was due to him because of his works."[5] But modern commentators are not the first who have attempted to avoid the simple statement that Isaiah saw Christ's glory in the Temple in his own day. Augustine, with the sobering experience of the Arian controversy behind him, writes: "Isaiah saw him not as he is, but in a symbolic manner."[6] C. H. Dodd faces the problem more directly; like Hoskyns and Davey, he sees the connection with 1.18, but he suggests that out of reverence John changed Isaiah's "I saw the Lord" to "he saw his glory".[7] This does not seem likely, since the glory of God or Christ means throughout the Gospel the manifestation of God's or Christ's true nature, and is not a reverential periphrasis in the Rabbinic manner. In 1.14 "we beheld his glory" is not merely a respectful way of saying "we beheld him". If anything, it increases the reality of the sight, rather than putting it at one remove. Dodd goes on to comment: "Christ as Logos, as Son of the Father, is invested with the nature, character, and power of the eternal from eternity ... the manifestation of this nature, character, and power, in time, takes place in the words and works of the incarnate Logos." This is very true, but it does not explain why John is here claiming that this manifestation took place in time seven hundred years before the incarnation.

The commentator who seems to come nearest to John's thought here is Bauer,[8] who says specifically that this is not an instance of Isaiah seeing the future Messiah, but the pre-incarnate Logos: "In the Temple vision of Isaiah, the Evangelist, looking at it from his conviction that no man has seen God at any time, discerns a meeting of the prophet with the pre-incarnate Logos." He also points out that John would read the *Kyrios* of the LXX as Christ. This is well said, but he too fails to bring these observations to their logical conclusion. And this we must now do by way of an examination of Isaiah 6 in the LXX. It will be sufficient for our pupose if we reproduce verses 1, 5, and 7-11:

> And it came to pass in the year in which King Uzziah died, that I saw the Lord seated on a high and lofty throne, and the house was full of his glory. . . . And I said, Alas for me! For I am appalled, because, being a man and having unclean lips, I dwell in the midst of a people of unclean lips and I have seen with my eyes the King, the Lord Sabaoth. . . .
>
> And he touched my mouth and said, Behold, this has touched thy lips, and it will take away thy transgressions and will cleanse thy sins. And I heard the voice of *Kyrios* saying, Whom am I to send, and who will go to this people? And I said, Behold, here am I. Send me. And he said, Go, and say to this people, You shall indeed hear and not understand; and you shall indeed see and not perceive. For this people's heart has grown fat, and they have covered their eyes, lest they should see with their eyes and hear with their ears and turn back, and I should heal them. And I said, Lord, how long? And he said, Until towns are abandoned because there are none to dwell in them, and houses also because there are no people, and the land is left empty.

We cannot claim that we have before us the LXX as John read it; indeed it is plain that his version of Isaiah 6.9,10 is different from ours, chiefly in that according to John the process of blinding and rendering deaf is attributed to Christ, while in our version it is something that the people do to themselves. But the main outlines are sufficiently clear to enable us to say with confidence that John had this passage in mind as he wrote 12.37-41. We notice first the startling claim in Isaiah 6.1: "I saw the Lord", reinforced in 6.5 by "I have seen with my eyes the King". We know that John interprets this as an instance of Isaiah seeing the pre-existent Word, Christ. We may therefore be confident that the same implication applies to John 1.18, and draw out the implications accordingly. The reference in Isaiah 6.1 to seeing God's glory quite sufficiently explains "he saw his glory" in John 12.41 and makes the suggestion of a reverential periphrasis quite unnecessary. Again, in Isaiah 6.5 John encounters a reference to "the King". This links up with the incident narrated in John 12.13–15, where the crowd greets Jesus as "the King of Israel". He was the king, John means, in a theocratic sense far beyond the intention of the crowd. It is even possible that "this shall take away thy transgressions" in Isaiah 6.7 would be understood by John as a prophecy of Christ's atonement.[9] The words in Isaiah 6.8 "I heard the voice of *Kyrios*" remind us of John 5.37:

> His voice you have never heard; his form you have never seen.

No man can hear the voice of God, any more than he can see him. But the Son is the voice (cf. Heb. 12.22–7; Acts 7.32; and our comment on these passages).

The prophet is then told to go and preach to the Jews, but his preaching is to take the form of a prophecy of their disobedience. In view of the quotation of Isaiah 53.1 in John 12.38 we can be quite sure that John would refer all this to the Jews in the time of Christ, and the terrible desolation of the land prophesied in the Isaiah passage would seem to him to have been fulfilled in his own day with the sack of Jerusalem by the Romans and the depopulation of Judaea. We may therefore examine the rest of the Gospel with the confident assumption that John accepts whole-heartedly the tradition, common to Paul, the author to the Hebrews, and Stephen, of Christ's activity in OT history.

John 1.14–18

> And the Word became flesh and dwelt among us, full of grace and truth (πλήρης χάριτος καὶ ἀληθείας); and we have beheld his glory, glory as of the only Son from the Father. (John bore witness to him and cried, "This was he of whom I said, 'He who comes after me ranks before me, for he was before me.'") And from his fullness have we all received, grace upon grace. For the Law was given through Moses; grace and truth came through Jesus Christ. (ὁ νόμος διὰ Μωϋσέως ἐδόθη, ἡ χάρις καὶ ἡ ἀλήθεια διὰ Ἰησοῦ Χριστοῦ ἐγένετο). No one has ever seen God; the only Son [mg.

the only God], who is in the bosom of the Father, he has made him known.

"No one has ever seen God." This is in itself a challenging statement. It is only a truism to those who have been brought up (as were all the nineteenth-century commentators) on Greek philosophy with its emphasis on the intellectual, non-material nature of God. To a well-instructed Jew it would occasion surprise: men in OT times are recorded as having seen God. Apart from Isaiah's experience, which we have just been discussing, three occasions seem to stand out in OT history on which specially favoured men did see God: Jacob saw God at Bethel, as recorded in Genesis 28; he also saw him at Penuel (Gen. 32); and Moses is described in Exodus 34 as seeing God on Mount Sinai. In fact, we find echoes of all these three occasions in the first chapter of John's Gospel, though we must confine ourselves to the last of the three as far as our present inquiry is concerned.

We note first John 1.15: why does John the Baptist use "before me" twice? In fact they are two quite separate phrases in the Greek. The first is *emprosthen mou* and the second is *prōtos mou*. Bauer refuses to take these words in a temporal sense, because in that case the second phrase would be tautologous. He suggests that they indicate superior rank, though he does, of course, see a reference to the pre-existence of the Logos. But does it not make better sense if we take the two phrases (deliberately ambiguous, no doubt) of pre-existent activity in OT history, and of eternal pre-existence respectively? He was before me in OT times (literally "became before me"), because he existed from all eternity (literally "was ahead of me"). If so, verses 16 and 17 will refer to the whole activity of the Logos: everything comes from him, Law, many blessings in OT history including grace outpoured, and now the greatest of all, the incarnation. Thus "we all" will be "we Jews". John the Baptist speaks on behalf of believing Jews, among whom of course were the first apostles who beheld the glory of the incarnate Word.

Then comes verse 17 with its reference to the giving of the Law, followed by the abrupt statement that no one has ever seen

God. We look for a passage in the OT where the giving of the Law is associated with man seeing God, and we find exactly such a passage in Exodus 33.12—34.9. Exodus 33.12,13 describes how Moses asked that God should accompany him, and God promises that "my presence will go with you" (33.14). The Hebrew is literally "my face will go".[10] The LXX avoids this anthropomorphism and translates "I myself will go before you." But we must not assume that this is what John's version of the LXX had. Indeed, we must not assume that John did not have access to the Hebrew. T. F. Glasson, in his very careful and learned study of the Fourth Gospel, writes: "And here I should like to say once and for all that in studying John, while the LXX should never be neglected, at times it is the Hebrew Bible that leads us to essential links and connections."[11] The truth of this is abundantly illustrated in the passage we are studying. Moses is then told that God will cause his "goodness" (33.19) and later his "glory" (33.22) to pass by. Moses is to have a partial vision of God: he will see God's back but not his face. The LXX translates both "goodness" and "glory" with the one word *doxa*. G. Quell in Kittel's *Biblia Hebraica* suggests that the LXX may have preserved the original reading, and that "glory" stood in both places. The first three verses of Exodus 34 then relate how Moses was commanded to hew out two more blocks on which the Law was to be written, and to bring them up to the top of Mount Sinai. Then the narrative continues (Ex. 34.4-6 LXX):

> And Moses took the two tables of stone, and *Kyrios* came down in a cloud and stood beside him there. And he called on the name of *Kyrios*. And *Kyrios* passed by before his face and called, *Kyrios* the merciful and compassionate God, long-suffering and full of mercy and true... (μακρόθυμος καὶ πολυέλεος καὶ ἀληθινός).

This is a pretty clear statement that Moses did see God. If we read to the end of the chapter, we find that Moses, having received a version of the Law, descends from the mountain with his face suffused with glory, from having seen the Lord. This in fact leads on to the very passage in which Paul shows so much interest in 2 Corinthians 3, and in which we detected the belief that it was Christ who spoke to Moses in the Tabernacle. It seems to me to be a very strong probability indeed that, according to John, it was the pre-existent Word, the Christ, whom Moses is described as seeing in Exodus 34.4–6. The very last phrase we quoted from Exodus, "full of mercy and true", is a translation of the Hebrew *rabh chesedh we'ᵉmeth*. It will at once be apparent that the phrase in John 1.14 is a rather more literal translation of these words: πλήρης χάριτος καὶ ἀληθείας. C. H. Dodd insists that the phrase χάριτος καὶ ἀληθείας can only represent the Hebrew phrase transliterated above, and he notes that in Hellenistic Judaism *charis* rather than *eleos* became the usual translation of *chesedh*.[12] The phrase occurs fifteen times in all in the Hebrew Bible;[13] *rabh chesedh* is also fairly frequent, eight times in fact (the LXX never uses *plērēs* for *rabh* here). In only one other place is *rabh chesedh we'ᵉmeth* used of God, in Psalm 86.15, where the LXX is πολυέλεος καὶ ἀληθινός. It is a Psalm of deep supplication to God for help out of trouble, and does not seem to have any relevance to John 1.14. We may therefore conclude with a high degree of certainty that in John 1.14 the author of the Fourth Gospel is deliberately echoing Exodus 34.6, and means to infer that it was the Word whom Moses saw in the scene described in Exodus 34. Whether he is using a different version of the LXX from ours, or translating direct from the Hebrew, we cannot say. The latter hypothesis is by no means to be ruled out, as Glasson has observed. John must have identified Christ with the "presence" of Exodus 33.14, whatever exact text of that verse he possessed. Admittedly in the Exodus passage it is clearly stated that Moses would not be permitted to see God's face, but John must have argued that to see God's face was to see God. This is impossible for men, therefore what Moses enjoyed was a vision of Christ. Now in Jesus that vision has been granted to men again, much more directly and compellingly. Once again we have the thought which we traced in 2 Corinthians 3, that Christians stand where Moses stood. It seems that the parallel between Exodus 34 and John 1.14 is too remarkable to admit of any other conclusion than that which we have put forward here. There is the well-known contrast between the indirectness of the Law and the directness of Christ's relation to those who meet him, whether in the old dispensation or in the new. Certainly *dia* with the genitive is used for both Moses and Christ in verse 17, but the verbs are different: the Law was given by the mediation of Moses, grace and truth came through Christ, because he *is* grace and truth (cf. 14.6). We have in fact precisely the same attitude to the Law *vis à vis* Christ as we have traced in Paul, in Hebrews, and in Stephen's speech.

G. H. C. Macgregor would avoid the difficulty of the OT theophanies by denying that Moses *really* saw God: "Nobody has ever seen God (a favourite Johannine thought; cf. 5.37; 6.46; 1 John 4.12,20) with the vision of sense, not even Moses, who prayed to be granted that vision (Ex. 33.18 sq.)."[14] Macgregor is here following the argument of Augustine and several of the Fathers before him.[15] But he cannot use their additional proof, that in seeing God Moses only saw *posteriora eius*, i.e. the things of his that were to come, the incarnation, and that therefore Moses' wish was only fulfilled at the Transfiguration. These Fathers were not in a position to ask impartially, what exactly did John mean? Augustine at least knew of the dangerous experiment of the Arianized Church during the generation before him, and he realized what disastrous conclusions resulted from identifying Christ with all OT theophanies. But we must press that question home, and in fact, if we try to read the OT as John read it, we cannot avoid the conclusion that Moses did see the Lord, and that, according to John, that Lord was Christ, the pre-existent Word.

Bultmann[16] has observed the parallel with Exodus 34.6, but he specifically rejects the conclusion that it has had any influence on John 1.14. His reason is that the meaning of *alētheia* ("truth") which runs all through the Fourth Gospel makes it impossible to understand the word here in the sense of *'emeth* in Exodus 34.6. But we may legitimately suggest that here Bultmann has been unduly influenced by his tendency to interpret the Fourth Gospel in Greek rather than Hebrew terms, and he makes no attempt in his commentary to reckon with the occasions in the OT when men are described as seeing God. Strathmann[17] notes a parallel only with Exodus 33.18–22, which he describes as an "OT prefiguration" (*Vorbild*) of the incarnation, and he emphasizes that in the Exodus account Moses did not dare to behold God's face. We would be inclined to question the idea of prefiguration here, as being too like those many other occasions on which commentators have escaped from a difficult NT interpretation of the OT by use of the magic concept typology. And if Moses did not dare to look on God, this is not at all the same thing as saying that he could not have seen God. The argument is: Moses is described as being in a position to see the Lord. But no man has seen God at any time, therefore he whom he did see (or at the very least could have seen) is not God the Father but God the Word. Of all scholars Glasson comes nearest to the view we have taken here, and yet surprisingly he does not see the astonishing conclusion that John is hinting at. He writes: "The phrase of John 1.14 'full of grace and truth' may reflect Exodus 34.6 'plenteous in mercy and truth', and it is at least interesting to observe that the very next verse in Exodus 34 says that God takes away (Heb. *nāsā'*) iniquity and transgression and sin. Like the one disclosed in Exodus 34, the Christ of God is full of mercy and truth."[18] This admirable comparison would gain immensely in force if we could say instead that Christ *is* the one disclosed in Exodus 34, and this surely is what John means.[19]

In 1 John 4.12 we meet again the sentiment "No man has ever seen God". Here the meaning is that God is to be seen in Christ alone for two reasons: first, because the love of God is manifested in Christ (verses 9, 20), and second because the author and his fellow witnesses have seen (same word as in John 1.14) that the Father sent the Son. Here is clearly stated that the Son is the visibility of the Father.

John 5.37–47

It will be sufficient if we reproduce verses 37–9 and 44–7:

> And the Father who sent me has himself borne witness to me. His voice you have never heard, his form you have never seen; and you do not have his word abiding in you, for you do not believe him whom he has sent. You search the scriptures because you think that in them you have eternal life; and it is they that bear witness to me. . . .
>
> How can you believe, who receive glory from one another, and do not seek the glory that comes from the only God? Do not think that I shall accuse you to the Father; it is Moses who accuses you, on whom you have set your hope. If you believed Moses, you would believe me, for he wrote of me. But, if you do not believe his writings, how will you believe my words?

It seems very likely that behind these verses lies some passage from the OT in which somebody *is* recorded as having seen the form of God and heard his voice. The cross-reference in the margin of the Bible Society Text is to Deuteronomy 4.12, where Moses reminds Israel of their experience on Mount Horeb:

> Then the Lord spoke to you out of the midst of the fire; you heard the sound of words, but saw no form; there was only a voice.

But this is hardly satisfactory, for here the form and the voice are not encountered together, but the one is emphasized and the other denied. Another possibility is Exodus 33.18–22, which we have already suggested lies behind John 1.14–18. There Moses asks to see God's glory, and is granted a certain revelation, a vision of God's back, but not of his face. Perhaps nearer to what we seek is Exodus 24.9–18, where Moses and Aaron and the elders of Israel go up the mountain and are described as seeing the God of Israel (24.10). But no word for "form" is used here, and though God speaks to Moses, he does not at this point utter the Law, but only gives instructions about the Tabernacle.

More appropriate than any of these is a passage which we have already detected as lying behind Hebrews 3.1–6. This is Numbers 12.6–8. The LXX is as follows (12.6b–8a):

> If there shall be a prophet of yours to *Kyrios*, in a vision I make myself known to him and in a dream shall I speak to him. Not so is

my minister Moses; in all my house he is faithful; face to face shall I speak to him [lit. "mouth to mouth"], in real form [*en eidei* and *eidos* is the word used for "form" in John 5.37], and not by riddles, and he has seen the glory of *Kyrios*.

Here we have all the elements we need: Moses is described as seeing God face to face, and "in real form"; although the word "voice" is not used, the fact of the Lord speaking personally to Moses is strongly emphasized. We cannot be at all confident that John had before him this version of the LXX. The last phrase is somewhat different in the MT. The RSV translates it:

clearly, and not in dark speech, for he beholds the form of the Lord.

The word translated "clearly" is not really appropriate in Hebrew, for it is the same as that translated "in a vision" in verse 6. Again, in the very last phrase the Hebrew "the form of the Lord" is rendered by the LXX "the glory of *Kyrios*". On the whole it seems likely that John was following something closer to our LXX than to our MT. That would give him both *eidos* meaning "real form" and "the glory of the Lord", and these both appear in Jesus' discourse here.[20]

If we take this passage from Numbers as most likely to be in John's mind here, then we can follow the subtle unfolding of his theme admirably. In 5.37 Jesus says that the Jews have never seen God's form or heard his voice. But Moses has seen the form of God and heard him speak. They search the Scriptures, which do indeed witness to Christ, for when Moses recorded in Numbers 12.1-8 the divine testimony to his intimacy with the Lord, he was in fact telling us that it was Christ whose form he had seen, Christ who spoke with him in the Tabernacle. In verse 30 Jesus says that the Jews will not come to him in order to have life, and in verse 44 what he says about them is

You do not seek the glory that comes from the only God.

Commentators have been a little puzzled about this phrase: How exactly are the Jews supposed to have seen the glory that comes from God? The point is that coming to Jesus for life eternal and seeking the glory that comes from God are the same thing. Moses sought the glory of God on the Mount and in the Tabernacle, and found it—or rather found him, for Christ is the glory: "and he has seen the glory of *Kyrios*" (Num. 12.8 LXX). It is therefore Moses who condemns them, for he wrote concerning Jesus, Not that he *prophesied* concerning Jesus. The favourite text from the Pentateuch which scholars quote in order to prove that Moses prophesied concerning Jesus is Deuteronomy 18.15 sq. (it is cited in the Bible Society Text margin here).[21] But that only points to a prophet like Moses; in Numbers 12.6,7 the notion of Moses being only a prophet is explicitly dismissed. A prophet can only see in a dream or a vision, but Moses saw face to face. It was Christ whom he saw, since no man can see the Father. So, when John says that Moses wrote concerning Jesus, he does not mean that Moses prophesied concerning Jesus. He means that Moses wrote about the Jesus whom he had seen on the Mount and in the Tabernacle. We may add that the author to the Hebrews seems to have found Christ in this passage also, and that this somewhat strengthens the case for assuming its presence behind this passage in the Fourth Gospel.

As we have observed, the commentators are a little embarrassed to explain how exactly Moses spoke of Christ. Bernard can only refer to Deuteronomy 18.15 and mention the brazen serpent. Barrett comments: "The Law rightly used should lead men not to unbelief, but to faith."[22] If this is so, to say "Moses wrote concerning me" is a rather awkward way of expressing this. Macgregor can get no farther than Deuteronomy 18.15. Bauer, besides quoting the obvious text from Deuteronomy, remarks: "For our evangelist the OT has passed completely into the possession of the Christian Church." We would claim that this had happened even more completely than he had imagined. Hoskyns and Davey have a different approach: they give a cross-reference to 2 Corinthians 3.13-16, though they do not see the full significance of that passage. Then they comment: "The reference here to what Moses wrote is therefore neither to any particular passage in the Pentateuch, such as, for example,

Deuteronomy 18.15, nor to some selection of so-called messianic passages; the reference is to the whole panorama of OT scriptures." John's allusion seems much too definite and particular for so vague and general a conclusion. Dodd seems to follow very much the same line of interpretation.[23] He paraphrases 5.46b thus: "You fail to see their true purport which would point to me as the real mediator of eternal life." The main point is that John does not here claim Moses as a prophet of the future Christ. He means that Moses witnessed to the Christ whom he himself had seen.

Two comments from the Fathers may throw further light on this. Irenaeus, writing about this very passage in John, says:

> Since therefore the writings of Moses (*litteras*) are the words (*verba*) of Christ, Christ himself said to the Jews, "If you had believed Moses, you would have believed me also. If therefore you do not believe his writings, you will not believe my words either." He manifestly indicates that Moses' writings are his utterances.[24]

This is coming very close indeed to saying that Christ spoke to Moses. Indeed we have already seen that Irenaeus would have had no difficulty about accepting this.

Augustine, as we have seen, is in the full tide of reaction against those who were only too ready to find the activity of the Word in OT history. He cannot therefore simply identify Christ with any one OT theophany. But even he has no doubt whatever that Christ spoke through various figures in the OT. This is what he says in *De Trinitate* III.11.26 about John 5.46:

> Indeed the Law was given to that people in the proclamations of angels [the reference is to Acts 7.53; Gal. 3.19]. But the coming of the Lord Jesus Christ is ordained and announced beforehand through the Law. And he himself as the Word of God was in the angels in a wonderful and inexpressible manner, in those angels by whose proclamations the Law itself was given. Consequently he says in the Gospel: "If you believed Moses, you would believe me, for he spoke concerning me."

John 6.30-40

We are concerned here only with the question: Who gave the manna? We need therefore only quote 6.30-3:

> So they said to him, "Then what sign do you do, that we may see, and believe you? What work do you perform? Our fathers ate the manna in the wilderness; as it is written, 'He gave them bread from heaven to eat'." Jesus then said to them, "Truly, truly, I say to you, it was not Moses who gave you the bread from heaven; my Father gives you the true bread from heaven. For the bread of God is that which comes down from heaven and gives life to the world."

Commentators have naturally pointed out that the Messiah was expected to call down the manna again. S-B gives several examples of this. On the other hand, nearly all the editors assume that Jesus' aim is to show the Father, not Moses, as the true giver of the manna. So Bernard, Temple, Heitmuller, Bultmann, Barrett, and R. H. Lightfoot.[25] The only exceptions to this rule are Bauer and Dodd. Bauer points out that Philo sees in the manna a type of the divine Logos. He does not conclude that, according to John, it was God who gave the manna, only that, because it was not Moses who gave it, it was not from heaven. But surely this is contradicted by Psalm 78.24, quoted by Jesus' Jewish opponents in order to prove the importance of the incident. Jesus does not deny that the manna was bread from heaven. Dodd is extraordinarily difficult to follow here, for he begins by assuming that, according to John, Moses did give the manna: "Again the manna given by Moses is contrasted with the true bread from heaven."[26] He suggests that the manna here symbolizes the Torah in John's mind, and he adds: "This bread of Moses is superseded by the real bread from heaven." Finally we read in a footnote: "The argument is somewhat complicated by the fact that the gift of the manna was expected to be restored by the Messiah." The argument, we may suggest, is not complicated but explicated by this fact, and it does not help to explain this passage if one begins by denying what Jesus asserts here—namely, that Moses did not give the manna. But, as we shall see, there is a certain truth in the suggestion that the manna here symbolizes the Torah. It stands at least for the old dispensation.

Strathmann follows the line of the majority of scholars in assuming that John wanted to show God as the giver of the manna, and he refers to Exodus 16.15. But there it is "the Lord", not God who gives it. This would have significance in John's eyes. Strathmann goes on to say that the manna lacked the two characteristics of the true bread from heaven: (*a*) it did not come down from heaven, and (*b*) it did not give life to the world. This is to misunderstand what John is trying to indicate here. The manna was from heaven: Scripture to this effect is quoted in 6.31. Also 6.49, which Strathmann refers to to prove that the manna did not give life, only says that it did not give eternal life. In a word, the contrast here is between two dispensations from Christ, and the inferiority of the first lies in the fact that it was temporary, material, and limited, not in the fact that it was not from Christ. To the list of orthodox interpreters of this passage we may add Glasson, who writes: "The gift of manna in the wilderness came not from Moses but from God."[27]

We return therefore to our original question: Who gave the manna? We must glance at two relevant passages from the OT. The first is Exodus 16. It is a long chapter, so we can only underline the essential points. In 16.4 (LXX) we read:

> And *Kyrios* said to Moses, "Behold I am about to rain loaves upon you from heaven."

In view of this it seems impossible to accept Bauer's suggestion that according to John the manna did not come from heaven. It is significant that in 16.10, when the people complain, we read:

> And they turned towards the wilderness, and the glory of *Kyrios* appeared in a cloud.

We have already seen good reason to believe that in John's mind the glory of the Lord is associated with Christ, and we remember that in Paul the pre-existent Christ is probably identified with the pillar of cloud. This verse would lead to a similar identification in John's mind. Finally comes 16.15, where Moses says to the people:

> This is the bread which *Kyrios* has given you to eat.

To these quotations we may add Psalm 78.24 (LXX 77.24), which is actually quoted by Jesus' opponents:

> And he rained manna upon them to eat,
> and gave them the bread of heaven.

It is not easy to say which of these passages is actually cited in John 6.31; but it does not make very much difference. In any case, the true answer to our question seems to be: it was Christ who gave them manna from heaven. A little farther on, in 6.49, Jesus reminds them that their fathers died even after they had eaten the manna, whereas the bread he gives them is the bread of life (cf. also 6.58). The cross-reference in the Bible Society Text at 6.49 is 1 Corinthians 10.5, where Paul reminds the Corinthians that their fathers were overthrown in the wilderness. But this is misleading: John is not trying to emphasize that the Israelites who ate the manna were punished, only that the manna did not give them eternal life. What we have here no doubt, then, is the contrast we have already noticed in Hebrews 12.22–7 between the old, temporary dispensation and the new, eternal one. As in Hebrews, so in John, Christ is the author of both.

Another cross-connection worth noting is the theme of protesting. In John 6.41–3 the Jews protest at Jesus saying that he is the bread that came down from heaven, and he tells them not to protest at this. In Exodus 16.2 the people protest, and in 16.8 Moses rebukes them, saying:

> your protests are not against us, but against God.

Perhaps John is suggesting that, just as the Jews protested against Christ in the wilderness of old, so they are doing now. On each occasion it is he who provided bread.

We maintain therefore that in John 6.32 the implication is this: it was not Moses who gave the manna in the wilderness, it was Christ. But that was an indirect gift. Now the Father gives life directly in the incarnate Word. It may even be that 6.36 refers to the appearance of the glory of the Lord in the pillar of cloud at the time of the giving of the manna:

> But I said to you that you have seen me and yet you do not believe.

The Jews of Jesus' time might be identified for the moment with their fathers of old. But of this we cannot be sure.

We have already pointed out that Paul in 1 Corinthians 10 identifies Christ by implication as the giver of the manna, the "supernatural food", literally "spiritual food". So John in making this identification is not a lone pioneer. Similarly we have quoted Melito as maintaining the same view, see p. 15. He writes, "He it was who gave thee manna from heaven", and Chrysostom in his exposition of 1 Corinthians 10, quoted on p. 20. rightly concludes that according to Paul it was Christ who gave the manna. It is interesting also to note that Philo identifies the Logos as the giver of bread, and Wisdom as the bread that was given. The last detail of course allegorizes away the historical element in true Philonic style, quite unlike John, who does not mean to deny that the manna in the wilderness afforded real material nourishment. We may say the same thing of Paul.[28]

If John is ambiguously portraying Christ as the giver of the manna in the wilderness, we would expect also to find traces of the belief that it was Christ who gave the water from the Rock. After all, this belief is explicit in Paul. It is not at all easy to find a reference, but it may be that Glasson has pointed one out. He suggests that the mysterious quotation from "the scripture" in John 7.37 is in fact a reference to the smitten Rock.[29] Glasson would translate verses 37 and 38 as follows:

> If any man thirst let him come to me,
> and let him who believes in me drink.
> As the Scripture says,
> Streams of living water shall flow out of his bosom [i.e. Christ's bosom].

This is of course a perfectly possible translation. The difficulty is that it still does not connect the scriptural quotation with any exact passage in the OT. Glasson supports his suggestion by another: he thinks that John 19.34,35, where blood and water flow from Christ's side, may be a reference to a Rabbinic tradition found in *Shemmoth* R. 1222a that Moses struck the Rock twice, and that the first time it gushed out blood and the second time water. The tradition is based on Psalm 78.20:

> He smote the rock so that water gushed out
> and streams overflowed.

This may possibly be the passage that John is referring to in 7.38, but there is no very close verbal parallel. The most we can say is that this may have been in John's mind. If it were so, it is likely that he follows Paul in meaning to suggest that the Rock *was* Christ, not, as Glasson maintains, that the Rock was a type of Christ.

Reverting for a moment to our interpretation of John 6.30-40, it may be relevant to suggest that there is another passage in the Fourth Gospel that lays itself open to similar treatment. We maintained that the thought behind 6.32 was of Christ as the giver of the manna in the wilderness. In 7.14-24 there is another obscure reference to Moses. The implication behind verses 14-18 is that Christ is teaching the real meaning of the Law, for that, it seems, is what "one who has studied the Law" means. Then comes verse 19:

> Did not Moses give you the Law? Yet none of you keeps the Law.

We will be suggesting an alternative translation presently, but for the moment we will be content to note that this is followed by verses 22 and 23, where we learn that circumcision was not given by Moses, and that it is only really fulfilled in the perfect wholeness to be found in Christ. I would suggest that verse 19 should be taken as intentionally parallel to 6.32, and translated:

> Moses did not give you the Law, and none of you keeps the Law.

A paraphrase of the whole passage would therefore run something like this: "Do the will of God by believing on me, and you will judge whether my teaching is from God. It was not Moses who gave you the Law, he only mediated it (cf. 1.17; Gal. 3.19; Acts 7.53), but it was I who gave it. But even so none of you keeps it. Why do you seek me, since it was I who gave you the Law?" The implication is that those who believe in Jesus will recognize that he is the author of the Law as well. Thus, the sense of 7.22-4 will be that Christ, who gave the partial and temporary Law of Moses, has every right to bring in the full, permanent dispensation of which his healings are the sign. There might also be another point in which 6.32 and 7.19 are parallel: in chapter 6, as we have seen, it was Christ who gave the manna, but even so those who received it protested. In chapter 7, it is Christ who gave the Law, but even so the Jews have not kept it.

John 8.30-59

As far as we are concerned, the crucial point of this chapter is not reached until verse 56:

> Your father Abraham rejoiced that he was to see my day; he saw it and was glad.

Plainly there is some reference to Abraham's experience here, but it is impossible to say with certainty which passage in Genesis forms the background to this verse. Several editors have pointed out that the Rabbis took the phrase "advanced in age" in Genesis 18.11 to mean "he entered into the ages to come", i.e. he was given foreknowledge of what was to come, and therefore they identify Genesis 18 as the passage which John has in mind.[30] If this be the case, we may suggest that Christ is identified with one of the three angels who visited Abraham, probably with the one whom Abraham addresses as "my Lord" in Genesis 18.3.[31] The difficulty about accepting Genesis 18 as the passage in question is that there is no hint in it of Abraham rejoicing; it is Sarah who laughs in 18.12. Again, according to this interpretation, Abraham is only shown the future Christ. The Words "he saw my day" imply that he actually saw Christ.

Another suggestion, therefore, is to take Genesis 17 as the passage John has in mind. This has the advantage that it contains a promise to Abraham about his posterity, and Abraham is described as laughing in 17.17. Moreover, there is evidence that this was traditionally understood as a sign of joy rather than incredulity.[32] Also there are references to Abraham's seed in 17.7. On the other hand, this is a passage from the Priestly narrative, and therefore "the Lord" occurs only in the first verse. There indeed the LXX has "*Kyrios* appeared", which might very well indicate Christ to John.[33]

Neither of these two passages can be rejected out of hand, but there is another that has an equal claim on our attention, Genesis 15. It begins in verse 1 with the words "the word of *Kyrios* came". It continues in verse 4 with (LXX)

> and at once the voice of *Kyrios* came to him saying . . .

We can confidently suggest that for John "the voice of the Lord" means Christ, for no man has ever heard the Father's voice.[34] There is also in this chapter a promise to Abraham's seed in verse 5. And verse 6 is very relevant:

> And he believed the Lord, and he reckoned it to him as righteousness.

This is surely the meaning of "what Abraham did" in 8.39. What Abraham did was to believe in Christ, and this is what God wills. See John 6.29:

> This is the work of God that you believe in him whom he has sent.

The RSV has obscured the parallel by translating "what Abraham did" in John 8.39. The Greek is literally "the works of Abraham". In 8.40 the Jews are accused of seeking to kill Jesus, who has spoken the truth to them. The difficulty about accepting this passage as the only one in John's mind is that there is no mention of Abraham's joy.[35]

In fact, there is no necessity for us to choose one of these three passages to the exclusion of the others. John probably had all three in mind, and perhaps the promise to Abraham in Genesis 12.1–7 also. If we put all these together we find all the details that John includes: the rejoicing in 17.17; the appearance of an angel in 18.1–15; Abraham's faith in 15.6; the prophecy of the future seed (who is Christ) in all of them. Thus John 8.56 contains not only the claim that Abraham was told all about the future incarnation, but also the claim that he actually saw Christ. The language is no doubt intentionally ambiguous, but we must understand that Abraham saw Christ, and was justified, like all Christians, through faith in Christ.

It is very relevant to quote a passage from Irenaeus here, in which he certainly sees in John 8.50 a cross-reference to Genesis 15.6. The quotation is from *Adv. Haer.* IV.10.2:

> Since therefore Abraham was a prophet, and he saw in the Spirit the comings of the Lord, and the plan concerning his passion whereby he himself and all should begin to be saved who believed in God as he believed, he rejoiced greatly. Therefore the Lord was not unknown to Abraham, since he longed to see his day, nor indeed was the Father of the Lord unknown; for he had learned from the Word of the Lord, and had believed on him; for this reason it was reckoned to him for righteousness by the Lord.

Compare also Hilary *De Trinitate* 4.27, where Hilary refers to John 8.56 and says that the God worshipped by Abraham was Christ.[36] Chrysostom suggests that John 8.56 refers to the sacrifice of Isaac: Abraham recognized in the type of the sacrifice of the ram Christ's self-offering which was to come.[37]

Both Bauer and Macgregor hold that Abraham saw Jesus in paradise. Macgregor writes: "He is not dead, as the Jews wrongly held (v. 52), but still consciously following the fortunes of his people", and he compares Mark 12.26. Quite apart from the fact that there is no trace of this idea in John, it would require "Abraham rejoices" not "rejoiced". Presumably Abraham would go on rejoicing in paradise during the whole period of the incarnation. Hoskyns and Davey do see a parallel with Hebrews 3.1-6. and they do suggest that Abraham's works were faith: "It was the distinction of Abraham to have received the emissaries of God with faith and obedience" (Gen. 18.2 sq.; 15.1 sq.). But they add "Abraham foresaw the advent of God". Very much the same approach to John 8.56 is taken by B. Lindars;[38] he takes Abraham's rejoicing to indicate joy at the birth of Isaac, in whose birth he saw the future seed, Christ. This is true, but not the whole truth. Abraham, according to John, both foresaw Christ's advent and spoke to Christ who was present with him. Bultmann insists that the Greek of "he rejoiced that he was to see my day" can only refer to the future, either "he yearned with rapture to see" or "he rejoiced that he should see". This is quite in accordance with our account of this passage. We may suggest that "he rejoiced that he was to see my day" may have Genesis 17.17 as its primary reference, and the words "he saw it" may refer primarily to chapter 18 of Genesis, where he recognizes the pre-existent Word in one of the three angels.

As we conclude our study of the Fourth Gospel, we may quote a penetrating remark by Jean Daniélou in *Sacramentum Futuri*, p. 139: "The Gospel of John shows the mystery of Christ unfolding itself on three planes, that of the Exodus which prefigures it, that of the Gospel which fulfils it, and that of the sacraments which prolong it." The three-tier plan is profoundly true, but we would not accept the word "prefigure". Christ is present in all three planes, as much really present in the first as in the other two. Perhaps we might substitute a paraphrase for Daniélou's first phrase: "Christ is present in the old dispensation, which anticipated the new in an indirect and impermanent fashion."

6

Christ in the Old Testament in the Catholic Epistles

The theme of the activity of the pre-existent Christ in OT history has proved to be so widespread in the NT that we are fully justified in looking for it in the Catholic Epistles. These Epistles, of course, have none of the internal homogeneity which we can take for granted in each of the three great NT traditions which we have examined so far, in the Pauline Epistles, the Hebrews-Acts 7 tradition, and in the Fourth Gospel. On the other hand, the three writings with which we are concerned in this chapter all probably belong to the later part of the NT. We do not propose to discuss the question of the respective dates of the Epistles of James, 1 Peter, and Jude. It will be sufficient for our purpose if we assume that they witness to the fact that the belief in the activity of Christ in OT times can be found in the later writings of the NT, thereby providing a bridge between the main traditions within the NT and the post-apostolic writers such as Ignatius and Justin, who also exhibit this belief with greater or lesser emphasis.

The Epistle of James

We have to deal with one long passage, James 5.7–15, and one isolated verse, 2.1. But if we actually reproduce 5.7,8; 10,11; 14,15, it will be enough for the moment:

> Be patient, therefore, brethren, until the coming of the Lord. Behold, the farmer waits for the precious fruit of the earth, being

patient over it until it receives the early and the late rain. You also be patient. Establish your hearts, for the coming of the Lord is at hand ... As an example of suffering and patience, brethren, take the prophets who spoke in the name of the Lord. Behold, we call those happy who were steadfast. You have heard of the steadfastness of Job, and you have seen the purpose of the Lord, how the Lord is compassionate and merciful (πολύσπλαγχνός ἐστιν ὁ κύριος καὶ οἰκτίρμων).... Is any among you sick? Let him call for the elders of the church, and let them pray over him, anointing him with oil in the name of the Lord; and the prayer of faith will save the sick man and the Lord will raise him up; and if he has committed sins, he will be forgiven.

In 5.7,8 we find two references to "the coming (*parousia*) of the Lord", both of which must refer to Christ. But there is no indication whatever that "the Lord" throughout this passage does not refer to the same person, Christ. Some scholars, however, perplexed by the fact that James seems to attribute so much to Jesus, have attempted to find a distinction of usage within this passage. Thus J. B. Mayor claims that when *Kyrios* is used here without the article it refers to the Father; when it is used with the article it refers to Christ.[1] But this is very difficult to maintain in view of verse 11. We would have to imagine a usage like this: verse 8 "the Lord" = Christ; verse 10 "*Kyrios*" = the Father; verse 11a "the purpose of *Kyrios*" (*telos*) = the Father; verse 11 b "the Lord" = Christ, and this in an OT quotation! But if it is once admitted that "the Lord" in the quotation in verse 11b refers to the Father, then the usage which Mayor maintains breaks down. Augustine and Bede[2] took the phrase "the purpose of the Lord" (literally "the end of the Lord") as a reference to Christ's passion and death. The great majority of editors, however, take both "*Kyrios*" and "the Lord" in verses 10 and 11 as referring to the Father, despite all the difficulties involved in this course.[3]

R. J. Knowling does indeed remark that some commentators take the prophets mentioned in verse 10 as NT prophets. This would make it possible to take "in the name of the Lord" in that verse as Christ's name. But here another difficulty is encountered: Would those who explain the verse in this manner be prepared to accept the OT quotation in verse 11 as referring to Christ? It seems very unlikely that they would. Again, there is no reason to think that NT prophets suffered any more than other Christians, and therefore they would not be especially suitable as examples of patience. Knowling points out that in verse 11 the Syriac reads "the end which the Lord made for him", and he mentions a theory held by some that there is an implied parallel between the appearance of God to Job and the appearance of Christ in the *parousia*. This is interesting, but we must defer consideration of this verse for a while.

David Daube in *The NT and Rabbinic Judaism*[4] definitely takes "in the name of the Lord" in verse 14 as a reference to Christ. If this be so, then it is impossible to deny that "in the name of the Lord" in verse 10 refers to Christ, and this in turn opens up the possibility that every mention of *Kyrios* or "the Lord" in this passage refers to Christ. When we look at James' use of *Kyrios* and "the Lord" outside this passage, we find in fact that it is ambiguous. In 1.1. "the Lord Jesus Christ" occurs. In 1.7 "the Lord" is completely ambiguous, with a slight balance of probability in favour of it meaning the Father, in view of "God" in verse 5. In 2.1 we have "our Lord Jesus Christ" (a verse we shall have to consider later). In 3.9 "the Lord and Father" is quite clear, and in 4.10 "the Lord" is ambiguous. "God" has been mentioned in verses 7 and 8, but in view of the eschatological tone of the verse, we might well decide that "the Lord" is Christ here. In 4.15 "if the Lord wills" is ambiguous; as we have already noted, "the coming of the Lord" in 5.7 and 8 must refer to Christ. We conclude therefore that James is perfectly capable of using both *Kyrios* and "the Lord" for Christ, and that the meaning in any given case can only be determined by the context.

When we look at James 5.7–15 in the light of this, we find that this could very easily be yet one more passage in which Christ's activities in OT history are taken for granted. The first such reference occurs in 5.10; the prophets spoke in the name of Christ, a doctrine for which we shall find confirmation presently when we come to examine 1 Peter 1.10–12, and which we can amply illustrate from the Fathers. Indeed it forms the main theme of our next chapter also. We would go on then to James 5.11, and take both "the end of the Lord" as a reference to Christ, and also apply to him the words "the Lord is compassionate and merciful". If so, there may be a deliberate intention to draw a parallel between the appearance of God to Job and the *parousia*. But of course the meaning would be that it was Christ who is the subject of the appearance on each occasion.

This thought, however, is hardly appropriate to the context, since God shows himself very far from being compassionate and merciful in Job 38, and the OT quotation certainly cannot be traced to the Book of Job. Where exactly the words do come from, it is not easy to decide. The Bible Society Text has a cross-reference to Psalms 103.8 and 111.4. Of these two the former is much closer to the text of James:

merciful and pitiful ($οἰκτίρμων$ $καὶ$ $ἐλεήμων$) is the Lord, long-suffering and compassionate ($μακρόθυμος$ $καὶ$ $πολυέλεος$).

Psalm 103.9 continues

he will not be angry for ever (*ouk es telos*).

(The LXX is numbered 102.8,9). This last verse may therefore account for the phrase "the end of the Lord" in James 5.11. We must not forget that Psalm 103 is attributed to David in the title, and James would have no hesitation in classing David as a prophet. On the other hand, in this context there is no suggestion of the prophet's having to endure persecution.

Another suggestion is that it is a quotation from Exodus 34.6, where exactly the same succession of epithets occurs in the LXX, translating exactly the same succession of words in the Hebrew as are found in Psalm 103.8,9.[5] Here also there is no difficulty in finding a reference to the prophets, for Moses would qualify for that category in James' eyes just as surely as David would. In this case "the end of the Lord" would be nothing less than the incarnation, with a hint that Christ had appeared to Moses of old. But once again we miss the note of suffering and patience which would make the reference completely appropriate.

We may therefore venture on a third suggestion: it might be a reference to Jonah 4.2, where the LXX runs:

> for Thou art pitiful and merciful, long-suffering and compassionate (ἐλεήμων καὶ οἰκτίρμων, μακρόθυμος καὶ πολυέλεος).

Here we find what is on the whole the most appropriate context yet for our James citation. We must assume that, according to James, Jonah is talking to Christ, and the prophet describes Christ in these terms. Jonah has just been prophesying to the Ninevites in Christ's name. What is more, the sequel could be described as waiting for "the end of the Lord". This is how Jonah is described in Jonah 4.5:

> Then Jonah went out of the city and sat to the east of the city and made a booth for himself there. He sat under it in the shade till he should see what would become of the city.

Admittedly there are no words in either Hebrew or Greek that would even remotely recall "the end of the Lord" or the thought of patience. But if James could sufficiently misunderstand the Book of Job to think that Job was a model of patience, he might sufficiently misunderstand the Book of Jonah to imagine that Jonah was the same.[6] We have already noticed the tendency to idolize OT characters in the NT.

We recollect the various references to Jonah in the Synoptic Gospels, which show that this prophet was of special interest to early Christians, as the Lord himself had referred to him. It is easy to imagine that they would look on Jonah as one who held converse with the pre-existent Christ. We can quote one or two passages from the Fathers which make exactly this claim. See Irenaeus, *Adv. Haereses* III.20.1:

> Thus from the beginning also the Lord had allowed that man should be swallowed by a great fish, that fish who was the author of deceit. This was not in order that man should be swallowed and perish altogether, but he was planning and preparing beforehand for the revelation of salvation. This revelation was carried out by the Word by means of the sign of Jonah for the benefit of those who had the same belief about the Lord as Jonah had, and who should confess

him and say, "I am a servant of the Lord, and I worship the Lord God of heaven, who made the sea and the dry land." The intention was that man, perceiving that his salvation was inseparable from God, should rise from the dead and glorify God, and utter that same sentence which was prophetically uttered by Jonah: "I cried to the Lord my God in tribulation and he heard me from the belly of hell."

We can see from this passage that, according to Irenaeus, it was Christ of whom Jonah spoke in Jonah 1.9, and Christ to whom he prayed in Jonah 2.2. Tertullian likewise hints at this belief, though he prefers to leave it as a hint. He writes:

> I perceive the Ninevites obtaining forgiveness of their crimes from the Creator—perhaps even on that occasion from Christ, since from the beginning he acted in the name of the Father.[7]

In fact, we must admit that the evidence is not sufficient for us to decide which OT passage exactly James had in mind when he wrote this passage. But we may certainly maintain that the most likely explanation lies in seeing it as an account of Christ's activity in OT history.

In view of this we must look again at James 2.1:

> My brethren, show no partiality as you hold the faith of our Lord Jesus Christ, the Lord of glory ('Ιησοῦ Χριστοῦ τῆς δόξης).

RSV is of course a paraphrase, and thereby inevitably an interpretation. The phrase is literally "our Lord Jesus Christ, the glory". NEB offers an even more extensive Targum: "our Lord Jesus Christ, who reigns in glory". All sorts of attempts have been made to avoid the simple juxtaposition of "the glory" with "our Lord Jesus Christ". The simplest is to insert "the Lord" before "of glory". But in fact when we compare this phrase with 1 Corinthians 2.8 and Acts 7.2, this does not really come to anything different from calling Christ "the glory". Ropes boldly cuts the knot by translating "our glorious Lord Jesus Christ". The Germans have devised a different method of cutting the knot, the theory of interpolation. For example, Hollmann and Bousset say that the only Lord of glory is God, and the words "our Jesus" must be an interpolation. Dibelius well points out that an interpolator would not have inserted the peculiar conjunction "our Jesus". He discusses every other solution, but his final word is, "But on the whole in this passage a hypothesis of interpolation is not absolutely necessary."

It seems simplest to take it as Hort[8] and Mayor do. Hort's discussion is particularly illuminating. He notes Acts 7.2, and thinks that the phrase there harks back to Psalm 29. He quotes as a parallel Titus 2.13 "the appearing of the glory of our great God and Saviour Jesus Christ", which he takes as meaning "the appearing of Jesus Christ, who is the glory of our great God, and who is our Saviour". Hort links the phrase in James 2.1 with the Sh^{e}kinah and the Memra' in the Targums. Mayor also refers to the Sh^{e}kinah.

In view of 5.7–15 we should have no hesitation in accepting this solution. Christ is here described as "the glory", meaning the Sh^{e}kinah, and James therefore seems to be revealing a link with 1 Corinthians 2.8, Acts 7.2, and John 1.14. The Epistle of James is thus less of an eccentric in the biblical writings than has at times been suggested, and the theory of an originally Jewish work interpolated by a Christian writer becomes to that extent less convincing.

1 Peter 1.10–12

In the light of all the NT passages we have so far examined, we can hardly fail to trace the activity of the pre-existent Christ in these verses from 1 Peter:

> The prophets who prophesied of the grace that was to be yours searched and inquired about this salvation; they inquired what person or time was indicated by the Spirit of Christ within them when predicting the sufferings of Christ and the subsequent glory (τὰ εἰς Χριστὸν παθήματα καὶ τὰς μετὰ ταῦτα δόξας). It was revealed to them that they were serving not themselves but you in the things which have now been announced to you by those who preached the good news to you through the Holy Spirit sent from heaven, things into which angels long to look.

This gives us a picture of the pre-existent Christ speaking through the prophets and foretelling his sufferings, death, resurrection, and ascension. Most editors accept this conclusion readily enough.[9] Gunkel remarks that according to NT writers "Christ had revealed himself in the course of history and revealed himself in the OT long before the man Christ". A number of editors, however, are not convinced that this conclusion necessarily implies a belief in the pre-existence of Christ on the part of the author of 1 Peter. R. Kühl, for example, thinks that it may imply no more than "the same Spirit as later anointed Christ for his messianic office".[10] Beare similarly writes: "But it is not necessary thus to read into the passage the implication of the pre-existence of Christ, the words may only mean that the Spirit of prophecy was the very Spirit that came upon him [sc. Christ] in the baptism." We will hardly be inclined to accept this as a likely explanation in view of our researches up to this point. Bigg goes to the other extreme in a manner reminiscent of Temple on St John: "Peter's view rests upon a perfectly unscholastic interpretation of Scripture. The Lord spoke to the prophets; Christ is the Lord; therefore Christ spoke to the prophets." This simple point-by-point identification of the ineffable *Adōnai* of the OT with Christ has its own difficulties, as we have already observed.

The one scholar who decisively rejects the conclusion that it was Christ who spoke in the prophets is E. G. Selwyn.[11] He understands the words as indicating Christian prophets, and both the sufferings and the glory to belong to contemporary Christians. He translates "the Spirit of Christ" as "the Messiah-Spirit" and "the sufferings of Christ" as "the sufferings of the Christ-ward road". He objects to applying the two verbs "searched and inquired" (ἐζήτησαν καὶ ἐξεραύνησαν) to OT prophets, on the ground that there is no example of this in the OT, and that the words imply research on written materials. He adds the undeniable truth that the OT prophets did not in fact prophesy primarily for the benefit of a distant epoch, but addressed their message to their own situation. We may, however, doubt whether this truth was really appreciated by the men who wrote the NT, and we must confess that his attempt to explain away "the Spirit of Christ" and "the sufferings of Christ" gives a rather Wardour Street rendering of what are fairly straightforward words. We cannot help agreeing with C. E. B. Cranfield when he dismisses Selwyn's interpretation with the words "this seems forced".[12]

Selwyn has however, in the course of discussing this passage, made a suggestion which may very well give us the clue we need for the interpretation of those words "searched and inquired". He refers to Habakkuk 2.1, and an examination of this passage in the LXX does seem to tell us what this phrase, that puzzled Selwyn so much, probably means. This is how Habakkuk 2.1-4 runs in the LXX:

> I shall stand on my watch and mount the crag and keep on the lookout to see what he will speak in me, and what I shall answer to my accusation. And *Kyrios* answered me and said. "Write the vision and (write it) clearly on a tablet, that he who reads the contents may overtake.[13] Because the vision is yet for a season, and it will rise to its end, and it will not be in vain. If it delays, wait for it, for a Coming One will arrive and will not delay. If he draws back, my soul will have no pleasure in him. But the Righteous One will live by my faithfulness."

As it stands, this passage has many of the characteristics of the prophetic activity described in 1 Peter 1.10-12. The prophet is searching and seeking for an answer, and when the answer comes it is in terms of waiting for a season till the oracle should be fulfilled. The prophet does not seek among written documents, but he is commanded to write his vision down. In 2.1 the prophet expects God to speak in him.[14] And we may note as well that this was probably considered a messianic passage. It is quoted twice by Paul and once by the author of Hebrews (Gal. 3.11; Rom. 1.17; Heb. 10.38).

The only problem remaining in connection with this passage is that strange phrase "things into which angels long to look". Naturally this has occasioned much speculation among scholars. Some would imagine fallen angels as wistfully contemplating from afar the salvation which they have forfeited. Thus Kühl compares Ephesians 3.10. Similarly Knopf refers to 1 Corinthians 2.7,8. But these are both examples of the elemental powers failing to recognize the Cross, of which there is no trace here. I would rather suggest that we compare passages such as Galatians 3.19; Acts 7.53; Hebrews 1.14—2.2. In all these passages we have emphasized the intermediary or subsidiary rôle of angels. The presence of the angels is a sign that this is not the direct, unmediated revelation of Christ, not in fact the new dispensation. Possibly, therefore, the suggestion here is that the angels are not parties to the dispensation of which Christ spoke through the prophets, not because there is any thought of rebellion on the side of the angels, but because the dispensation of which Christ speaks is to be direct, unmediated, an incarnation. We might venture our own translation of Hebrews 2.16 and say "for it is not angels that he lays hold of, but he lays hold of the seed of Abraham".

Jude 5, 6

We give the RSV translation of these two verses, even though it is based on a reading different from that adopted by the Bible Society Text, and on a reading which, if correct, would make the ensuing discussion unnecessary:

> Now I desire to remind you, though you were once for all fully informed, that he who saved a people out of the land of Egypt, afterwards destroyed those who did not believe. And the angels that did not keep their own position but left their proper dwellings have been kept by him in eternal chains in the nether gloom until the judgment of the great day.

We should take the question of the right reading first. The RSV would seem to be based on the reading *ho sōsas*, for which there is no MS. support at all. But it may be a method of avoiding a decision as to which is the right reading to put a non-existent reading in the text and give all the alternatives in the margin. The choice seems to lie between "*Kyrios*", "the Lord", and "Jesus" as the subject, for the variant "God" is not strongly supported, and is probably a conflation from 2 Peter 2.4.[15] If we could be sure that "Jesus" was the original reading, it would clear the matter up.[16] Even if not original, it may well be a correct gloss. As far as context is concerned, we find ourselves in very much the same position as we did with James 5.7–15. If it were not for the startling nature of the assertion, we would naturally take both *Kyrios* and "the Lord" in this passage as Christ, since "our only Master and Lord, Jesus Christ" has occurred at the end of the last verse, with no mention of a change of subject in between. When we look at Jude's use of *Kyrios* in the rest of the Epistle, the case for its meaning Christ in this passage is confirmed: he uses *Kyrios* four times with "Jesus Christ", and twice in quotations from apocryphal works, verses 9 and 14. Kühl argues in fact *Kyrios* without the article must mean God the Father, since whenever it occurs with the article it is accompanied by the words "Jesus Christ".[17] But two of three occurrences of *Kyrios* without the article are in quotations. It is interesting to note that the author of 2 Peter, in reproducing this passage from Jude, changes the *Kyrios* of Jude 5 to "God" (see 2 Pet. 2.4 sq.), though he does not reproduce the actual reference to the Exodus. This would suggest that he at least understood Jude 5 to refer to God and not to Christ. But we might also draw the conclusion that he found the passage ambiguous.[18]

Bigg as easily assumes that Christ is intended here as he did in expounding 1 Peter 1.10–12. Knopf writes: "It is not out of the question that 'Jesus' is the original reading." Hollmann and Bousset make no reference to a possible christological meaning, but make the interesting suggestion that the author may have had baptism in mind when he mentions the deliverance from Egypt.

This suggests a link with 1 Corinthians 10, and indeed when we compare the two passages we see a remarkable resemblance. In both Christ is associated with the deliverance from Egypt; in both the intention seems to be to warn the readers that being recipients of Christ's benefits is no guarantee of ultimate salvation; in both the writer seems to be reminding his readers of what they should know already. Paul says, "I want you to know, brethren", which usually denotes a reminder of what they are supposed to know already. Jude's phrase is even more definite: "I desire to remind you." When we connect with these two passages Hebrews chapters 3 and 4, where the author of Hebrews is also drawing admonitory lessons for his readers from the events of the wilderness period, with Christ envisaged as active in these events, we seem to discern the outlines of a piece of early Christian catechesis.

We have therefore good cause for accepting the hypothesis that it is Christ who is referred to in this passage in Jude. If so, we are left with the remarkable conclusion that three separate actions in OT history are here ascribed to the pre-existent Christ:

He saved the people from Egypt.
He destroyed those who did not believe in the wilderness.[19]
He guards in prison the rebellious angels.

We to-day find it sufficiently bizarre that Christ should be envisaged as active in the legendary days of the Patriarchs and the wilderness sojourn without having to accept the additional burden of imagining him as taking part in incidents only narrated in apocryphal or para-apocryphal literature. We may be very grateful that we are under no obligation to accept Jude's word for it that the events connected with the angels to which he refers actually took place, and we may express a certain amount of relief that Jude is probably one of the later books of the NT to be written, and is on the periphery rather than at the heart of the record of revelation.

With this we conclude our exposition of the theme "Christ in OT history" in the NT. It will be fully apparent by now that this theme is not confined to one or two places in Paul, but is in fact an assumption underlying a great deal of NT exegesis of the OT. Speculation as to how this belief originated is not in place at this point, but we can at least be sure that it was no individual quirk of Paul's. It must have been part of a well-established tradition. We now turn to a consideration of some aspects of Paul's understanding of the OT which have been laid bare by our conclusions arrived at in what we have been studying up to this point.

7

Prophetic Prayer and Dialogue in Paul

We have now explored the theme of Christ in the OT so far that we may look on it as one which formed a quite considerable part of Paul's thinking about the OT. In implying, as he does in several passages, that Christ was active in OT times, he was only developing what must have formed part of the tradition of Christianity which he received. We are justified, therefore, in using this conclusion as a means of exploring further Paul's use of the OT. This is what we propose to do in this chapter. We shall not be so much concerned with examining passages in which Paul presupposes the activity of Christ in OT times, but rather concentrating our attention on places where Paul seems to envisage Christ as speaker, or as spoken to, in OT passages. Our previous study should have convinced us that this sort of understanding of the OT is fully in line with Paul's thought, and we need not, for instance, spend any time in wondering whether Christ could have spoken through Psalmists or prophets in Paul's view. We know that this was perfectly possible, even likely, in view of what we have already noted about Christ's activity in OT times. We shall find, as we explore the four passages that we have chosen in Paul's Letters, that his understanding of Christ's utterances in the OT can throw a surprising amount of light on what Paul believed about Christ. The question we shall be considering, of course, will not be whether Paul was justified in finding utterances of Christ in the OT, but whether he did or not. And if it proves that he did, we can certainly treat those utterances as evidence for what Paul thought Christ could have said, and therefore as evidence for what Paul thought of Christ. If we can view this conclusion in perspective, it should not seem very novel: since Paul drew so much of his theological concepts and vocabulary from the Septuagint, it is not really surprising that some passages in the Septuagint should tell us something about Paul's christology.

We have called this chapter "Prophetic Prayer and Dialogue in Paul". This does not mean that we are going to present Paul himself as a prophet or as one who conducted dialogues with others. It means that we are going to explore those passages in Paul's writings where he seems to be envisaging the pre-existent Christ as having uttered prophetic prayer, or conversed with God the Father, through the mouth of Psalmist or prophet, and we intend to show that Paul is equally capable of representing the Son as taking part in dialogue with others, perhaps with the Father, perhaps with angelic powers, through the mouth of OT characters. Both these activities of the pre-existent Son can be easily found in the Epistle to the Hebrews. Indeed, there we have just the reverse of the situation we find in Paul. In Paul's writings the activities of Christ in OT history actually appear on the surface at least once, but his uttering prophecy through the mouth of OT characters is below the surface. In Hebrews the places where the pre-existent Christ is represented as active in OT history are not at all obvious, and have to be carefully examined before they can be said to be proved, whereas the author of Hebrews seems to take for granted that all his readers will understand his habit of quoting Psalms as if they were prophetic dialogues between the Father and the Son. Thus at the very beginning of his work in 1.5, 7–13 we have the Father addressing the Son in Psalms. In 2.12,13 we find the Son addressing the Father. In 5.6,7 the Father addresses the Son in the words of Psalms 2.7 and 110.4. And in chapter 10 of Hebrews the very nerve centre of his argument concerning the nature of Christ's work is expressed in a Psalm quotation in which the Son addresses the Father. What we are doing in this chapter, therefore, could be described as tracing in Paul's writings a feature which is very much to the fore in the Epistle to the Hebrews. It will surely go to confirm our belief in the unity of the NT that one and the same method of using the OT should prove to be common to both great traditions inside the NT itself.

1 Corinthians 2.6–9

Yet among the mature we do impart wisdom, although it is not a wisdom of this age or of the rulers of this age (τῶν ἀρχόντων τοῦ αἰῶνος τούτου), who are doomed to pass away. But we impart a secret and hidden wisdom of God, which God decreed before the ages for our glorification. None of the rulers of this age understood this; for if they had, they would not have crucified the Lord of glory (τὸν Κύριον τῆς δόξης). But, as it is written, "What no eye has seen, nor ear heard, nor the heart of man conceived, what God has prepared for those who love him."

Who are "the rulers of this age"? One view is that it is a straightforward reference to the rulers of Palestine in the year of the crucifixion, Pontius Pilate, Caiaphas, etc. The other view is that it refers to the elemental powers whom Christ overcame by his Cross and Resurrection, the "principalities, the powers, the world rulers of this present darkness, the spiritual hosts of wickedness in the heavenly places" (Eph. 6.12). This second view is not incompatible with the first, for the secular rulers may have been thought of as the instruments of the spiritual powers. Most older English commentators, because of their reluctance to allow that Paul could be so bizarre in his theological conceptions, tend towards the first view. Thus, on this side we find Hodge, McFadyen, Edwards, Robertson and Plummer, and Goudge. On the other side are nearly all the continental scholars, Allo, Lietzmann, Bousset, Héring. Moffat alone sides with the continentals.[1]

I suggest that a consideration of the OT background to this passage makes it quite clear that the second view is correct, and that the rulers are primarily elemental powers. Behind this passage lies Psalm 24 in the LXX (where it is numbered Psalm 23). In the

LXX of this Psalm we find just those elemental powers whose activities Paul seems to be referring to here. This is how Psalm 24.8-10 runs in the LXX:

> Lift up your gates, your rulers, (ἄρατε πύλας, οἱ ἄρχοντες ὑμῶν)
> and be lifted up, eternal gates,
> and the king of glory (ὁ βασιλεὺς τῆς δόξης) shall come in.
> Who is this king of glory?
> *Kyrios* mighty and powerful,
> *Kyrios* powerful in war.
> Lift up your gates, your rulers,
> and be lifted up, eternal gates,
> and the king of glory shall come in.
> Who is the king of glory?
> The Lord of powers, he is the king of glory.

There is no mention of the rulers in the Hebrew. The LXX translator has in fact misunderstood the word for the "heads" or "bars" of the gates to mean "heads" in the sense of "rulers". As we look at these verses from Paul's point of view, we see how many points would appeal to him as appropriate to the Messiah: there is a suggestion of uncertainty as to the identity of the king of glory, which fits in exactly with this passage in 1 Corinthians; there is the emphasis on the power of the king of glory, a power whose real character Paul has just been describing in terms of the Cross; and perhaps in the last line of the Psalm Paul would see a reference to Christ's conquest of the elemental powers which is surely implied in the words of 1 Corinthians 2.6 "who are doomed to pass away" (*tōn katargoumenōn*—it is the very word with which we had so much trouble in 2 Corinthians 3). Paul must have thought of the Psalm as giving us a description of Christ's entry into heaven after the victory brought about through his death and resurrection. The powers who had (by the hands of Pilate and Caiaphas) engineered his death ask in wonder: Who is this that enters the eternal city? The reply tells them that he is stronger than they, and that the crucified Jesus is none other than the Lord of Hosts. If we accept this explanation of the passage, we do not have to look further afield than the LXX for the phrase "the Lord of glory".[2] It is a conflation from the LXX of Psalm 24, such as would naturally occur to one who identified the "king of glory" of Psalm 24 with the Lord Jesus. Thus we find in this Psalm as interpreted by Paul a clear example of the prophetic dialogue: the victorious Son engages in dialogue with the elemental powers, a dialogue which is prophetic because it was uttered (as Paul believed) through the lips of David a thousand years before the event, but one which nevertheless tells us something of how Paul understood the work of Christ.

It is by no means irrelevant to point out that this is very much the interpretation of Psalm 24 which we find in Justin Martyr. In his *Dialogue with Trypho* he first quotes the Psalm in full, and then comments as follows:

> It is therefore demonstrated that the Lord of hosts is not Solomon, but when our Christ has risen from the dead and ascended into heaven, the rulers in the heavens appointed by God are commanded to open the gates of the heavens, in order that he who is the king of glory may enter.... For when the rulers in heaven saw that he had an unattractive, dishonoured, and inglorious appearance, not recognising him, they asked: "Who is this king of glory?" And the Holy Spirit answers them, either in the person of the Father or in his own person: "The Lord of hosts, he is the king of glory."[3]

Compare also *Dialogue* 85.1 and *Apology* I.51, where the same interpretation is put forward. It is impossible to say whether Justin is merely expounding 1 Corinthians 2, or is using a traditional Christian interpretation of Psalm 24. In neither the *Dialogue* nor the *Apology* could he usefully have cited Paul as an authority that would carry weight with those whom he was addressing. In any case, it is significant that his interpretation of the Psalm coincides so closely with that which we have traced in this passage from 1 Corinthians.

Another problem connected with this passage is the source of the quotation in verse 9. There are three possibilities, Isaiah 64.4, Isaiah 65.17, and Jeremiah 3.16. None of them exactly fits it, but on the whole Isaiah 64.4 seems to come nearest to it. The LXX (which is numbered 64.3) runs thus:

From eternity we have not heard, neither have our eyes seen, any God but Thee, and thy works which Thou performest for them who await mercy.

This does not exactly represent the Hebrew, and is most astray in the last phrase.[4] It is even possible that the LXX as we have it is in some respects nearer the original Hebrew than our MT.

If we read on in the LXX from Isaiah 64.3, we meet a passage of deep penitence and misery, and eventually reach at 65.1,2 a passage which Paul quotes in Romans 10.20,21. We have already suggested in chapter 2 that Paul applies Isaiah 65.1,2 to God's act in Christ, and specifically to the Cross. It is therefore possible that Paul looks on the whole section Isaiah 64.1—65.2 as a sort of meditation on the Cross. We shall be expounding another long section from Isaiah in a very similar sense presently. The verse he quotes in 1 Corinthians 2.9 prophesies the strange act of God, never guessed at by man's mind; the next few verses express the misery of mankind from which the Cross was to save them, or even possibly the misery of God's people when they failed to recognize their Messiah. Then comes Isaiah 65.1 with its account of the revelation of God in Christ to the Gentiles as well as to Israel. This was the culmination of God's strange act. If this is so, then 1 Corinthians 2.9 is not a description of the joys of heaven, or of the glories of the *parousia*. It is a description of the love of God manifested in his saving act through Christ on the Cross. The unexpected and inscrutable character of what God has prepared does not lie in the fact that our experience of the life to come is ineffable anyway, but in the fact of the crucifixion of the Messiah, the death, resurrection, ascension, and proclamation to the Gentiles of the Lord of glory. At least there is good reason to suspect that behind this passage in 1 Corinthians 2 lies the exegesis of an OT text in terms of the pre-existent Christ engaged in prophetic dialogue.[5] Paul is in fact here not indulging in gnostic speculations about the hidden demiurge. He is using OT scripture to illuminate the death, resurrection, and entering into glory of Christ.

2 Corinthians 4.11–15

For while we live we are always being given up to death for Jesus' sake, so that the life of Jesus may be manifested in our mortal flesh. So death is at work in us, but life in you. Since we have the same spirit of faith as he had who wrote (ἔχοντες δὲ τὸ αὐτὸ πνεῦμα τῆς πίστεως, κατὰ τὸ γεγραμμένον), "I believed, and so I spoke", we too believe, and so we speak, knowing that he who raised the Lord Jesus will raise us also with Jesus and bring us with you into his presence. For it is all for your sake, so that as grace extends to more and more people it may increase thanksgiving, to the glory of God.

I have already treated this passage at some length in *The Pioneer Ministry*, pages 76–8. The line of interpretation follows that suggested by Goudge and repeated by R. P. C. Hanson. The question is: What exactly does Paul mean by "according to that which is written"? This is a literal translation of the Greek. The RSV, by translating "the same spirit of faith as he had who wrote", commits itself to one school of thought, that which interprets Paul as meaning he had the same spirit of faith as the Psalmist. This interpretation is followed by Windisch, Bousset, Lietzmann, and Allo. Strachan suggests that Paul claims the same spirit of faith as his readers, which seems completely irrelevant to the context. The objection to the RSV rendering is that it would have little point unless Paul indicated who he thought the Psalmist was. The answer to this question is almost certainly David. But the contents of the Psalm do not seem at all appropriate to David's situation, and indeed the appeal to the faith of the Psalmist of old is more reminiscent of modern homiletic methods than of Paul's interpretation of the OT. When we follow Goudge and R. P. C. Hanson in their theory that it is Christ who is envisaged here as speaking through the words of Psalm 116, then we find much light on this passage. I reproduce here my translation of the LXX of Psalm 116.10–19 (it appears as a separate Psalm, no. 115, in the LXX):

> I believed, therefore did I speak,
> but I was greatly humbled.

I said in my excitement,
"Every man is a liar".
What shall I repay unto the Lord
in return for all he has rewarded me?
I will take the cup of salvation,
and I will call upon the name of *Kyrios*.
Valuable before *Kyrios*
is the death of his holy ones.
O *Kyrios*, I am thy servant (*doulos*),
thy servant and the son of thy handmaid.
Thou hast broken my bonds asunder.
I will sacrifice to thee the sacrifice of thanksgiving.
I will repay my vows to the Lord
before all his people,
in the courts of the house of *Kyrios*,
in the midst of thee, Jerusalem.

It is very easy to trace the points of similarity with Christ's situation which Paul would find in this Psalm, his precious death, his life of service, his victorious resurrection whereby he burst the bonds of death, all these details of Christ's career would strike Paul at once as he studied this Psalm. Moreover, once we recognize it as an utterance of the Messiah, we can see how relevant it would be to Paul's purpose in this part of 2 Corinthians. He has just been speaking about the identification of the ministers with the life of the Church through their reproducing the life and death of Jesus in their lives. Their strenuous life is a kind of death and may well lead to actual death. But as Christ held firmly to his faith in the God who would rescue him from all his perils, so do the ministers of the new covenant. And as Christ gives thanks in the Church for his resurrection, the work of God, so do the ministers believe that God will raise them up in Christ. Paul would consider the ending of the Psalm as representing an act of praise by Christ in the Church (Jerusalem) for his resurrection. That is why Paul passes naturally from a mention of Psalm 116 to an assertion of his hope in the resurrection. So these words "I believed, and so I spoke" are no passing echo of a half-remembered phrase. They are a definite reference to a specific passage in Scripture which illumines Paul's meaning, and which he intends his readers to understand as he does. There is no question here of a list of *Testimonia*; S-B remarks that no passage in ancient Rabbinic literature deals with Psalm 116.10.

We can hardly fail to be impressed with the instruction about Christ which Paul must have found in this Psalm. In it Christ gives thanks to God in the Church, acknowledges himself as the recipient of salvation, and above all is held up as the great example of faith. Here surely is remarkable evidence on what Paul believed about Christ's human nature. It is impossible also to pass over in silence the significance of 2 Corinthians 4.15 for our theology of the Eucharist. Christ giving thanks to God in the Church brings it about that "as grace extends to more and more people it may increase thanksgiving (*eucharistian*) to the glory of God". If Paul could express the Church's offering of praise in terms of Christ praising God in the Church, it is entirely appropriate that we find the Church of a hundred years later allowing the offering of thanksgiving a central place in its worship.[6]

2 Corinthians 5.16—6.2

From now on, therefore, we regard no one from a human point of view; even though we once regarded Christ from a human point of view, we regard him thus no longer. Therefore, if anyone is in Christ, he is a new creation; the old has passed away, behold, the new has come. All this is from God, who through Christ reconciled us to himself and gave us the ministry of reconciliation; that is, God was in Christ reconciling the world to himself, not counting their trespasses against them, and entrusting to us the message of reconciliation ($\tau\grave{o}\nu$ $\lambda\acute{o}\gamma o\nu$ $\tau\hat{\eta}s$ $\kappa\alpha\tau\alpha\lambda\lambda\alpha\gamma\hat{\eta}s$). So we are ambassadors for Christ, God making his appeal through us. We beseech you on behalf of Christ, be reconciled to God. For our sake he made him to be sin who knew no sin, so that in him we might become the righteousness of God. Working together with him, then, we entreat you not to accept the grace of God in vain (*eis kenon*). For he says (*legei gar*), "At the acceptable time have I listened to you, and helped you on the day of salvation." Behold, now is the acceptable time; behold now is the day of salvation.

We hope to show that behind this passage lies a considerable section from the LXX of Isaiah, and that Paul is consciously meditating on the Isaiah passage as he writes. First, however, it will be helpful to give a sort of précis of the passage in 2 Corinthians in its context:

> God has renewed all things through the unique agency of Christ. He has in fact reconciled the world to himself in Christ, showing thereby his divine forgiveness. Christ was adjudged a sinner by the Law, but now, vindicated by God, appeals through us ministers of the new covenant to you that you should accept God's reconciliation. What God said to the Messiah of old has now proved true of Christians as well.

This paraphrase obviously takes much for granted, in particular the interpretation of verse 21. I have already worked out what I believe to be the right explanation of this difficult verse in *The Wrath of the Lamb*, pp. 80–2.[7] Christ was adjudged to be sin by the Law, because he refused to live by the Law but followed the way of faith instead. But he was not condemned in God's eyes; on the contrary, we have in Scripture the prediction of his vindication by God, and that prediction was fulfilled in the resurrection. This brings us to the OT citation in 6.2, and to that we must turn.

When we do so, we find that the context in which the quotation occurs could not fail to have had great significance for Paul. We must therefore translate it from the LXX. This is how Isaiah 49.1–9 runs in the LXX as we have it:

> Listen to me, islands,
> and attend, Gentiles;
> it shall stand for a long time, says *Kyrios*,
> from the womb of my mother he has called my name,
> and has made my mouth like a sharp sword,
> and under the covering of his hand has he hidden me;
> he has fashioned me as a chosen weapon,
> and has kept me covered in his quiver,
> and has said to me "My slave (*doulos mou*) art thou,
> Israel, and I will be glorified in thee."
> And I said, "In vain have I laboured (*kenōs ekopiasa*),

and have spent my strength for vanity and nothing.
Therefore my judgement is with *Kyrios*
and my labour is before my God."
And now, thus says he who formed me from the womb as his slave[8]
to gather Jacob and Israel to him—
I shall be gathered[9] and I shall be honoured before *Kyrios*,
and my God shall be my strength—
And he said to me, "It is a great thing for thee to be called my servant
(*paida mou*),
to establish the tribes of Jacob,
and to bring back the dispersed of Israel.
Behold, I have appointed thee as a covenant of the people,[10]
as a light of Gentiles,
that thou shouldest be a salvation to the ends of the earth."
Thus says *Kyrios*,
the God of Israel, who rescued thee:
"Sanctify him who abhors his own soul,[11]
who is loathed by the Gentiles, the servants of the rulers.
Kings shall see him and stand up,
rulers, and they shall worship him,
because of *Kyrios*, because he is faithful,
the Holy One of Israel, and I have chosen thee."
Thus says *Kyrios*,
"In an acceptable time have I heard thee,
and in a day of salvation I have helped thee,
and given thee for a covenant of Gentiles to establish the land
and to cause the desolate heritage to be inhabited,
saying to those in chains, Come forth,
and to those in darkness, Appear."

As we read over this passage, we notice that, besides the quotation in 6.2, Paul has echoed another phrase from it in 6.1

we entreat you not to accept the grace of God in vain.

This is an echo of Isaiah 49.4:

And I said, "In vain have I laboured".

Paul quotes the same phrase in Philippians 2.16:

I did not run in vain or labour in vain (*oude eis kenon ekopiasa*).

The fact that in Isaiah 49.4 the LXX has *kenōs* rather than *eis kenon* is not very significant.[12] It is quite possible that Paul's text of the LXX had *eis kenon* in Isaiah 49.4. Paul was not therefore quoting from a list of *Testimonia*; he had the whole passage before him.

Paul sees that passage as a dialogue between God and the Messiah. First God declares that he has prepared his servant the Messiah for his task (49.1–3). Then the Messiah protests that his work has been in vain, but immediately receives the reply from God that his judgement is with God, not (it is implied) with man or with any other power. It is God's plan to use him for reconciling the whole of humanity to himself, Gentiles as well as Jews (49.4–6). Indeed verses 4–6 would in Paul's eyes apply very exactly to God's reconciling work in Christ as he describes it himself in 2 Corinthians 5.19–21. Christ's judgement was apparently one of complete condemnation, even to the point of being adjudged a sinner. But his true judgement was with God, who vindicated him. His labour was not in vain, though it seemed to be so at the time. That word "labour" in the LXX of Isaiah 49.4 would speak to Paul of Gethsemane and the Cross.[13] Isaiah 49.5–8 gives an account of the reconciling work of the servant; he has not only to reconcile Israel to God, but also to be a covenant of the people. This phrase reminds us of Paul's description in this very Epistle of the ministers of the new covenant, and in 5.20,21, Paul refers to the activity of these ministers. Finally, in Isaiah 49.8 comes God's full answer to the servant's plea. God has heard him and saved him, and once again we find a mention of the covenant which the servant is to inaugurate. Paul would see this as the assurance from God to the Messiah of salvation from the ordeal through which he is to pass in the passion and crucifixion.

In 2 Corinthians 6.2 the quotation is applied to us Christians, but to us as in Christ. The Isaiah passage shows that the Messiah was first himself to undergo the experience of frustration, appeal for help, and salvation before we could undergo it; we only experience "the day of salvation" because Christ has first experienced it. Paul would find in this passage an identification of the servant with Israel, particularly in 49.3. This would not puzzle him as it has puzzled so many modern commentators; he would have no difficulty in identifying Israel with Christ. It would signify to him that Christ's experience of struggle and salvation was one which was ultimately to be shared with the members of his Church; and this is in fact what he means by the citation in 2 Corinthians 6.2. In short, Paul saw the passage Isaiah 49.1–13 as a *logos katallagēs,* a message of reconciliation itself. In it was predicted in dialogue form the reconciliation that God was to effect in Christ. What the Isaiah passage brings out in addition is that, according to Paul, Christ himself experienced that same conflict and salvation which we Christians are to experience in him. As we read the passage in Isaiah, and then Paul's meditation on it in 2 Corinthians 5.16—6.2, we cannot fail to be impressed by the boldness and depth of his thought about the incarnation, a boldness only equalled by Mark and the author to the Hebrews. Everything that God is described as doing in this passage in 2 Corinthians (reconciling, entreating, entrusting the ministry of reconciliation) Christ is also represented as doing. And everything that man is described as experiencing (being made the righteousness of God, fearing that the labour may have been in vain, being heard by God when he cries for help, receiving the needed salvation) that also Christ is envisaged as experiencing. Christ is proclaimed as the perfect mediator, fully God and fully man, in a way that effortlessly transcends the fumbling efforts of the Chalcedonian Fathers to express.

Commentators on the whole have missed the point, because they have assumed that Paul in 6.2 is merely quoting Scripture in an illustrative or homiletic manner. McFadyen dismisses the quotation thus: "He availed himself of the ancient words probably only because they happily expressed his meaning." It would be difficult to imagine a more un-Pauline approach to the OT. Plummer makes the artless suggestion that in a modern work the quotation would be in a footnote; and Lietzmann actually claims that it is cited without regard to its context in Isaiah as a maxim useful for exhortation. All these scholars have read into Paul the approach to the OT favoured in their own day and have not attempted to read the OT through Paul's eyes. Three scholars, however, have gone deeper: Hodge's pre-critical literalism keeps him in many respects closer to Paul's outlook, and he can write quite simply: "The 49th chapter of Isaiah, whence this passage is taken, is addressed to the Messiah." But he does not pursue this theme, and he makes the suggestion, echoed by several later editors, that the *dexasthai* ("accept") of 6.1 suggested to Paul's mind the *dektō* ("acceptable") of 6.2. Windisch actually hints at the connection between *eis kenon* of 6.1 and the *kenōs* of Isaiah 49.4: "Paul by the quotation might have intended to suggest what the sequel to 'not to accept the grace of God in vain' would be, since earlier on in Isaiah 49.4 'in vain have I laboured' occurs", and he refers to a work by A. Klöpper where the same suggestion is made. There is no attempt, however, to work out the implication of the Isaiah passage for Christ in Paul's mind. Goudge also writes: "Thus St. Paul probably interprets the words of the glorified Christ 'heard for his godly fear' and saved out of death (Heb. 5.7), his perfect acceptance by the Father being established by the resurrection." But he applies the Isaiah citation to Paul's own experience, not Christ's, and he fails to work out the implications of this remarkable conclusion that according to Paul Christ also underwent the experience of salvation. We might also cite a good comment by Bousset: "He [sc. Christ] is the reconciler and himself becomes reconciled, both in a wonderful way."[14]

Thus an examination of the OT background to 2 Corinthians 5.6 has shown us not only Christ and the Father engaged in prophetic dialogue about the redemption that was to take place in the end time, but it has also shed a considerable amount of light on what Paul actually believed about Christ. In 2 Corinthians 4.13 we found Christ presented as the exemplar of faith. Here we find him as the pioneer in experiencing salvation. Surely it is not going far beyond the evidence to suggest that, in Paul's theology, Christ himself was the first to be justified by faith?

Romans 15.2-9

Let each of us please his neighbor for his good, to edify him. For Christ did not please himself; but, as it is written, "The reproaches of those who reproached thee fell on me." For whatever was written in former times was written for our instruction, that by steadfastness and by the encouragement of the scriptures we might have hope. May the God of steadfastness and encouragement grant you to live in such harmony with one another, in accord with Christ Jesus, that together you may with one voice glorify the God and Father of our Lord Jesus Christ. Welcome one another, therefore, for the glory of God. For I tell you that Christ became a servant (*diakonon*) to the circumcised to show God's truthfulness, in order to confirm the promises given to the patriarchs, and in order that the Gentiles might glorify God for his mercy. As it is written, "Therefore I will praise thee among the Gentiles, and sing to thy name."

This passage would seem peculiarly suitable to our purpose, not only because of the wealth of OT citations which it provides (there are three more in verses 10-12), but also because Paul actually comments on the use of the OT for Christians. C. H. Dodd suggests that Paul found the Psalm quotation in verse 3 in a list of *Testimonia*.[15] But it seems a very odd quotation to use as a proof text, and one not very likely to carry conviction without a lot of explanation. As Jülicher points out, it is not a very appropriate quotation, as the Psalmist is thinking of abuse intended for God falling on the devotee, whereas in fact Jesus incurred abuse from those who refused to believe in him. We must therefore look at the Psalm as a whole, in order to find out what Paul had in mind when he quoted it.

It is Psalm 69, and Paul quotes verse 9. This is one of the Psalms whose title includes the phrase "to the chief musician",[16] a phrase translated by the LXX as *eis to telos* "for the end". We have already suggested in connection with Psalm 19 that this in itself might be an indication to an early Christian that here was messianic material to be found. The Psalm in fact largely consists of a prayer for help. Perhaps Paul saw it as the prophetic prayer of the Messiah for salvation from the dangers that surrounded him. Indeed, it is difficult to see how Paul could have read it any other way, for his argument depends on the assumption that the words which he cites were uttered by Christ. That the second person singular in the quotation must indicate God is certain; it cannot indicate mankind, as Sanday and Headlam suggest (see my *Wrath of the Lamb*, pp. 98 sq.). In the course of the Psalm we can find one or two notes that are repeated by Paul in this passage in Romans. We have the note of hope in verse 3 of the Psalm.[17] The LXX has

> My eyes grow dim with hoping for my God.

Again we find the note of steadfastness, for in Psalm 69.6,20 we find the verb *hupomenein*, corresponding to the *hupomonē* of Romans 15.4. Psalm 69.7-9 deserves translating from the LXX, as it may well have spoken to Paul of the atoning work of Christ:

> For it is for thy sake that I have suffered reproach,
> that shame has covered my face.
> I have become a stranger to my brethren,
> an alien to my mother's sons.
> For zeal for thy house has consumed me,
> and the insults of those who insulted thee have fallen on me.

Here Paul would find an account of Christ's vicarious suffering. It is important to bear in mind that Paul has already quoted this Psalm in this very Epistle. (See Rom. 11.9, where Ps. 69.22,23 is quoted.[18]) Even more significant is the fact that verse 9a, the first line of the verse which Paul actually cites, is quoted in John 2.17, where there can be no doubt at all that Christ is thought of as the speaker. All this goes to show that the Psalm was certainly considered as a messianic one by early Christians, but not of course that either Paul or John was merely using proof texts without regard to the context from which the quotation comes. There is indeed a confession of sin in verse 5 of the Psalm, but we may suggest that Paul would interpret this as a vicarious confession; like the suffering, it was part of Christ's voluntary self-identification with men. The Psalm ends with a burst of praise in verses 30-4, and here Paul would no doubt see the Messiah praising God for the salvation which he has experienced.

When we read the Psalm in this light, Romans 15.4–6 begins to take on a deeper meaning. Paul exhorts the Roman Christians to show steadfastness and to maintain hope, because this is what Christ has done in the Psalm he has just quoted. The phrase in Romans 15.5 is not a mere platitude: "live in such harmony with one another, in accord with Jesus Christ". They are to show steadfastness and hope because that is in accord with Jesus Christ: the frame of mind implied in "live in harmony" is described in Psalm 69. And the act of praising God referred to in Romans 15.6 is also in accord with Christ, for the Psalm represents the Messiah as praising God at the end. Indeed Paul reverts to this very theme in Romans 15.9. It seems clear, then, that Paul's citation of Psalm 69 in Romans 15.3, far from being a mere passing reference, governs the thought of the passage that ensues. It looks as if we have another example of what we traced in 2 Corinthians 5.16—6.2, a passage in a Letter of Paul's that is in fact a sort of meditation on an OT passage.

We find Paul's observations on Scripture that follow in verse 4 full of significance in view of all this. What was written in the OT, he says, was written for our instruction (*didaskalian*). This is the same word as Paul uses in Romans 12.7, no doubt of Christian catechesis. So Paul is saying in effect that Psalm 69 can give us teaching about the Messiah. It looks as if he did not value the Psalm exactly as an instance of prophecy fulfilled, though no doubt it is this, but rather as a piece of information about Christ's own work uttered by Christ himself. It is an interpretation of his sufferings, given us by the Messiah himself. Thus Paul deliberately foregoes the advantage of claiming an argument from prophecy in what later became the traditional Christian sense. If he looks on this Psalm as an utterance of Christ, it would be pointless for him to say: "See how wonderfully the inspired prophet David has foretold what would later come to pass." He prefers to concentrate on the element of "instruction". It is a passage that will help Christians to understand the meaning of the Messiah's life and death. Thus, through Paul's use of the Psalms as the utterances of Christ, we can catch a glimpse both of a piece of early Christian catechesis, and of one aspect of Paul's christology.[19]

E. E. Ellis well remarks of passages such as this one, "The stress of Pauline quotations is not upon predictive prophecy as such, but upon the application of principles enunciated in the OT."[20] This certainly gets away from what we have called the Victorian approach to this subject, but we might question the word "principles", at least as far as this citation of Psalm 69 is concerned. It is not that Paul finds in this Psalm principles which he also traces in the events concerning Jesus; the connection is more personal than this: Paul sees Christ personally speaking in the Psalm, describing his passion. B. Lindars writing of this Psalm, says: "It is clear that it was found useful as a whole by the early Christians."[21] This is very true, and is a useful warning against the tendency in some quarters to represent the NT writers as having taken their OT citations almost exclusively from alleged lists of *Testimonia*. But Fr Lindars tends rather to suggest that the Psalm was used for apologetic by the early Church, whereas in this context at least Paul is using it for instruction. It is for use inside the Church, not for ammunition against outsiders.

Romans 15.7,8 could be considered as a sort of summary of Paul's interpretation of Psalm 69: Christ has so identified himself with God's people that he actually became their servant. The Psalm describes the sufferings that formed the climax of the incarnation. Paul draws the typically Christian lesson that Christians should likewise serve one another. In the light of this we can have little doubt about the meaning of verse 8. It means that the Messiah became "a servant of the Jewish people" as the NEB translates it. Some of the older editors have attempted to take the phrase as meaning that in some sense Christ became a minister of the rite of circumcision. Thus, Sanday and Headlam explain it as meaning that Christ came "to carry out the promises implied in that covenant the seal of which was circumcision", and Kirk even more elaborately "Christ is a minister of circumcision even to Gentiles, because he had admitted them to all the privileges promised to the Jewish Church, of which circumcision, though now abolished for Christians, may be still regarded as the symbol". Here is Burghley's nod indeed! Surely any explanation that is simpler than this has first claim on our attention.

The reference, we take it, is to the incarnation, whereby Christ, coming as an humble servant to his own people, received them into fellowship with himself, and thus with God and with each other. But this act of bringing into fellowship was not confined to Jews: as was foretold by Christ in the OT, Gentiles also were brought into this fellowship by Christ. In order to prove this, Paul quotes the OT. Of the four citations that follow, the last three do not really concern us; they are intended so show that the accession of the Gentiles was foretold in Scripture. It is the first with which we are concerned. Paul quotes Psalm 18.49 (= 2 Sam. 22.50). It is a well-known Psalm, and is possibly also cited in Hebrews 2.13, though the reference there may be to Isaiah 8.17. It is worth noting that the title of Psalm 18 contains the phrase *eis to telos* in the LXX, which may have been taken by early Christians as a sign of messianic significance. The Psalmist, like his fellow in Psalm 69, gives thanks for salvation from peril. There is in this Psalm a verse which in the LXX would seem to an early Christian to contain an explicit reference to the Messiah, for verse 50b (LXX 17.51b) runs:

and one [sc. God] who performs mercy for his Christ (τῷ Χριστῷ αὐτοῦ).

Paul actually quotes the previous verse, so there can be very little doubt indeed that the verse which he does quote is believed by him to be an utterance of the pre-existent Christ. Christ gives thanks in the Church for the deliverance which he is to experience at God's hands. If we were to ask Paul, "in what Church?", I doubt if he would have understood our question. There is only one, continuous from Abraham to Apollos, the same Church in which David sang, Isaiah prophesied, Christ was born, and the Roman Christians rejoiced (so Paul hopes) to serve one another. Thus, in these two Psalms (69 and 18) we have clear instances of

Christ speaking through the mouth of David, experiencing salvation, and worshipping God in the Church. Paul's use of the OT has at least told us something of value about Paul's estimate of Christ.

This passage from Romans bears a remarkable resemblance to two other passages in the Epistles, one Pauline and one not. These are Philippians 2.1-11 and Hebrews 2.5-18. We may isolate the following points of resemblance:

1. In all three Christ's humiliations are mentioned (Rom. 15.8; Phil. 2.6-8; Heb. 2.8,9).
2. In all three his fellowship with us is the result of this (Rom. 15.7; Phil. 2.1; Heb. 2.10).
3. In all three the incarnation is made the basis for encouragement for Christians (Rom. 15.8,9; Phil. 2.6-8; Heb. 2.17,18).
4. In all three the glory of Christ or God is also stressed (Rom. 15.7,9; Phil. 2.8-11; Heb. 2.9).
5. In two of them Christ is depicted as praising God in the Church, perhaps in the same words (Rom. 15.9; Heb. 2.12).
6. In two of them Christ is envisaged as speaking in the OT (Rom. 15.3,9-12; Heb. 2.12,13.).

It is even possible that we have an example of Christ speaking in the OT in Philippians 2.10,11. In those verses Paul quotes Isaiah 45.23. If one reads the paragraph Isaiah 45.18-25 in the LXX, it is difficult to resist the conclusion that to Paul this would be an utterance of the pre-existent Christ. This conclusion is denied by C. F. D. Moule, who writes: "He [sc. Paul] is still not using it [sc. the OT citation] as a proof that these are the attributes of Christ. He is (on the other grounds) affirming these divine attributes and borrowing ready made phrases to describe them."[22] Is this not perhaps an example of the Victorian school of interpretation which we have noted previously? One verse in particular from Isaiah 45 would surely seem to Paul to be of great significance as it appears in the LXX. It is Isaiah 45.25:

> From *Kyrios* shall be justified and in God shall be glorified the whole seed of the children of Israel.

If we take *Kyrios* as Christ, this could be accepted as a rough and ready summary of Paul's theology of the atonement.

It is quite possible, therefore, that Romans 15.2–9 gives us an example of instruction, of which the other two passages already mentioned are also examples. It may well have been Paul's custom to use the incarnation as a basis for exhortation in order to deepen Christian fellowship. It is not rash to suggest that such teaching may have formed a basic part of Christian catechesis. At the root of this teaching is what we should to-day call the doctrine of the incarnation, anachronistic though that term is in the context of the NT. Embedded also in it is the conception of Christ speaking through the OT, and of Christ praising God in the Church. These ideas, then, are no brilliant invention of Paul's, but a basic part of the early Church's message for intending members.

We may be permitted one more observation before we close our review of Paul's use of the OT as far as concerns Christ. Again and again we have noticed that the clearest light on his thought comes from a study of those passages in the LXX which seem to lie behind his writings. And again and again what seemed at first to be difficult and even exotic has proved to be based upon a Christian interpretation of the LXX. It would be no exaggeration to say that Paul got his theological vocabulary, and therefore much of his theological thought, from the LXX. Of course, this does not in itself exclude the possibility of extraneous elements having entered his theological system. The very fact that he interpreted the LXX differently from his fellow Jews suggests that some sort of extraneous influence was operating. We can only guess at the reasons which made the LXX translators treat the Hebrew as they did. They themselves were not working in watertight compartments, whatever legend may say. But when all is said and done, the overwhelming impression we gain from our study of Paul is that the primary source of his theological thought is the LXX itself, and not any other influence acting directly upon him. If we add up the facts about Jesus, Christian tradition as received by Paul, and Paul's own study of the LXX, we shall not, it may be suggested, find very much remainder if we want to account for the sources of Paul's thought. This might well be borne in mind when we are asked to believe that Paul adopted this or that gnostic myth, or that he consciously adapted to Christian use some particular element in the Rabbinic tradition.

8

Jesus
in the Old Testament

To what extent did the writers of the NT identify Jesus with the *Adōnai* of the OT? We have noticed that scholars on the whole have given an unsatisfactory answer to this question, in so far as they have faced it at all. They have tended to go to one of two extremes: either they have denied the identification completely, or else they have suggested that wherever the Tetragrammaton occurs it is understood by the writers of the NT as indicating the pre-existent Jesus. In fact it seems that the situation is more complicated than either of these views would indicate. None of the writers whom we have been studying has any hesitation in identifying Jesus with the *Kyrios* of the OT in certain contexts. On the other hand none of them ever dreamed of suggesting that wherever the Tetragrammaton occurred in the Scriptures it really meant Jesus. All one can do is to examine briefly the usage of our three main traditions. We begin with Paul.

We can assert at once that there is no question here of a point-by-point identification of Jesus with *Kyrios* or "the Lord" in the LXX. One can point to many places where Paul quotes *Kyrios* in the OT in the sense of God the Father. To give two examples from many: in Romans 9.28 and 11.3 occur OT citations where there is no reason at all to imagine that Paul takes *Kyrios* to mean anything but God the Father. Again, in two of the passages we examined in the last chapter, 2 Corinthians 4.11–15 and 5.16—6.2, we have claimed that Paul based his instruction on two OT passages, one from a Psalm, and one from Isaiah. In both those OT passages, if our exposition is right, Paul must have taken *Kyrios* throughout as referring to God. Otherwise we have no dialogue or prophetic address left. But it is equally certain that Paul very often reads *Kyrios* of the LXX as Jesus, and that he was quite capable of maintaining this equation through long passages of the OT. We may wonder therefore what was the clue by which Paul thought he could distinguish between *Kyrios* = the Father and *Kyrios* = Jesus. This is where at first sight typology might seem to have its use. The answer might seem to be that Paul was ready to identify the *Kyrios* of the LXX with Jesus when he thought that an OT situation or utterance offered a parallel to an event in the life of Jesus or of the Church, or that it was fulfilled in such an event. This definition has to be carefully phrased, because the notion of fulfilment in itself was not always necessary for this purpose. Thus, Paul hoped that the punitive strokes in the wilderness would not be fulfilled in the life of the Corinthian Church, though he undoubtedly saw a parallel situation. I would prefer therefore not to use the word "typology" at all; it seems to me that the two phrases "parallel situation" and "fulfilment of prophecy" adequately cover all the passages in which Paul uses *Kyrios* of the LXX as indicating Jesus. If we use the word "typology", we are importing misleading suggestions, such as the idea that Christ was less really present in OT situations than in his incarnate life, or even that certain incidents in OT history took place primarily in order to point forward to NT times—both of which ideas are quite absent from Paul's thought, though not from the thought of the Fathers.

There is likewise no reason to think that either the author to the Hebrews or Stephen identified *Kyrios* with Jesus wherever the name occurred in the LXX. Hebrews indeed begins by asserting that God had spoken in the prophets to the fathers, and goes on in 1.8 sq. to represent the Father as speaking to the Son in Psalm 45, and (in all likelihood) as addressing him as "God".[1] There cannot be any suggestion that God, according to the author to the Hebrews, was incapable of revealing himself except through Christ, or that *Kyrios* must mean Jesus wherever it occurs in the

LXX. In the same way, in Acts 7.49 we find God, not Jesus, represented as speaking in a citation from Isaiah 66.1. I would seriously suggest that there is an allusive reference to Jesus in this citation: I believe he is indicated by the phrase "the place of my rest,"[2] but this very fact shows a distinction in Stephen's mind between God and Jesus. God is not here eclipsed by the pre-existent Jesus, but actually speaks about him.

At the same time we cannot, it seems to me, give the same explanation for Hebrews' OT christophanies as we gave for Paul's. In the case of Paul, "parallel situation" and "prophecy of NT events" accounted for all his examples of finding Christ in the OT. These two categories will not explain all the occasions on which the author finds Jesus acting or speaking in the OT. They will cover some undoubtedly: the reason why he thought Melchisedech was the pre-existent Son is clearly Melchisedech's resemblance to Christ as priest revealed in the NT dispensation. Again in 2.6,7 he does see Psalm 8 as referring to the future humiliation and exaltation of the Son. But in other places we must surely admit that other motives are at work. There is no obvious "parallel situation" interpretation which can be applied to our author's understanding of Numbers 12.1-8 in 3.1-6. It seems much more likely that what prompted the author of Hebrews to find Jesus there was the fact that *Kyrios* is in that Numbers passage described as appearing to Moses face to face. Again; in chapters 3 and 4 of his Epistle, we suspect that he finds Jesus in Psalm 95 because of the prominence in that Psalm of the Voice. Very much the same might be said of Hebrews 12.18-28, where we have traced an identification between Jesus and the Voice on Sinai. And in this respect the author of the Stephen speech in Acts appears to be of exactly the same mind: Jesus is allusively identified with the God who appeared to Abraham, with the angel who who appeared to Moses in the burning bush, and with the angel who spoke to Moses at the theodicy on Sinai (Acts 7.38). There are of course signs of the "parallel situation" theme also: perhaps we may find them in the story of Joseph, more probably in Moses' career. A prophecy about Jesus is quoted from

Deuteronomy 18.15 in Acts 7.37, so direct prophecy is also to be found.

But both the Epistle to the Hebrews and Stephen differ from Paul in their marked tendency to identify Jesus with both the *eidos* ("appearance") and the *phōnē* ("voice") of God in the OT. Here undoubtedly we may trace the influence of Philo, and here is something of an argument for an Alexandrian provenance for both these documents. Their authors did indeed incline to believe that "no one has ever seen God", and would no doubt assent to John's corollary that no one has ever heard his voice either. Though it cannot be proved, yet it seems very likely that both writers would trace an appearance of Jesus wherever God is represented as either appearing visibly or speaking audibly in the OT.

This is certainly John's belief, derived perhaps from Philo or the tradition of Philo. No one has ever seen God, so whenever in the OT God is described as appearing or being heard it is in fact Jesus, the pre-existent Word, who was seen or heard. But this is by no means the same thing as saying that John identified Jesus with the *Adōnai* of the OT. On the contrary, John as much as Paul could envisage God as speaking to Jesus in the OT. The clearest example of this occurs in John 10.34,35 where Jesus quotes Psalm 82. It seems likely that John envisages this Psalm as a dialogue between God, who speaks verses 2–4, and the Word (John 10.35), who utters verses 6–8. Thus the notion that God, according to John, could not speak in the OT because God speaking was always the Word, is ruled out by this citation. It is interesting to see that the notion of prophetic dialogue between the pre-existent Jesus and God is probably to be found in the Fourth Gospel also.

Charles Wesley, in one of his finest passion hymns, has a verse which runs:

> Jehovah in thy person show,
>   Jehovah crucified!
> And then the pardoning God I know,
>   And feel the blood applied.[3]

This daring address to Christ is justified by the material we have been examining through this work. The NT writers do indeed put before us, indirectly, it is true, and implicitly, but nevertheless undeniably, the amazing, shocking idea, Jehovah crucified. It is so startling that the writers themselves as it were hold their breath. They will not utter it audibly; but there it is, and we may not ignore it if we are to understand their message about Jesus. They are saved, however, from patripassionism by the very fact which we have been emphasizing: Jehovah, in so far as the name corresponds to the *Kyrios* of the LXX, is not identical at every point with Jesus. The ineffable Name indicates sometimes the Father and sometimes the Son. But we may not doubt that he who was crucified in history was, according to the writers of the NT, in his essential nature one with God, and therefore entitled to be called by the ineffable Name revealed to Moses in the burning bush.

We must now examine the converse of the theme "Jehovah crucified": What exactly is the significance of the claim that Jesus appeared in OT history? We have tended, in speaking about christophanies in the OT, to use the name Christ. It is much more natural for a modern Christian to say that Christ, or the Word, or the Son, appeared to Moses or Isaiah, and not Jesus. But the usage of the NT writers is very remarkable in this respect. Neither Paul, nor the author of Hebrews, nor John has any hesitation in using the name Jesus on occasion for the pre-existent Being whom they declare took part in OT history. The clearest example comes perhaps from 2 Corinthians 8.9, where Paul writes quite incidentally,

> For you know the grace of our Lord Jesus Christ, that though he was rich, yet for your sake he became poor, so that by his poverty you might become rich.

But "Christ" here is put in brackets by the latest Bible Society edition of the Greek NT.[4] Paul thus speaks quite calmly of the pre-existent Jesus. Likewise in Philippians 2.5-11, when Paul is writing his great hymn of the incarnation, the subject is "Christ Jesus" in 2.5, and at the end he echoes Isaiah 45.23, substituting "at the name of Jesus every knee shall bow" for "to me every knee shall bow" of the original. It looks very much as if he would say quite simply that it was Jesus who uttered these words. Similarly we have argued in chapter 7 that the subject of the quotation in 2 Corinthians 4.13 is the pre-existent Son. But he is referred to as "Jesus" throughout that passage. Of course, Paul does frequently use "Christ" of the pre-existent Son, as in 1 Corinthians 10.4, where he actually says that the Rock was "the Christ". So also in Romans 15.3. But in 15.7, having used "the Christ", he immediately refers to him as "Christ" in the next verse, so it must remain very doubtful whether Paul can ever be thought of as having written of the Messiah as such participating in OT history. At least no one has yet had the courage to translate 1 Corinthians 10.4 as "and that Rock was the Messiah".

Exactly the same attitude is reflected in the Epistle to the Hebrews. In Hebrews 2.9 Jesus is plainly identified with the figure referred to in Psalm 8, and he is described as having been made a little lower than the angels, so it is Jesus who is the subject of an incarnation. In 3.1 Jesus is the subject of the passage based on Numbers 12, where we have maintained that he is thought of as having appeared to Moses in the tabernacle. In 4.8 we have actually traced a play on words, whereby Joshua is eclipsed by Jesus. In 12.23–7 Jesus is identified with the Voice that spoke on Sinai. The author can of course use both Christ and "the Christ" in a pre-existent context (e.g. 3.6; 5.5), but he seems to use it as a name rather than as a title. The only place where "the Christ" looks like a title is in 11.26, "abuse suffered for the Christ"; but this is in a citation from a Psalm.

The evidence for the usage in the Fourth Gospel is not so easy to assess. The first time that pre-existent activity in OT history, as opposed to the eternal pre-existence of the Word, is hinted at, is in John 1.14,17, where Christ is first called the Word, and then in verse 17 called Jesus Christ. But in 12.37–41 John begins a sentence "When Jesus had said this . . .", and then goes on to refer to him as the Lord to whom Isaiah spoke in Isaiah 53.1, and whom the prophet saw in the Temple. It does not seem likely therefore that John would have had any difficulty in stating that Isaiah saw the pre-existent Jesus.

It seems to me very probable, therefore, that not only the author of the First Gospel (Matthew 1.21), but also all the writers with whom we have been dealing in this book saw a special significance in the name Jesus, and indeed looked on it as a title meaning Saviour. We have come very near to this in our discussion of Hebrews 4.8. It is interesting to note that R. P. C. Hanson[5] suggests a deliberate play on words in the Jesus-Joshua equation of Acts 7.45. The fact that all these writers can quite casually, or even carelessly, use Jesus for the pre-existent Son suggests that they thought of the name as a title. We certainly cannot suspect that they believed the man Jesus of Nazareth was pre-existent. It seems to follow that they used Jesus as a title meaning Saviour. Is there perhaps some connection between this and the fact that the actual title *Sōtēr* occurs very rarely in the books we have been examining, but very frequently in the Pastorals and in 2 Peter, writings in which we have found no trace of the pre-existent activity of Christ in OT times?

What is the significance of this doctrine of the pre-existent activity of Jesus? We with our inborn tendency to interpret things in terms of their origin and development, are compelled to speak of "the doctrine of the pre-existent Messiah". But it must be confessed if we are honest that there is not very much evidence for such a doctrine in the NT. There is much evidence for a belief in the pre-existence of Jesus, of Jesus Christ, we may say. The strongest impression we gain is of the continuity of the person of Jesus in OT history, in the period of the incarnation, and in the life of the Church. If we may put it crudely: scholars strive to find traces in pre-Christian Judaism of belief in a pre-existent office, the Messiah. The NT writers give abundant evidence of belief in a pre-existent person, Jesus. We may surmise that they identified the one with the other, but that does not seem to be the way they approached it. They knew of Jesus who had lived and died and risen from the dead, and who was present with them in the Church's life. They find essentially the same characteristics of that Jesus in the history of the Jewish people before the incarnation.

An outstanding characteristic of Jesus in the OT period is that he inspires faith or is the occasion of unbelief, exactly as in the days of his flesh. Thus in Romans 10.16 we read

> But they have not all heeded the gospel; for Isaiah says, "Lord, who has believed what he has heard from us?"

Isaiah addressing the pre-existent Jesus reports the unbelief of Israel. The same theme meets us in Hebrews 4.2:

> For good news came to us just as to them; but the message which they heard did not benefit them, as it did not meet with faith in the hearers.

The message was the message of Christ. Similarly in Hebrews 11.24-7 Moses by faith chooses to be afflicted with the Jesus whom he has seen in the burning bush. The vision has called forth faith in him. Again in John 8.39,40 Abraham's works consist in the fact that he believed in the Jesus who appeared to him, as the Jews in the days of Jesus' flesh did not. We might even point to Jude 5, where Jesus is apparently envisaged as having destroyed those who did not believe after the exodus from Egypt.

The pre-existent Jesus is likewise the source of grace and mercy: Paul in 1 Corinthians 10 represents him as providing spiritual food and drink for the Israelites in the wilderness. In John 1.14-18 grace and truth come from him in his incarnation, as they did when he appeared to Moses whom he had hidden in the cleft of the rock, and as they have been coming from him all through Israel's history, grace upon grace. And perhaps in James 5.11 we are meant to understand that we can learn from the Scriptures of the OT about the compassion and mercy of the Lord Jesus.

Jesus also judges in OT times. Indeed, this element in his nature is perhaps emphasized more when the NT writers read his activity back into the OT than when they think of him in their own day. He was not pleased with the fathers in the wilderness, says St Paul in 1 Corinthians 10, consequently many thousands

JESUS IN THE OLD TESTAMENT

of them died. Paul even thinks of the fathers as having attempted to put Jesus to the test, with dire results. Perhaps this is why in 10.22 he asks indignantly

> Shall we provoke the Lord to jealousy? Are we stronger than he?

The same warning is uttered in Hebrews 12.25-7, where those who showed themselves unwilling to hear Jesus' voice on Sinai were terribly punished. The author of Jude actually appears to make the pre-existent Jesus responsible for incarcerating the rebellious angels, and perhaps for destroying Sodom and Gomorrah (Jude 6-7).

Object of faith, source of grace, agent of divine judgement—all this and more was true of the pre-existent Jesus according to the writers of the NT. What then is left for the incarnation? Both Ignatius and Irenaeus ask this question. Ignatius writes as follows:

> Christ is the door of the Father by which enter Abraham and Isaac and Jacob and the prophets and the apostles and the Church ... But the gospel has something peculiar to itself, the presence (*parousia*) of the Saviour, our Lord Jesus Christ, his passion, his resurrection. For the beloved prophets proclaimed with him in view.[6]

Plainly Ignatius thought of the Patriarchs and prophets as already conversant with Jesus. Irenaeus' comment is this:

> If some such thought as this should occur to you "What did the coming of the Lord add?", then you must know that he brought complete renewal, since he brought himself, who had been announced ... For the coming of a king is announced beforehand by slaves sent to prepare and equip those who are to receive their Lord.[7]

The note of renewal, characteristic of Irenaeus, is found here, but more important is the emphasis on Jesus' presence in the flesh, exactly the same emphasis as we found in Ignatius.

But newness is also part of what the NT writers believed about the incarnation. As they had no notion of a developing revelation in the OT, what they believed about Christ in the OT tells us something of what they believed about him in the new dispensation also. The newness came through the incarnation, not through the revelation of the Son as such. What was new was not grace, or faith, or rejection, or love, or Son, or Word, but God the Word incarnate, God the Son incarnate. Thus, a fuller appreciation of what the NT writers believed about Jesus in the OT, far from depreciating the importance of the incarnation, throws the incarnation into bold relief. It was the taking of flesh as such, the act, the event in history, culminating of course in death and resurrection, that was unique, supreme, new.

A natural consequence of this is that Jesus' own human nature and career is now seen to be of absolutely central importance for Paul and for the author to the Hebrews, contrary to the conclusions of some modern scholars. Jesus' own faith, his relation to the Father (often as reflected in the Psalms), his experience of prayer, suffering, and salvation are now seen to have been in the background of the thought of these writers while they were composing their respective Letters. It is true that the method by which they came to understand the importance of these features of the incarnate life is one which moderns must find extremely difficult to accept. But the actual result should not present any difficulty: because the entering into human life as such stands out in such bold contrast to the appearances of Jesus believed to have taken place during OT history, the writers of the NT were bound to have a special interest in the details and the experiences of that life. Their way of evincing that interest seems strange to us, but we can no longer deny that they were interested. Thus, by a paradoxical set of circumstances, the very element in Paul's writings that the old Liberal scholars found so impossible to understand, his method of interpreting the OT, has when explored brought us face to face with the very subject which they most condemned him for ignoring, the incarnate career and experience of the Lord Jesus Christ.

Incidentally, our studies should also have thrown some light on a question which has been brought up recently in a book of no small reputation, *Honest to God*. The question, as far as we are concerned here, is this: Why does St Paul refrain from applying the word "God" to Jesus? The Bishop of Woolwich has brought the question up in the wider context of the NT as a whole and in particular of the Fourth Gospel. But if we can answer it for Paul, the same reasons will be seen to apply to the other traditions in the NT.[8] Paul believed, as we have maintained, that the pre-existent Jesus had appeared at certain points in OT history and had taken an active part in Israel's destiny. He came to this belief because he identified the *Kyrios* of the LXX with Jesus in certain passages. Now Paul must have known that the name *Kyrios* in Greek represented the Tetragrammaton, that name which we wrongly pronounce "Jehovah", and more accurately (but still iconoclastically) pronounce "Yahveh". Paul of course like all devout Jews would never have dreamed of attempting to pronounce it at all. But, to put the matter in our crude modern terminology, Paul believed that at certain points in the OT the name "Jehovah" hid the identity of the pre-existent Jesus.

Thus, Paul found himself with two distinguishable heavenly Beings active in OT history and referred to frequently in the OT. What was he to call them? The pre-existent Jesus he called *Kyrios* or "The Lord". But what of the other, the Father? There was only one possible way of referring to him that would distinguish him from "the Lord". He must be called *Theos*, and *Theos* must normally be reserved for him, or else inextricable confusion would follow. In a word, Paul avoids attributing the name *Theos* to Jesus because, if he did so, or did so indiscriminately, he would be involved in the deepest confusion of the Persons—to use later Trinitarian phraseology. But Paul distinguished the Persons of the Father and the Son. The whole difficulty no doubt goes back to the fact that by Paul's time, and long before it, the Jews had come to see that God must not have a name, because that would imply that he is one of a class. But God is unique, therefore he does not need a name to distinguish him from other members of the same class. It was only during the earlier period of henotheism that Israel's God needed a name in order to distinguish him from Moab's god and Ammon's god.[9]

As far as theology is concerned, Paul undoubtedly believed in what we mean to-day when we talk of "the divinity of Christ". Indeed, paradoxically enough, it is precisely because he identified Jesus with certain appearances of God in the OT that he refrains from applying the word *Theos* to him. He wanted to reserve that name for the Father, who also, Paul held, revealed himself in the OT. Paul was not nervous of applying *Theos* to Jesus because he doubted Jesus' divinity, nor was he willing, like Justin and Theophilus of Antioch, to interpret every appearance of God in the OT as a christophany. He held at least a Binitarian theology, and, I would add, a Trinitarian theology in the making.

At the beginning of this book we suggested that, if our thesis concerning the doctrine of Christ in the OT as understood by the NT writers were correct, some modifications would have to be made in what has recently been put forward about the place of typology in the NT. It must be obvious by now that, if the evidence brought forward in the intervening chapters is accepted, typology can no longer be regarded as the normative method by which the NT writers interpreted the OT. Indeed, typology has proved not to be central at all in the NT: the central affirmation is that the pre-existent Jesus was present in much of OT history, and that therefore it is not a question of tracing types in the OT for NT events, but rather of tracing the activity of the same Jesus in the old and in the new dispensation. In many (perhaps most) places where typology has been found in the NT we should prefer to say that the real presence of Christ is to be found and not a type.

But there is a residue of typology, or something like it, in the NT when all this has been admitted. What we must do now is to look at all the words for "type" that occur in the NT and try to decide whether they really convey what the later Church meant by typology. We begin, of course, with *tupos*. There are only four relevant uses in the NT. We have already dealt with one, that which occurs in 1 Corinthians 10.6, and have decided that to translate it "type" there is to miss the sense. This applies also of course to *tupikōs*. Two more of the four examples have also been dealt with, by implication at least. In Hebrews 8.5 and Acts 7.44 *tupos* does not mean the OT type of which the NT reality is the fulfilment. It means the heavenly reality, of which Moses made an imperfect copy. It is perhaps reminiscent of Plato, but certainly not what is normally meant by typology.[10] This leaves us with Romans 5.14, where Adam is described as τύπος τοῦ μέλλοντος, "a type of the one who was to come", as the RSV translates it. On this E. Kenneth Lee well comments: "There is clearly no thought of imitation but simply a partial resemblance, and that not of moral characteristics, but of function."[11] If Adam was a type of Christ, he was nevertheless quite unlike him in certain vital respects. Also, we are not justified in regarding *tupos* here as necessarily referring only to the future. After all, according to Paul Jesus existed long before Adam did. Perhaps we would be as well justified in rendering the whole phrase as "an imperfect copy of him who was to appear". Far from portending what was to happen, he imperfectly reflected him who was always the true image. The future reference lies in the fact that the true image was only to be displayed fully in the future.

Another word that might fall into the category of "type" is *antitupos*. It occurs in Hebrews 9.24, where the holy place made with hands in the old dispensation is described as "a copy of the true one" (ἀντίτυπα τῶν ἀληθινῶν). Here *antitupos* seems to mean an imperfect copy of a reality already existing in heaven, rather than a type which points forward to the future reality. We are still in the realm of Plato. It is very remarkable that *antitupos* is used in exactly the opposite sense in I Peter 3.21, where baptism stands as the *antitupos* of the Ark. This does seem to imply typology: the Deluge is seen as the type of baptism, but the fact that *antitupos* can be used for very nearly logically opposite terms within the NT shows how far the NT writers were from having worked out a systematic typology.

Two other words in Hebrews would seem to fall into the same category as *antitupos*; these are *skia* ("shadow") and *hupodeigma* ("pattern, example"). In Hebrews 8.5 *skia* in used in much the same sense as *antitupos* above; it seems to indicate the OT sanctuary as an imperfect copy of an already existing heavenly reality. But in Hebrews 10.1, the Law is described as having "but a shadow of the good things to come", and this does seem like typology, though we must point out that the Law, like Adam, was different in many vital respects from that which it foreshadowed. In Hebrews 4.11 *hupodeigma* is used as a warning example, very similar to *tupos* in 1 Corinthians 10.6. It is not a "type" here at all. Very much the same may be said of the same word in James 5.10 and 2 Peter 2.6. In the first place the prophets are an example of patience to Christians; in the second the fate of the cities of the plain is an "example to those who were to be ungodly". On the other hand in Hebrews 8.5 and 9.23 *hupodeigma* is used as *skia* is in Hebrews 8.5, i.e. a copy of a heavenly reality. E. Kenneth Lee well translates *hupodeigma* in these two places as "a glimpse". But it is a glimpse of what is now existent in heaven rather than of what is to come.

If we want a word in the NT that means "type" in the later sense, we will find a much more likely candidate in *parabolē* as used by the author to the Hebrews. He uses it twice, in 9.9 and 11.19. In 9.9 the OT sanctuary is described as "symbolic for the present age" (παραβολὴ εἰς τὸν καιρὸν τὸν ἐνεστηκότα); and in 11.19 it is said of Abraham's sacrifice of Isaac "figuratively speaking, he did receive him." (ὅθεν αὐτὸν καὶ ἐν παραβολῇ ἐκομίσατο). The word is unique in this sense in the NT. Everywhere else it means a parable, or a proverb. Grimm-Thayer's attempt to eliminate the typological sense by translating "by risking him" will hardly stand.[12] The only element in common between the "parable" of Jesus and the "parable" of Hebrews is that both require faith in order that they should be understood.[13] Melito also uses *parabolē* in exactly this sense (*Homily* 40). He says of Israel under the Law,

> The people therefore was a blueprint for the Church (προκέντημα τῆς ἐκκλησίας) and the Law a document of prefiguration (γραφὴ παραβολῆς).

But we should notice that in each place where *parabolē* is used in

JESUS IN THE OLD TESTAMENT

Hebrews it refers to an event (11.19) or a recurring series of events (9.9), not exclusively to an object or a person. Hauck in TWZNT says of Hebrews 11.19: "The restitution of Isaac to Abraham was a symbol that points beyond itself. It represented the future resurrection from the dead." D. Kaufmann refers to a Jewish tradition that Isaac was the author of the end of the second of the Eighteen Benedictions: "Blessed art Thou, o Lord, who bringest the dead to life."[14] So the author of Hebrews may have had Rabbinic precedent for his speculations in 11.19.

It remains to suggest one more word in the NT that may have at least led the way towards typology: *sēmeion*. We refer to Matthew 12.38–41, the sign of the prophet Jonah. There are of course two explanations of this sign furnished in the Gospels. The first is found both in Luke 11.29,30 and in Matthew 12.38–41. The second is found in the Matthew passage only. According to the first explanation, the sign of the prophet Jonah means that, as Jonah was himself unwilling to listen to God's call, and also preached to Gentiles who did accept that call, so the Jews in Jesus' day were proving unwilling to listen to God speaking to them by Jesus, whereas the Gentiles would listen and obey. In this explanation of the sign one can hardly trace typology, only that "parallel situation" phenomenon which, as we have suggested, inspired Paul to trace Christ's activity in the OT. But the second explanation of the sign of Jonah is much more like typology: as Jonah was three days and nights in the whale's belly, so will the Son of Man be three days and nights in the earth. In other words, Jonah's experience is a type of the death and resurrection of Christ. May we not suggest that, in these two alternative explanations of the sign of Jonah, we are actually witnessing the birth of typology (or a birth of typology) inside the NT? It is not therefore arbitrary to conclude, as many do, that the explanation common to Luke and Matthew may well go back in origin to Jesus himself, while the explanation peculiar to Matthew is the product of the early Church's study of the OT.[15] It is possible that *sēmeion* is also used in this sense by implication in the Fourth Gospel: B. Lindars points out that in Numbers 21.8,9 the pole on which Moses fixed the brazen serpent is described in the LXX as a *sēmeion*.¹⁶ In John 3.14,15 this incident is represented as foreshadowing Christ's death. Very probably John thought of it as what would later be called a type of the Cross. But no word is used for "type", and we are left to draw the conclusion ourselves.

We may then distinguish four levels on which the OT is interpreted by NT writers, each one degree farther removed from history. These are

1. Real Presence of Christ in OT history.
2. Prophecy.
3. Typology.
4. Allegory.

By "Real Presence" we mean the method of interpretation which sees the pre-existent Jesus actually present in OT events. It will at once be obvious that levels 1 and 2 are the really significant ones as far as the christology of the NT is concerned. We have produced many examples of Christ's real presence in the OT according to NT writers, and have been able to draw from them some conclusions about NT christology. In the same way prophecy is a category which the NT writers use for interpreting the OT, and from it, too, considerable doctrinal significance can be drawn. In many places we have seen Christ prophesying his incarnation, suffering, and death in the OT, according to the NT writers with whom we have dealt. But it is important to realize that the significance of prophecy very often lies in the fact of its being uttered by Christ, not just about Christ. This is why it is essential that we should not be misled by the attribution in the NT of a prophecy to this or that OT character, Moses, David, Isaiah, or some other prophet. All that this means in most cases is that the writer is giving the OT reference, and the writer is quite capable of treating the prophecy as if it had been uttered by Christ. Thus prophecy is not a mode of interpretation that casts everything necessarily into the future. It often tells us as much about the relation of the pre-existent Son to the Father as about what was to take place in the messianic era.

JESUS IN THE OLD TESTAMENT

Typology is not therefore central to the NT exegesis of the OT, it could be more accurately described as peripheral. Where it does occur, it consists in treating the OT event as foreshadowing a NT event. For example, in Hebrews 11.18,19 Abraham receiving back Isaac on Mount Moriah is thought of as a type of the resurrection. The sacrifice of Isaac is, of course, a very common type in the Fathers, but always as a type of the Cross. In Hebrews it is a type of the resurrection. One might conjecture, however, that if the author had enlarged on this theme, he would probably have said that Abraham offering his only son and receiving him back is a type of God giving his only Son and receiving him back through the resurrection of Jesus. Similarly in John 3.14 Moses lifting up the serpent in the wilderness is a type of Christ's being lifted up on the Cross. In each case an OT event, not a person or a thing, is a type of an event in the new dispensation. It is probable, in my opinion, that Hebrews chapter 11 contains a good deal more cryptic typology, if we could have had a fuller explanation from the author. Perhaps behind 11.21 lies the belief that in some way Jacob's rod foreshadowed the Cross; we might even guess that Joseph's care for the disposal of his bones indicated according to our author a belief in the resurrection that was to come. Indeed, in some ways it is Hebrews that seems to lead the way towards the later traditional doctrine of typology which we find in the Fathers. But the author was not to know this. Far more important, in his opinion, was his speculation about the occasions on which the pre-existent Jesus had actually (not typically) appeared in OT history. There is also in Hebrews the category of prophecy; many examples can be found in the first two chapters alone. The point is that the first two categories of interpretation, Real Presence and Prophecy, are the dominating and controlling ones in the NT. Typology is marginal (though tending to increase), and is not invested with any great christological significance. Allegory is rare, incidental, and used for illustration rather than proof.

We may therefore claim that in the last analysis the "Real Presence" method of interpretation of the OT kept the NT writers closer to history and reality than if they had given way to typological or allegorical urges, as they have often been unjustly accused of doing. Moderns cannot fail to find their methods of exegesis bizarre and startling at times, but it meant that again and again they found in the pages of the OT the living God speaking to them, meeting men face to face in mercy and judgement, demanding from them decision, calling out from them belief or unbelief. This is what many theologians are rightly urging Christians to do to-day, and this fact should bring us nearer to, rather than further from, the writers of the NT as we strive to see the relevance of the whole Bible for our condition.

Notes

CHAPTER 1

[1] J. Agar Beet (ed.), *Romans* (London 1900, 5th ed.).
[2] H. Rashdall, *The Idea of the Atonement in Christian Theology* (London 1919), pp. 131–2.
[3] R. Bultmann, *Theology of the NT*, E.T., Vol. 1 (London 1952), p. 116.
[4] Paris 1950.
[5] London 1959.
[6] London 1961, p. 15. See also E. E. Ellis, *Paul's Use of the OT* (Edinburgh 1957).

CHAPTER 2

[1] Throughout this book translations of the LXX are my own; no further indication of this will be given in the text. Κύριος is always transliterated, but ὁ Κύριος is translated "the Lord". Kyrios is used as the transliterated form of Κύριος owing to its familiarity to readers, otherwise the Greek υ becomes the English "u".
[2] *From First Adam to Last* (London 1963), p. 50.
[3] Hans Lietzmann (ed.) 1 and 2 Corinthians in *Handbuch z. NT*, Vol. IX, 2nd ed. (Tübingen 1923). In future after the first citation of the commentary it will be assumed that all further references can be found *in loc.*, and there will be no further references in the notes to that work.
[4] *Theology* XLVIII, pp. 173–7, August 1945, art. "Moses as a Type of Christ".
[5] H. L. Goudge (ed.), *1 Corinthians*, Westminster Comms. (London 1913).
[6] Jean Héring (ed.), *La Première Épître de St. Paul aux Corinthiens* (Neuchâtel and Paris 1949).
[7] A. Robertson and Alfred Plummer (eds.), *1 Corinthians*, ICC (Edinburgh 1911).

[8] Cambridge 1939, pp. 57 sq.
[9] E. J. Goodspeed (ed.), *Dialogue* in *Die Altesten Apologeten* (Göttingen 1914), my tr.
[10] Section 84. Ed. Campbell Bonner as No. XII in *Studies and Documents*, ed. Kirsopp Lake and Sylvia Lake (London and Philadelphia 1940), my tr. In future it may be assumed that all trs. from the Fathers are mine unless it is stated otherwise.
[11] Ed. and tr. from the Armenian by Joseph Smith, s.j., section 46 (Westminster, Maryland and London 1952).
[12] It runs ὁ δὲ ἐγὼ ἕστηκα πρὸ τοῦ σε ἐκεῖ ἐπὶ τῆς πέτρας ἐν χωρήβ A* supplies ἐλθεῖν instead of ἐκεῖ. The Hebrew is quite straightforward: "Behold, I will stand before thee on the Rock at Horeb."
[13] J. E. McFadyen (ed.), *1 and 2 Corinthians* in Interpreter's Comm. (London 1911).
[14] L. Venard art. "Citations de l'AT dans le NT" in *Dictionnaire de la Bible*, Supplement to the 2nd volume ed. J. Pirot (Paris 1934).
[15] E.-B. Allo (ed.), *Première Épître aux Corinthiens* (Paris 1934).
[16] J. Bonsirven, *Exégèse Rabbinique et Exégèse Paulinienne* (Paris 1939), p. 303.
[17] *Sacramentum Futuri*, p. 159.
[18] That moderns are not the only commentators who misinterpret Paul's thought in terms of typology is shown by the following quotation from Basil, *De Spiritu Sancto*, chap. 31 (ed. C. F. H. Johnston, Oxford 1892): "The type is a revelation of things expected, shewing beforehand by means of imitation the future demonstratively, as Adam was a type of him who was to come, and the Rock was Christ typologically, and the water from the Rock was a type of the living power of the Word ... and the manna was a type of the living bread that came down from heaven, and the serpent fixed on the standard was a type of the saving passion fulfilled through the Cross."
[19] From *Theology of the NT*, pp. 36 and 312 of Vol. 1.
[20] E. E. Ellis, *Paul's Use of the OT* (Edinburgh 1959), p. 121.
[21] G. W. K. Lampe and K. J. Woollcombe, *Essays in Typology* (London 1957), p. 114.
[22] T. C. Edwards (ed.), *1 Corinthians* (London 1885).
[23] In art. πέτρα in TWZNT, Vol. VI, p. 96.
[24] *Homily XXIII on 1 Corinthians* in Migne, PG, Vol. LXI, Tome X (Paris 1859).
[25] *Allegory and Event*, pp. 79–80.

NOTES TO CHAPTER TWO

26 Charles Hodge (ed.), *1 Corinthians* (modern reissue London 1958).
27 Wilhelm Bousset (ed.), 1 Corinthians in *Die Schriften d. N.T.*, Vol. II (Göttingen 1917).
28 S-B, Vol. III (Munich 1926); T. F. Glasson, *Moses in the Fourth Gospel* (London 1963), p. 59. Both these authorities quote the passage as from the *Tosephta Sukka* 3.11 sq.
29 Quoted from the Midrash M^{e}khiltha on Ex. 17.6.
30 I have already made this point in my book *The Pioneer Ministry* (London 1962), p. 37.
31 *From First Adam to Last*, p. 50.
32 *A Christian Theology of the OT* (London 1959), p. 216.
33 It is supported by $\mathfrak{P}^{46}$ DG *pm* latt sy$^{p\ h}$ co Marcion Irenaeus Clem. Alex Origen.
34 A. Plummer (ed.), *2 Corinthians*, ICC (Edinburgh 1915); R. Strachan (ed.), *2 Corinthians*, Moffatt Comms. (London 1915).
35 Torch Comms. (London 1954).
36 It is suggested by R. P. C. Hanson, but amplified here.
37 The suggestion that *anakaluptomenon* is acc. absl., which I defended in *The Pioneer Ministry*, p. 70, ought to be abandoned on linguistic grounds; see Blass-Debrunner 242, p. 219 (F. Blass and H. Debrunner, *A Greek Grammar of the NT*, etc., Eng. tr. and ed. R. W. Funk (Cambridge and Chicago 1961), based on 9th and 10th German eds.).
38 The word must mean "beholding" not "reflecting", despite the strong temptation to take it in this latter sense. No one has yet been able to produce an example of the middle of *katoptrizō* meaning "reflect".
39 Quoted S-B from Jerusalem Targum I.
40 Quoted from Midrash P^{e}siqtha Rabbathi, uttered by R. Jehoshua of Sikhim (*c.* A.D. 330) in the name of R. Levi (*c.* 300).
41 Hans Windisch (ed.), 2 Corinthians, *Krit.-Exeg. Komm. z. d. NT*, Vol. VI, Book 9 (Göttingen 1924).
42 J. Jeremias, art. Μωϋσῆς in TWZNT, Vol. IV, p. 873.
43 Johannes Munck, *Paul and the Salvation of Mankind* (E.T., London 1959, of German ed., 1952), pp. 58–61.
44 *Paul and Rabbinic Judaism* (London 1948), p. 148.
45 W. W. Harvey (ed.), *S. Irenaei Libros V adv. Haereses* (Cambridge 1857), IV.34.9.
46 Tertullian *Adv. Marcionem* V.11.6 ed. A. Kroymann, Tertulliani

Opera Omnia, Corpus Christianorum (Series Latina), Vol. I (Turnhout 1954). See also IV.22.15 where it is clear that it was Christ's glory that Moses reflected.

[47] W. C. Sanday and A. C. Headlam (eds.), *Romans*, ICC (Edinburgh 1912).

[48] A. Nygren (ed.), *Romans* (E.T., London 1952).

[49] Op. cit., p. 39. Cf. his comment on Romans 10.18 (p. 38): "The apostle certainly does not cite the Scripture here as an authority; he simply expresses a well-known fact in terms borrowed from the OT."

[50] See *The Wrath of the Lamb* (London 1957), pp. 73 sq.

[51] K. E. Kirk (ed.), *Romans*, Clarendon Bible (Oxford 1937).

[52] H. Lietzmann (ed.), Romans in *Handbuch z. NT*, Vol. III, Book 2 (Tübingen 1919).

[53] C. H. Dodd (ed.), *Romans*, Moffatt Comms. (London 1942 edition).

[54] Adolf Jülicher (ed.), Romans in *Die Schriften d. NT*, Vol. II (Göttingen 1917).

[55] *Dialogue* 114.2.

[56] The verses in the LXX are numbered one more than in the English, so this comes as verse 6, and so on.

[57] A. W. F. Blunt (ed.), *Justin's Apology* (Cambridge 1911).

[58] *Exégèse Rabbinique, etc.*, p. 330.

[59] There is nothing in the Hebrew to correspond to "the rage of", but it may have been in the original text.

[60] *Paul's use of the OT*, p. 23.

[61] J. B. Lightfoot (ed.), *The Apostolic Fathers* (London 1891); *Ep. Barnabas* 12.4.

CHAPTER 3

[1] *St. Paul and the Church of the Gentiles*, p. 122.

[2] B. F. Westcott (ed.), *Hebrews* (London 1892).

[3] Hans Windisch (ed.), Der Hebräerbrief in *Handbuch. z. NT* (Tübingen 1913).

[4] In Heb. 11.7 the word is used of Noah building the ark and in 9.2,6 of Moses erecting the tabernacle. Moulton and Milligan give more examples of the word meaning "erecting" than "creating". But Spicq quotes several instances of this latter meaning from the LXX. In Classical Greek the word is regularly used of things which

NOTES TO CHAPTER THREE 183

require a good deal of preparation, like a bridge or a ship. The Vulgate is therefore most misleading in translating verse 4: "Omnis namque domus fabricatur ab aliquo; qui autem omnia creavit, Deus est."

[5] The sense is the same whether we read οὗ οἶκος with 𝔓[13] ABI, or ὅς οἶκος with 𝔓[46] D*M 1739.

[6] James Moffatt (ed.), *Hebrews*, ICC (Edinburgh 1924).

[7] A. S. Peake (ed.), *Hebrews*, Century Bible (London 1902).

[8] Otto Michel (ed.), Der Brief an die Hebräer in *Krit.-Exeg. Komm. ü. d. NT*, Vol. XIII, Book 8 (Göttingen 1949).

[9] My attention was drawn to the significance of this passage by a footnote in R. P. C. Hanson's *Allegory and Event*, p. 97, n. 2.

[10] Georg Hollmann (ed.), Der Hebräerbrief in *Die Schriften d. NT*, Vol. II, 2nd ed. (Göttingen 1917).

[11] T. Robinson (ed.), *Hebrews*, Moffatt Comms. (London 1933).

[12] C. Spicq (ed.), *L'Épître aux Hébreux* (Paris 1953, 2nd ed.).

[13] J. Bonsirven, *Le Judaisme Palestinien au Temps de Jésus-Christ*, Vol. I, p. 81 (Paris 1934, 2nd ed.): "Christian theology has seen in Moses one of the types (Fr. *figures*) of Christ", and he refers to Heb. 3.2–5.

[14] *Theology of the NT*, Vol. I, p. 111: "Christ was pre-depicted in Moses as the one faithful in all God's house (Heb. 3.1-6), and in Melchisedech as the High Priest (7.1-10)."

[15] *N.T. Studies*, Apr. 1962, Vol. 8, No. 3, pp. 236 sq.; cf. also E. L. Allen in *Expository Times*, Vol. 67, 1955–6, p. 104, art. "Jesus and Moses in the NT", where he is puzzled at the author applying θεράπων to Moses. The explanation is to be found in Num. 12.1-15. It should be noted that Dr Aalen's case partly depends on the undeniable fact that the author of Hebrews quotes 2 Sam. 7.14 in 1.5 as the Father speaking of the Son.

[16] F. C. Synge, *Hebrews and the Scriptures* (London 1959), p. 21.

[17] *Sacramentum Futuri*, p. 204. Cf. R. P. C. Hanson's suggestion in *Theology*, Vol. LI, No. 332, p. 142, April 1947, art. "Studies in Texts, Acts 6.13", that μετὰ Ἰησοῦ in Acts 7.45 carries the same ambiguity.

[18] *Ep. Barnabas*, 12.8.

[19] This verse may well have influenced Paul in connection with I Cor. 10.

[20] Irenaeus Fragment XIX in A. Stieren *Irenaei Op. Omn.*, Vol. II, p. 837 (Leipzig 1853). Tertullian, *Adv. Marcionem* III.16.3-4. Eusebius, *Eccl. Hist.*, ed. K. Lake, Loeb Ed., I.iii (London and New York 1926,

Vol. I). F. C. Synge (op. cit., pp. 19–20) notes both the reference to Joshua and Justin's comment, but still calls Joshua a type of Jesus in Hebrews.

[21] J. P. Migne, *Origenis Op. Omn.*, *Selecta in Genesim* (PG, Vol. II, Paris 1957).

[22] A. P. Bruce, *The Epistle to the Hebrews* (Edinburgh 1899), p. 153.

[23] Incidentally, we may note that he can refer to Ps. 95 as the utterance of the Holy Spirit (3.7) or as Christ speaking in David (4.7).

[24] D^{e}bhar hashsh^{e}mu'ah.

[25] M. Rissi in an art. "Die Menschlichkeit Jesu nach Heb. 5.7–8" (*Theologische Zeitschrift* 1955, pp. 28 sq.) agrees on the basis of *keklēromēken* in 1.4 that Christ was appointed high priest at a certain point in time. He concludes that the author thought of him as high priest throughout his incarnate life, and that his sonship and highpriesthood were coterminous. He takes *prosagoreutheis* in 5.10 not as an act of appointment, but as an act of proclamation in heaven of the priesthood which had been veiled on earth. This hardly seems to fit in with our author's time schedule, suggesting as it does that *prosagoreutheis* actually refers to a time after the incarnate ministry.

[26] A. Nairne, *The Epistle of Priesthood* (London 1913), p. 334; E. C. Wickham (ed.), *Hebrews*, Westminster Comms. (London 1910); F. Boylan (ed.), *Hebrews*, Westminster Version (London 1931).

[27] *Exégèse Rabbinique, etc.*, p. 305; the word he uses is "ébauche".

[28] J. van der Ploeg, art. in *Révue Biblique* liv, 1947, p. 187, "L'Exégèse de l'AT dans l'Épître aux Hébreux". The quotation occurs on p. 216.

[29] Wm. Manson, *The Epistle to the Hebrews* (London 1951), p. 113.

[30] J. Héring (ed.), *L'Épître aux Hébreux* (Neuchâtel-Paris 1954).

[31] M. Simon in art. mentioned in n. 33 below says that M. was an embarrassing figure for the Rabbis. The genealogy from Shem was partly an attempt to furnish him with a respectable lineage.

[32] Hippolytus, *Refut. Omn. Haer.* VII.36.1 in P. Wendland, ed. *Hippolytus Werke* Vol. III in *Die Griechischen Schriftsteller der ersten drei Jahrhunderte* (Leipzig 1916).

[33] Art. "Melchisedech dans la polemique entre juifs et chrétiens et dans la legende" in *Révue d'Histoire et de le Philosophie Réligieuses*, 1937, pp. 58 sq. The pseudonymous work is called *De Melchisedecho*.

[34] Epiphanius, *Adv. Haer.* 67.6 in Migne, PG, Vol. XLII, pp. 181 sq.

[35] *Paul and the Church of the Gentiles*, p. 123.

[36] The substance of the section on Melchisedech formed part of a

paper delivered at the Second Congress for the Study of the NT held at Christ Church, Oxford in 1961.

[37] W. Michaelis, in art. "ἀόρατος" in TWZNT, Vol. V, p. 369, asserts that the author was not interested in the question whether Moses saw God or not. But he has not considered the parallel with Acts 7.

[38] This point is well made by Estius; see next note.

[39] G. Estius, *Comm. in NT*, Vol. III, ed. J. Holzammer (2nd. ed., Mainz 1859).

[40] Estius is no doubt influenced here by Augustine; see Augustine, *De Trinitate* III.11.24 in *Éditions Bénédictines*, M. Mellet et Th. Camelot ed. *De Trinitate*. (Paris 1955, Vol. I).

[41] Michel's exposition agrees largely with Spicq, and he compares 2.2. I examine this passage in the next chapter, and so postpone discussing it till then. There is a variant reading in verse 25 concerned with the position in the text of the words τὸν ἐπὶ γῆς, but I have not discussed it, as it does not seem to me to make any difference to the exegesis which of the three variants is accepted.

[42] Incidentally, the fact that our author quotes Hag. 2.6 and not 2.7 is a slight indication that he is not relying here on a list of *Testimonia*. Hag. 2.7, with its reference to "the desired things of all the Gentiles", is a much more obvious messianic prophecy than the one he quotes. Canon Synge (op. cit., p. 39) seems to me to have missed the point of this passage. What made the people refuse to hear God's voice was not reverence, as he suggests, but fear.

[43] G. Bardy and J. Sender (ed.), *Théophile d'Antioche: Trois Livres à Autolycus* in *Sources Chrétiennes* (Paris 1948).

[44] I originally suggested a christological interpretation of Heb. 12.24–7 in *The Wrath of the Lamb*, p. 139. But the detailed exposition given above was first worked out in the paper for the Oxford Congress of 1961 referred to in n. 36 above.

CHAPTER 4

[1] *Allegory and Event*, p. 94.

[2] For the sake of convenience I shall refer to Stephen as the author of this speech throughout, without prejudice to the question of authenticity.

[3] The Hebrew is "And he makes them dance like a calf of Lebanon",

but the original may have been "And he makes Lebanon to dance like a calf".

[4] He has read $w^e\!siry\bar{o}n$ as $w\bar{\imath}shur\bar{u}n$.

[5] F. F. Bruce (ed.), *Acts* (London 1951); E. Preuschen (ed.), Apostelgeschichte in *Handbuch z. NT*, Vol. II (Tübingen 1912), 9th ed.

[6] H. H. Wendt (ed.), Apostelgeschichte in *Krit.-Exeg. Komm. ü. d. NT*, Vol. II, 9th ed. (Göttingen 1913).

[7] C. S. C. Williams (ed.), *Acts*, Black's Comms. (London 1957).

[8] *Adv. Haer.* IV.12.1.

[9] F. J. Foakes-Jackson and Kirsopp Lake, *The Beginnings of Christianity*, Part I, Vol. II, Comm. on text by K. Lake and H. J. Cadbury (London 1933).

[10] This is a reference to the LXX translation of Isa. 9.6, where the LXX translates part of the phrase "Wonderful Counsellor, Mighty God" as "angel of great counsel".

[11] Chrysostom, *Comm. in Acta*, Homily XVI, ed. Migne in PG, Vol. LX, Tome IX (Paris 1859).

[12] Jerome, *Comm. in Ep. ad Gal.*, ed. Migne in PL, Vol. XXVI, Tome VII (Paris 1845).

[13] E.T. London 1957.

[14] The Hebrew seems to mean "like aloes that the Lord has planted". But the word for "aloes" is an obscure one. Not only the LXX, but also the O.L., the Vulgate, and the Targum read "tents".

[15] F. Rendall (ed.), *Acts* (London 1897).

[16] The reference is to *Antiquities* XV.5.3.

[17] R. H. Charles, *Apocrypha and Pseudepigrapha of the OT*, Vol. II, Book of *Jubilees* (Oxford 1913).

[18] *Le Judaisme Palestinien*, p. 232.

[19] The Bible Society Text prefers the reading "give to you". The authorities seem fairly equally divided, but with the balance in favour of "you".

hēmin ADE pm lat sy; *humin* אB al p co Ir.

[20] *St. Paul and the Church at Jerusalem*, pp. 44, 55, n. 33 (Cambridge 1925).

[21] There is no specific reference to angels in the MT, and it is not obvious how the words entered the text of the LXX. They may have been originally a gloss on the previous line.

[22] E. E. Ellis (op. cit., p. 66) suggests that Ps. 68.17,18 (LXX 67.17,18) is the source of Stephen's references to the angels on Mount Sinai. This

seems to me unconvincing. A comparison of Ps. 68 with Deut. 33 seems to tell definitely in favour of the latter.
[23] *Comm. in Acta,* Homily XVII.3.
[24] *Comm. in Ep. ad Gal.,* ed. Migne in PG, Vol. LXI, Tome X (Paris 1859).
[25] S-B in Gal. 3.19.
[26] H. Lietzmann (ed.), An die Galäter in *Handbuch z. NT,* Vol. II, 2nd ed. (Tübingen 1923).
[27] Heinrich Schlier (ed.), Der Brief an die Galäter in *Krit.-Exeg. Komm. ü. d. NT,* Vol. VII (Göttingen 1949).
[28] *The Formation of Christian Dogma,* pp. 79–81.
[29] *Theology of the NT,* E.T., Vol. I, p. 268.
[30] R. B. Rackham (ed.), *Acts* in Westminster Comms. (London 1901).
[31] *Essays in Typology,* p. 19

CHAPTER 5

[1] C. H. Dodd, *The Interpretation of the Fourth Gospel* (Cambridge 1960), p. 247. A variant reading here should be noticed. Instead of τὴν δόξαν αὐτοῦ, Θ f13 one Old Latin MS. and the Coptic read τὴν δόξαν τοῦ Θεοῦ and D reads τὴν δόξαν τοῦ Θεοῦ αὐτοῦ. This is not sufficient MS. evidence in itself to stand against the testimony of the rest, and in any case it would give a very rough sort of syntax: περὶ αὐτοῦ in verse 41 would have to refer to God, and εἰς αὐτὸν in verse 42 to Christ, without any indication of a change of subject. The alternative reading must have originated in a mistaken gloss.
[2] J. H. Bernard, *St. John,* ICC (Edinburgh 1928).
[3] Wm. Temple, *Readings in St. John's Gospel* (Oxford 1960, paperback ed.).
[4] E. C. Hoskyns and F. N. Davey, *The Fourth Gospel* (London 1947, 2nd ed.).
[5] R. Bultmann (ed.), Das Evangelium des Johannes in *Krit.-Exeg. Komm. ü.d. NT* (Göttingen 1962, 6th imp.), p. 347 n.
[6] *Comm. in Johan.* in loc. quoted in J.-L. Maier, *Les Missions Divines selon St. Augustine* (Fribourg 1960), p. 115.
[7] *Interpretation of the Fourth Gospel,* pp. 207, 260.
[8] K. Bauer (ed.), Das Johannesevangelium in *Handbuch z. NT,* Vol. VI (Tübingen 1925, 2nd ed.).

⁹ The Hebrew is "Your guilt is taken away and your sin forgiven". The LXX has changed the past tenses into the future.

¹⁰ The MT is *pānai yēlēkhu*. The Syriac appears to have read *lᵉphānai lēkh* "go before me", which may have given rise to the LXX tr.

¹¹ T. F. Glasson, *Moses in the Fourth Gospel* (London 1963), p. 63.

¹² *Interpretation of the Fourth Gospel*, pp. 82, 175.

¹³ *chesedh weʾemeth* of God Ex. 34.6; 2 Sam. 2.6; Ps. 25.10; 40.11,12; 57.3,10; 61.7; 86.15; 89.14; 108.4; 115.1; 117.2; 138.2. *rabh chesedh* of God Ex. 34.6; Num. 14.18; Joel 2.13; Jonah 4.2; Ps. 86.5,15; 103.8; Neh. 9.17.

¹⁴ G. H. C. Macgregor (ed.), *The Fourth Gospel* in Moffat Comms. (London 1928).

¹⁵ See Augustine, *De Trinitate* II.16,17; cf. also Irenaeus, *Adv. Haer.* IV.34.9; Tertullian, *Adv. Marcionem* IV.22.15.

¹⁶ Op. cit., p. 50 n.

¹⁷ Hermann Strathmann (ed.), Das Evangelium nach Johannes in *Das NT Deutsch* (Göttingen 1951).

¹⁸ Op. cit., p. 97.

¹⁹ J. A. T. Robinson in an art. called "The Relation of the Prologue to the Gospel of St. John" in *NT Studies*, Jan. 1963 (Vol. 9, No. 2) seeks to prove that the Prologue is a later addition, fitted on by the author to a Gospel which originally began with the Baptist's mission. I find his arguments wholly unconvincing. If the evidence produced above is valid, he is on the wrong track altogether, and in particular his claim that 1.15 is anomalous and inappropriate in its context is quite baseless. According to the exposition given above, it provides the essential link in the argument.

²⁰ The MT of Num. 12.8abc is

peh ʾel-peh ʾᵃdhabēr bō
ūmarʾeh wᵉlō bᵉchīdōth
uthᵉmunath ʾAdonai yabīt

The trouble is that *marʾeh* is exactly the word used in verse 6 to mean "a vision" and not "face to face". This latter place is tr. in the LXX ἐν ὁράματι. The LXX may have deliberately tr. *thᵉmūnath ʾAdonai* as τὴν δόξαν κυρίου from motives of reverence, or else it may have had some such phrase as *kᵉbhōdh ʾAdonai* in its Hebrew text.

²¹ It is true that Deut. 18.15 sq. is cited in Acts 3.22; 7.37, and the latter is from Stephen's speech. Both are cited as prophecies of Christ.

My point is that here John is not concerned with prophecies, but with an actual appearance of Christ to Moses.

[22] C. K. Barrett (ed.), *The Gospel according to St. John* (London 1955). He seems here to be largely reproducing W. Heitmuller (ed.), Das Johannesevangelium in *Die Schriften d. NT*, Vol. IV (Göttingen 1918, 2nd ed.).

[23] *Interpretation of the Fourth Gospel*, p. 266.

[24] *Adv. Haer.* IV.3.1.

[25] R. H. Lightfoot (ed.), *The Fourth Gospel* (Oxford 1959).

[26] *Interpretation of the Fourth Gospel*, p. 83.

[27] *Moses in the Fourth Gospel*, p. 45.

[28] Philo, *Quis Rerum Div. Haeres?* XXXIX, ed. Colson and Whitaker, Loeb ed. of *Philo Op. Omn.*, Vol. IV, p. 279 (London 1949, 2nd reprint).

[29] *Moses in the Fourth Gospel*, pp. 28, 54.

[30] The phrase occurs also in Gen. 24.1. This suggestion is made by C. K. Barrett and C. H. Dodd, *Interpretation*, etc., p. 261.

[31] For patristic references to Christ as one of these three angels, see Justin, *Dialogue* 56.1; 57.2; Irenaeus, *Adv. Haer.* III.6.1; IV.36.3; *Proofs*, etc., 44; Tertullian, *Adv. Marcionem* III.1.6; Eusebius, *Eccl. Hist.* I.ii.6–7; Hilary, *De Trinitate* 4.25 sq. (Migne, PL, Vol. X, p. 63). Cf. also Wisd. 10.6, where it is Wisdom that rescues Lot from Sodom. See also Plate 42 in N. Zernov, *Eastern Christendom* (London 1962). It reproduces an ikon in which the three angels visiting Abraham appear as the three Persons of the Holy Trinity. This represents Augustine's view, *De Trin.* II.2.10–12.

[32] According to C. K. Barrett this is how Philo takes it.

[33] This is the source favoured by R. H. Lightfoot.

[34] The LXX has "the voice of *Kyrios*" here, where the MT has merely "the word of the Lord", so the point would be clearer in the LXX.

[35] This point is well made by E. E. Ellis, op. cit., p. 87.

[36] Quoted Maier, op. cit., p. 56.

[37] Migne, PG, Vol. LII, Tome CV, Chrysostom, *Homiliae in Genesim*, Hom. XLVIII (Paris 1862).

[38] B. Lindars, *New Testament Apologetic* (London 1961), p. 227

CHAPTER 6

[1] J. B. Mayor (ed.), *The Epistle of James* (London 1910).

[2] Quoted in R. L. Knowling (ed.), *The Epistle of James* in Westminster

Comms. (London 1904), and in Martin Dibelius (ed.), *Der Brief des Jakobus* in *Krit.-Exeg. Komm. ü. d. NT*, Vol. XV, Part 7 (Göttingen 1921).

[3] *Sic* Knowling; J. M. Ropes (ed.), *The Epistle of James* in ICC (Edinburgh 1916); G. Hollmann and W. Bousset (ed.), *Der Brief des Jakobus* in *Die Schriften d. NT*, Vol. III (Göttingen 1917), and Dibelius.

[4] London 1956, p. 236. He has a theory that James is an originally Jewish work, Christianized by a later hand; but this need not concern us here.

[5] But in Ex. 34.6 the MT adds $w^{e'}emeth$ at the end, which the LXX translates καὶ ἀληθινός.

[6] In fact, the LXX slightly tones down God's rebuke in Jonah 4.4 and 9.

[7] Tertullian, *Adv. Marcionem* IV.10.3. It will be remembered that Marcion denied the identity of the Creator with God the Father.

[8] F. J. A. Hort (ed.), *Epistle of James* (London 1909, unfinished).

[9] *Sic* C. Bigg (ed.), *1 Peter* in ICC (Edinburgh 1901); R. Knopf (ed.), 1 Petrus in *Krit.-Exeg. Komm. ü. d. NT*, Vol. XIII, Part 7 (Göttingen 1912); H. Gunkel (ed.), 1 Petrus in *Die Schriften d. NT*, Vol. III (Göttingen 1917); F. W. Beare (ed.), *1 Peter* (Oxford 1947); E. Stauffer, *NT Theology*, pp. 102-6 (E.T. London 1955).

[10] R. Kühl (ed.), 1 Petrus in *Krit.-Exeg. Komm. ü. d. NT*, Vol. XII, Part 6 (Göttingen 1897).

[11] E. G. Selwyn (ed.), *The First Epistle of Peter* (London 1946), in loc. and pp. 259 sq.

[12] In Peake's Comm. on the Bible (rev. ed., London 1962).

[13] The LXX translator has misunderstood the Hebrew, which is "that he who runs may read".

[14] The LXX has translated the MT literally; it probably only means "what he shall speak to me".

[15] It is represented by one hand in Codex Claromontanus, a few Greek minuscules, the Philoxenian Syriac, and Clem. Rom.

[16] It is found in Alexandrinus, Vaticanus, a few OL MSS., the Coptic, and Origen. R. M. Grant in *An Historical Introduction to the NT* (London 1963), p. 50 much prefers this reading.

[17] For reference see under 1 Peter; as also for Knopf, Bigg, and Hollmann and Bousset.

[18] I assume with the great majority of editors that 2 Peter is dependent on Jude and not *vice versa*.

[19] Did Paul mean to identify Christ with "the Destroyer" in 1 Cor. 10.10? I have not ventured to suggest this in chapter 2, but I think it by no means impossible.

CHAPTER 7

[1] James Moffatt (ed.), *1 Corinthians* in Moffatt Comms. (London 1938).
[2] Héring traces it to the Book of Enoch.
[3] *Dialogue* 36.5–6.
[4] The Hebrew of the last line is literally "he [sc. God] works for him who waits for him". The LXX translator seems to have repeated "he works", and thus got his phrase "thy works". Where he got his word "mercy" from is a mystery. Equally mysterious is Paul's substitution of "those who love him" for the LXX "those who wait for mercy". Indeed a conflation of Paul's reading with the LXX would give us "those who wait for him", which is very nearly the MT. It is worth noting that R. Kittel (in *Bibl. Hebr.*) actually suggests that we should read "those who wait for him", instead of the singular "him who waits", and this reading is adopted by the RSV (without any indication that it is in fact a departure from the MT).
[5] The element of dialogue is of course underlined if the whole of Isa. 64.1—65.2 is within Paul's purview here.
[6] Charles Wesley's magnificent paraphrase of Ps. 116.12 to end appears in the modern Methodist Hymn Book under "Dedication" (no. 339). But it would be even more appropriate as an introit to the Eucharist. N.B. This passage in 2 Corinthians I have expounded rather more in detail in my Inaugural Lecture, "Paul's Understanding of Jesus" (Hull 1963).
[7] The explanation, as far as concerns Gal. 3.6–14, is repeated and amplified in the Lecture referred to above.
[8] This does not at all represent the Hebrew, which runs: "Adōnai has called me from the womb; from the belly of my mother he has made mention of my name."
[9] The Greek has by mistake repeated the word "gather" from the previous line.
[10] The words "as a covenant of the people" are not in the MT.
[11] The Greek has misunderstood the Hebrew, which runs: "the

God of Israel, the Redeemer, his Holy One, to one despised, one loathed by the nations, a servant of rulers".

[12] The Hebrew phrase lying behind it is *lᵉrīq*. If we include *lārīq*, it occurs five times, and is translated three times by εἰς κενόν, once by κενῶς, and once by διὰ κενῆς (εἰς κενόν in Lev. 26.20; Job 39.16; Isa. 65.23; κενῶς in Isa. 49.4; διὰ κενῆς in Lev. 26.16).

[13] The Hebrew is better rendered "recompense", but we must assume that Paul was using the LXX.

[14] Wilhelm Bousset (ed.), 2 Corinthians in *Die Schriften d. NT*, Vol. II (Göttingen 1917).

[15] The suggestion is made in his *Comm. on Romans* in loc.

[16] For an alternative suggestion as to what this really means see p. 42.

[17] The LXX is as usual one behind in the Psalm numeration, but it is also one ahead in the verse numeration, so this is Ps. 68.4 in the LXX.

[18] In Rom. 11.9 the words are attributed to David, but, as we have maintained in chapter 2, this is no bar in Paul's mind to the Psalm having been uttered by Christ. Indeed this Psalm is also attributed to David in the title, but this does not prevent Paul finding in it the utterance of the Messiah.

[19] On the question of prediction see the judicious remarks of van der Ploeg in art. cit. What he calls the *sensus plenior* is very much what we have been outlining here.

[20] Op. cit., p. 126.

[21] Op. cit., p. 99.

[22] *The Birth of the New Testament* (London 1962), pp. 77–8.

CHAPTER 8

[1] I am aware that this is disputed, but it seemed to me the more likely interpretation of the passage.

[2] The LXX sometimes uses *topos* as a method of toning down an anthropomorphism; cf. Ex. 24.10, where the LXX reads "and they saw the place where the God of Israel stood". Philo, following the LXX of course, identifies the *topos* here with his Logos; see *De Confus. Linguarum.* xx.9.7; cf. also *De Somniis* (I).xi.62.

[3] The first line is "With glorious clouds encompassed round", no. 172 in the modern Methodist Hymn Book; but a squeamish modern generation has omitted the verse quoted here. I cite it from the ed. of 1875, where it is no. 128.

NOTES TO CHAPTER EIGHT

[4] It is omitted by Vaticanus and the Sahidic version.
[5] In art. cit., "Studies in Texts: Acts 6.13".
[6] *Philadelphians* 9.
[7] *Adv. Haer.* IV.64.1.
[8] See *Honest to God* (London 1963), pp. 70–1. The question has also been brought up in an acute form by Martin Werner (op. cit., pp. 127–8 et al.). He gives a much more specific answer than does the Bishop of Woolwich, and one which is based, I am sure, on a complete misunderstanding of Paul's approach to the pre-existent Jesus.
[9] It was a most unfortunate coincidence that the missionary expansion of the last century took place before the name "Jehovah" had been discredited. One consequence is that in many Indian languages we still have a version of the Bible that translates the Tetragrammaton as "Jehovah". I have heard Telugu congregations singing hymns to "Jehovah our shepherd". Presumably they thought that "Jehovah" was the name of the Christians' God, as "Vishnu" or "Krishna" was the name of a god of the Hindus.
[10] I cannot follow K. J. Woollcombe (op. cit., p. 64 n) when he writes of Heb. 8.5: "In Hebrews [sc. *tupos*] is obviously used in the sense of something secondary. The author's purpose in quoting Ex. 25.40 was to show that Moses' tent was at best a *tupos*, i.e. something inferior to the true archetype. *Tupos* and *antitupos* are synonymous in Hebrews." But *tupos* in this passage means the archetype. How can it be equated with *antitupos*?
[11] In art. "Words denoting Pattern in the NT" in *NT Studies*, Vol. 8, No. 2, pp. 166 sq., Jan. 1962.
[12] *Greek-English Lexicon of the NT*, 4th ed. (Edinburgh 1905).
[13] Bonsirven notices this use of *parabolē*, though he equates it with the use of *tupos* in Paul, which we can hardly accept. (*Exégèse Rabbinique, etc.*, p. 269.)
[14] Art. "Sens et Origine des Symboles Tumulaires de l'AT dans l'Art Chrétien primitif" in *Révue des Études Bibliques* xiv, pp. 33 sq. and pp. 217 sq., 1887.
[15] Ignatius calls the bishop the *tupos* of God, and the presbyteral college the *tupos* of the apostles (*Magn.* 6; *Trall.* 3). This is not far from Rom. 5.14, but of course there is no future reference. In exactly the same sense in the *Didache* slaves are exhorted to obey their masters as the *tupos* of God (ed. H. de Romestin, London 1885, IV.11; cf. also *Ep. Barn.* 19.7). Hermas uses *tupos* as "symbol". See *Vis.* iv.2.5:

"This beast is a *tupos* of the coming affliction"; cf. also *Sim.* i.9. He can use it simply to mean "explanation"; see *Vis.* lv.11.4: "You have the explanation (*tupos*) of the first vision." See M. Whittaker (ed.), *Der Hirt des Hermas* (Berlin 1956). In *Ep. Barn.* OT persons and things are frequently described as *tupoi* of NT persons and things. The most remarkable example occurs in 12.9–10, where Joshua is described as being "the Son of God manifested in the flesh by means of a type". In 2 Clement XIV.3 the flesh is described as the *antitupos* of the spirit. (J. B. Lightfoot (ed.), *Apostolic Fathers*, London 1893.)

[16] Op. cit., p. 266.

Bibliography

BOOKS REFERRED TO IN THE TEXT

E.-B. Allo (ed.), *Première Épître aux Corinthiens* (Paris 1934)
C. K. Barrett (ed.), *The Gospel according to St. John* (London 1955)
—— *From First Adam to Last* (London 1963)
K. Bauer (ed.), Das Johannesevangelium in *Handbuch z. NT*, Vol. VI (Tübingen 1925, 2nd ed.)
F. W. Beare (ed.), *1 Peter* (Oxford 1947)
J. Agar Beet (ed.), *Romans* (London 1900, 5th ed.)
J. H. Bernard (ed.) *St John*, ICC (Edinburgh 1928)
C. Bigg (ed.), *1 Peter*, ICC (Edinburgh 1901)
F. Blass and A. Debrunner, *A Greek Grammar of the New Testament, etc.*, Eng. tr. and ed. F. W. Funk (Cambridge and Chicago 1961 based on 9th and 10th German eds.)
J. Bonsirven, *Le Judaisme Palestinien au Temps de Jesus-Christ*, Vol. I Paris 1934, 2nd ed.)
—— *Exégèse Rabbinique et Exégèse Paulinienne* (Paris 1939)
W. Bousset (ed.), 1 Corinthians in *Die Schriften d. NT*, Vol. II (Göttingen 1917)
—— (ed.), 2 Corinthians in *Die Schriften d. NT*, Vol. II (Göttingen 1917)
F. Boylan (ed.), *The Epistle to the Hebrews*, Westminster Version (London 1931)
A. P. Bruce, *The Epistle to the Hebrews* (Edinburgh 1899)
F. F. Bruce (ed.), *The Acts of the Apostles* (London 1951)
R. Bultmann (ed.), Das Evangelium des Johannes in *Krit.-Exeg. Komm. ü. d. NT* (Göttingen 1962, 6th imp.)
—— *Theology of the New Testament*, Eng. tr. Vol. I (London 1952)
H. J. Cadbury (ed.), Text of Acts in *The Beginnings of Christianity* with K. Lake (London 1953)
R. H. Charles, *Apocrypha and Pseudepigrapha of the OT*, Vol. II, Book of Jubilees (Oxford 1913)
C. E. B. Cranfield (ed.), 1 Peter in Peake's Comm. on the Bible (rev. ed. London 1962)

J. Daniélou, *Sacramentum Futuri* (Paris 1950)
D. Daube, *The NT and Rabbinic Judaism* (London 1956)
W. D. Davies, *Paul and Rabbinic Judaism* (London 1948)
M. Dibelius (ed.), Der Brief des Jakobus in *Krit. Exeg. Komm. ü. d. NT*, Vol. XV, Part 7 (Göttingen 1921)
C. H. Dodd (ed.), *Romans*, Moffat Comms. (London 1942 ed.)
—— *Interpretation of the Fourth Gospel* (Cambridge 1960)
T. C. Edwards (ed.), *1 Corinthians* (London 1885)
E. E. Ellis, *Paul's Use of the OT* (Edinburgh 1959)
G. Estius, *Comm. in NT*, Vol. III, ed. J. Holzammer (2nd ed. Mainz 1859)
F. J. Foakes-Jackson and K. Lake, *The Beginnings of Christianity* (London 1933)
T. F. Glasson, *Moses in the Fourth Gospel* (London 1963)
H. L. Goudge (ed.), *1 Corinthians*, Westminster Comms. (London 1913)
—— (ed.), *2 Corinthians*, Westminster Comms. (London 1927)
R. M. Grant, *A Historical Introduction to the New Testament* (London 1963)
Grimm-Thayer, *Greek-English Lexicon of the New Testament* (Edinburgh 1905, 4th ed.)
H. Gunkel (ed.), 1 Petrus in *Die Schriften des NT*, Vol. III (Göttingen 1917)
A. T. Hanson, *The Wrath of the Lamb* (London 1957)
—— *The Pioneer Ministry* (London 1962)
R. P. C. Hanson, *Allegory and Event* (London 1959)
—— (ed.), *2 Corinthians* in Torch Commentaries (London 1954)
W. Heitmuller (ed.), Das Johannesevangelium in *Die Schriften d. NT*, Vol. IV (Göttingen 1918)
J. Héring (ed.), *L'Épître aux Hébreux* (Neuchâtel-Paris 1954)
—— (ed)., *La Première Épître aux Corinthiens* (Neuchâtel-Paris 1959)
C. Hodge (ed.), *1 Corinthians* (modern ed. London 1958)
—— (ed.), *2 Corinthians* (modern ed. London 1959)
G. Hollmann (ed.), Der Hebräerbrief in *Die Schriften des NT*, Vol. II (Göttingen 1917)
G. Hollmann and W. Bousset (ed.), Der Brief des Jakobus in *Die Schriften des NT*, Vol. III (Göttingen 1917)
F. J. A. Hort (ed.), *Epistle of James* (London 1909, unfinished)
E. C. Hoskyns and F. N. Davey, *The Fourth Gospel* (London 1947, 2nd ed.)

BIBLIOGRAPHY

A. Jülicher (ed.), Der Römerbrief in *Die Schriften des NT*, Vol. II (Göttingen 1917)
K. E. Kirk (ed.), *Romans* in Clarendon Bible (Oxford 1937)
G. A. F. Knight, *A Christian Theology of the Old Testament* (London 1959)
R. Knopf (ed.), 1 Petrus in *Krit.-Exeg. ü. d. NT*, Vol. XIII, Part 7 (Göttingen 1912)
R. J. Knowling (ed.), *Epistle of James* in Westminster Comms. (London 1904)
W. L. Knox, *St. Paul and the Church at Jerusalem* (Cambridge 1925)
—— *St. Paul and the Church of the Gentiles* (Cambridge 1939)
R. Kühl (ed.), 1 Petrus in *Krit.-Exeg. Komm. ü. d. NT*, Vol. XII, Part 6 (Göttingen 1897)
G. W. K. Lampe and K. J. Woollcombe, *Essays in Typology* (London 1957)
H. Lietzmann (ed.), Der Römerbrief in *Handbuch z. NT*, Vol. III, Book 2 (Tübingen 1919)
—— (ed.), An die Galäter in *Handbuch z. NT*, Vol. II (Tübingen 1923, 2nd ed.)
—— (ed.), 1 and 2 Corinthians in *Handbuch z. NT*, Vol. IX (Tübingen 1923, 2nd ed.)
R. H. Lightfoot (ed.), *The Fourth Gospel* (Oxford 1959)
B. Lindars, *NT Apologetic* (London 1961)
J. E. McFadyen (ed.), *1 and 2 Corinthians*, Interpreters' Comm. (London 1911)
G. H. C. Macgregor (ed.), *The Fourth Gospel* in Moffat Comms. (London 1928)
J.-L. Maier, *Les Missions Divines selon S. Augustin* (Fribourg 1960)
W. Manson, *The Epistle to the Hebrews* (London 1951)
J. B. Mayor (ed.), *The Epistle of James* (London 1910)
O. Michel (ed.), Der Brief an die Hebräer in *Krit.-Exeg. Komm. ü. d. NT*, Vol. XII, Book 8 (Göttingen 1949)
J. Moffatt (ed.), *Hebrews*, ICC (Edinburgh 1924)
—— (ed.), *1 Corinthians* in Moffatt Comms. (London 1938)
C. F. D. Moule, *The Birth of the New Testament* (London 1962)
J. Munck, *Paul and the Salvation of Mankind* (Eng. tr. London 1959; German ed. 1952)
A. Nairne, *The Epistle of Priesthood* (London 1913)
A. Nygren (ed.), *Romans* (Eng. tr. London 1952)
A. Peake (ed.), *Hebrews*, Century Bible (London 1902)

A. Plummer (ed.), *2 Corinthians*, ICC (Edinburgh 1915)
E. Preuschen (ed.), Apostelgeschichte in *Handbuch z. NT*, Vol. I, Book 1, (Tübingen 1912, 9th ed.)
G. Quell (ed.), Exodus in Kittel's *Biblia Hebraica* (Stuttgart 1949, 4th ed.)
R. B. Rackham (ed.), *Acts* in Westminster Comms. (London 1901)
H. Rashdall, *The Idea of the Atonement in Christian Theology* (London 1919)
F. Rendall (ed.), *Acts* (London 1897)
A. Robertson and A. Plummer (ed.), *1 Corinthians*, ICC (Edinburgh 1911)
J. A. T. Robinson, *Honest to God* (London 1963)
T. Robinson (ed.), *Hebrews*, Moffatt Comms. (London 1933)
J. M. Ropes (ed.), *The Epistle of James*, ICC (Edinburgh 1916)
W. C. Sanday and A. Headlam (ed.), *Romans*, ICC (Edinburgh 1912)
H. Schlier (ed.), Der Brief an die Galäter in *Krit.-Exeg. Komm. ü. d. NT*, Vol. VII (Göttingen 1949)
C. Spicq (ed.), *L'Épître aux Hébreux* (Paris 1953, 2nd ed.)
E. Stauffer, *New Testament Theology* (Eng. tr. London 1955)
R. H. Strachan (ed.), *2 Corinthians*, Moffat Comms. (London 1915)
H. Strathmann (ed.), Das Evangelium nach Johannes in *Das NT Deutsch* (Göttingen 1951)
F. C. Synge, *Hebrews and the Scriptures* (London 1959)
W. Temple, *Readings in St. John's Gospel* (Oxford 1960, paperback ed.)
H. H. Wendt (ed.), Apostelgeschichte in *Krit.-Exeg. Komm. ü. d. NT*, Vol. II (Göttingen 1917, 9th ed.)
B. F. Westcott (ed.), *Hebrews* (London 1892)
E. C. Wickham (ed.), *Hebrews*, Westminster Comms. (London 1910)
C. S. C. Williams (ed.), *Acts*, in Black's Comm. (London 1957)
H. Windisch (ed.), 2 Corinthians in *Krit.-Exeg. Komm. ü. d. NT*, Vol. VI, Book 9 (Göttingen 1924)
—— (ed.), Der Hebräerbrief in *Handbuch z. NT* (Tübingen 1913)
N. Zernov, *Eastern Christendom* (London 1962)

ARTICLES REFERRED TO IN THE TEXT

S. Aalen, "'Reign' and 'House' in the Kingdom of God" in *NT Studies*, April 1962, Vol. 8, No. 3, pp. 236 sq.
E. L. Allen, "Jesus and Moses in the NT", in *Expository Times*, Vol. 67, 1955–6, p. 104

O. Cullmann, πέτρα in TWZNT, Vol. VI, p. 96

R. P. C. Hanson, "Moses as a Type of Christ" in *Theology*, XLVIII, August 1945, pp. 173–7

—— "Studies in Texts: Acts 6.13" in *Theology*, LI, April 1947, p. 142

F. Hauck, παραβολή in TWZNT, Vol. V, p. 741

J. Jeremias, Μωϋσῆς in TWZNT, Vol. IV, p. 873

D. Kaufmann, "Sens et Origine des Symboles Tumulaires de l'AT dans l'Art Chrétien primitif" in *Révue des Études Bibliques*, xiv, 1887, pp. 33 sq., 217 sq.

E. Kenneth Lee, "Words denoting Pattern in the NT" in *NT Studies*, Vol. 8, No. 2, January 1962, pp. 166 sq.

W. Michaelis, ἀόρατος in TWZNT Vol. V, p. 369

M. Rissi, "Die Menschlichkeit Jesu nach Heb. 5.7–8" in *Theologische Zeitschrift*, 1955, pp. 28 sq.

J. A. T. Robinson, "The Relation of the Prologue to the Gospel of St. John" in *NT Studies*, Vol. 9, No. 2, January 1963

M. Schmidt, θρησκεία in TWZNT, Vol. III, p. 155

M. Simon, "Melchisedech dans la polemique entre juifs et chrétiens et dans la legende" in *Révue d'Histoire et de la Philosophie Réligieuses*, 1937, pp. 58 sq.

J. van der Ploeg, "L'Exégèse de l'AT dans l'Épître aux Hébreux" in *Révue Biblique*, liv., 1947, p. 187

L. Venard, "Citations de l'AT dans le NT" in *Dictionnaire de la Bible*, Supplement to the 2nd. vol., ed. J. Pirot (Paris 1934)

EDITIONS OF THE FATHERS REFERRED TO IN THE TEXT

Augustine, "De Trinitate", ed. M. Mellet et Th. Camelot in *Éditions Bénédictines* (Paris 1955), Vol. I

Barnabas, Epistle of, ed. J. B. Lightfoot in *The Apostolic Fathers* (London 1891–3)

Basil, *De Spiritu Sancto*, ed. C. F. H. Johnston (Oxford 1892)

II Clement, See *Ep. of Barnabas*

Chrysostom, *Homiliae in Genesim*, ed. Migne, PG, Vol. LII, Tome CV (Paris 1862)

—— *Comm. in Acta*, ed. Migne in PG, Vol. LX, Tome IX (Paris 1859)

—— *Homiliae in 1 Corinth.*, ed. Migne, PG, Vol. LXI, Tome X (Paris 1859)

—— *Comm. in Ep. ad Gal.*, ed. Migne, PG, Vol. LXI, Tome X (Paris 1859)

Didache, ed. H. de Romestin (London 1885)

Epiphanius, *Adv. Haer*, ed. Migne, PG, Vol. XLII, Tome II, pp. 181 sq.

Hermas, Shepherd of, ed. M. Whittaker, *Der Hirt des Hermas* (Berlin 1956)

Hilary, *De Trinitate*, ed. Migne, PL, Vol. X, Tome II, p. 63

Hippolytus, *Refut. Omn. Haer.*, ed. P. Wendland, *Hippolytus Werke*, Vol. III, in *Die Grieschischen Schriftsteller der Ersten Drei Jahrhunderte* (Leipzig 1916)

Ignatius, ed. J. B. Lightfoot in *The Apostolic Fathers* (London 1891)

Irenaeus, *Fragmenta*, ed. A. Stieren in *Irenaei Opera Omnia*, Vol. II, p. 837 (Leipzig 1853)

—— *Adv. Haereses*, ed. W. W. Harvey (Cambridge 1857)

—— *Proof of the Apostolic Preaching*, ed. and tr. from the Armenian by Joseph Smith (Westminster (Maryland) and London 1952)

Jerome, *Comm. in Ep. ad Gal.*, ed. Migne in PL, Vol. XXVI, Tome VII (Paris 1845)

Justin, *Apology*, ed. A. W. F. Blunt (Cambridge 1911)

—— *Dialogue with Trypho*, ed. E. J. Goodspeed in *Die Ältesten Apologeten* (Göttingen 1914)

Melito, *Homily on the Passion*, ed. Campbell Bonner as No. XII in *Studies and Documents* (ed. Kirsopp and Sylvia Lake, London and Philadelphia 1940)

Origen, *Selecta in Genesim*, ed. Migne, PG, Vol XII, Tome II (Paris 1857)

Philo, *Opera Omnia*, ed. Colson and Whitaker, Loeb ed. Vol. IV, p. 279 (London 1949, 2nd reprint)

Tertullian, *Adv. Marcionem*, ed. A. Kroymann in *Corpus Christianum* (Series Latina), Vol. I (Turnhout 1954)

Theophilus of Antioch, *Trois Livres à Autolycus*, ed. G. Bardy and J. Sender in *Sources Chrétiennes* (Paris 1948)

Index of Biblical References

OLD TESTAMENT

Genesis
12.1–9	86, 124
15.1–6	124
15.1	125
15.7	86
17.7	124
17.17	124, 126
18.1–15	124
18.2	125
18.3	123, 126
18.11	123
18.12	123
24.1	189
28.13	109
32.30	109

Exodus
2.9,10	74
3.1–10	87
3.7,8	74
3.12	86
13.21,22	11
14.19	11
14.24	12
14.30	12
14.31	11, 13
16.2	120
16.4	119
16.8	120
16.10	119
16.15	119, 120
16.15,16	16
17.1–7	16, 17, 24
17.2	17
17.6	17, 23

17.9	19
20.18–21	77
20.22	76
23.20,21	14, 62, 87
24.9–18	114
24.10	192
24.18	54
25.40	66, 193
31.18	54
33.8–11	92
33.11	34
33.12—34.9	110–13, 114
33.14	92
33.21	34
34.5	109
34.6	130, 188, 190
34.27–35	26–7
34.34	29,

Leviticus
18.5	38
26.16	192
26.20	192

Numbers
12.1–15	48–57, 183
12.1–8	114–16, 163, 166
14.18	188
21.4–9	24
21.8,9	175
21.17–19	22
24.4	96
24.6	90
24.16	96

17.9 — 62–3

INDEXES

Deuteronomy	
4.10	92
4.12	114
4.36	76
5.23,24	77
8.3	16
9.10	92
18.15	53, 116, 117, 163, 188
18.16	92
30.11–14	36
30.12	2
30.14	38
32.15	85
32.18–21	44
32.20	45
32.43 (LXX)	95
32.47	95
33	98, 99
33.2–5	94
33.2	95
33.5	85, 103
33.9	96
33.26	85

Joshua	
5.3	62

2 Samuel	
2.6	188
7.12–14	56, 57
7.14	183
22.50	157

1 Chronicles	
17.10–12	56, 57

Nehemiah	
9.17	188

Job	
38	130
39.16	192

Psalms	
2	71, 72
2.7	140
8	163, 166
18.1	157
18.49	157
19.4	2, 37, 42
19.5	44
19.9	43
24	83, 141–3
25.10	188
29	85, 87, 133
29.3	84
29.5–8	84
40.6–8	60, 140
40.11,12	188
45.6,7	162
57.3	188
57.10	188
61.7	188
68.17,18	186
69	153–7
69.3	154
69.5	154
69.6	154
69.7–9	154
69.9	153
69.20	154
69.22	154
69.23	154
69.30–4	154
78.20	122
78.24	118, 120
82	164
86.5	188
86.15	111, 188
89.14	188
95	58, 59, 60, 61, 163, 184
99.7	15
103.8	130, 188
108.4	188
110	65, 70, 71, 72
110.4	70, 140
111.4	130
115.1	188
116.10–19	145–7
117.2	188
138.2	188

INDEX OF BIBLICAL REFERENCES 203

Isaiah		26.2 (LXX 33.2)	77
6.1	107–8	29.23 (LXX 36.23)	77
6.5	107–8		
6.7–11	107–8	Daniel	
8.17	157	3.25	69
9.6	186		
44.2	85	Joel	
45.18–25	158	2.13	188
45.23	158, 165		
45.25	158	Jonah	
49.1–9	148–52	1.9	132
49.4	192	2.2	132
52.7—53.1	42	4.2	131, 188
52.7	37, 40, 41	4.4	190
52.10	41	4.5	131
52.13	41	4.9	190
52.15	41		
53.1	40, 41, 59, 105, 108, 166	Habakkuk	
53.8	69	2.1–4	135
64.4	143–4		
65.1,2	45, 46, 144	Haggai	
65.1	41	2.2,3	79
65.17	143	2.5	79
65.23	192	2.6,7	185
66.1	163	2.6	76, 80
Jeremiah		Zechariah	
3.16	143	3.1–5	81

APOCRYPHA AND INTERTESTAMENTAL
LITERATURE

Wisdom		Jubilees	
9.8	90–1	1.27	92
10.6	189	2.1	92
10.15–18	15	49—50	92
11.1–7	15		
11.4	15	Philo	
		Quis Rer. Div. Haer. xxxix	189
4 Maccabees		De Conf. Ling. xx9.7	192
17.24	3	De Somniis (I) xi.62	192
Wisdom of Ben Sira		Josephus	
24.4	15	Antiquities XV.5.3	186

INDEXES

NEW TESTAMENT

Matthew		12.41,42		187
1.21	167	12.41		25, 49, 82
12.38–41	175	14.6		112
17.17	45	19.34,35		122

Mark		Acts	
2.19	43	3.22	188
4.12	29	6.13	183, 193
9.19	45	7.2	83–6, 132, 133
10.5	93	7.27–34	74
12.26	125	7.30–5	75, 86–8
16.20	100	7.31	84
		7.32	108
Luke		7.35	95, 102, 103
11.29,30	175	7.38,39	54
24.21	87	7.38	91, 92, 95, 100, 163
		7.44	72, 87, 89–91, 173
John		7.45	167, 183
1.14–18	108–13, 114, 168	7.46–50	72
1.14	8, 31, 106, 133, 166	7.49	163
1.15	188	7.53	91, 94, 96, 99, 122, 136
1.17	123, 166		
1.18	106, 107	Romans	
3.14,15	176, 177	1.17	135
3.29	43	3.2	96
5.37–47	113–17	3.25	3
5.37	108, 112	5.14	33, 173, 193
6.29	124	6.13–19	36
6.30–40	118–23	7.2	28
6.41–3	120	7.24	12
6.46	112	9.25,26	46
6.49	119, 120	9.28	39, 161
6.58	120	10	35–47
7.14–24	122–3	10.4	28
7.37,38	121, 122	10.6	2
8.30–59	123–6	10.16	168
8.39,40	168	10.16,17	59
8.52,53	70	10.18	2, 182
8.56	106	10.20,21	144
10.34,35	164	11.3	39, 161
12.37–41	7, 61, 104–8, 166	11.7	29
12.38	59	11.9	154
12.39,40	29	11.25	29

INDEX OF BIBLICAL REFERENCES

Romans continued—
11.26	12
12.7	155
15.2–9	153–60
15.3	166
15.7,8	166
15.10–12	153

1 Corinthians
1.6	43
1.9	43
1.18	43
1.30	37
2.6–9	141–4
2.8	83, 85, 132, 133, 136
10	71, 87, 121, 137, 168
10.1–13	58, 63
10.1–11	10–25
10.2	8, 55
10.4	7, 82, 95, 166
10.5	120
10.6	172, 174
10.9	44
10.10	191
10.22	44, 169
13.8	27
13.9	50

2 Corinthians
1.18–22	43
3.7–18	25–35
3.13–16	116
3.17	21
4.6	31
4.11–15	145–7, 161
4.13	166
5.16—6.2	147–52, 155, 161
5.18–21	52
8.9	61, 165
11.2	43

Galatians
3.2	59
3.6–14	191
3.11	135

3.12	38
3.19,20	13, 91, 97
3.19	54, 92, 96, 99, 100, 122, 136
3.20	98

Ephesians
1.6	85
2.15	27, 30
3.10	136
5.22–33	43
6.12	141

Philippians
2.1–11	158
2.5–11	165
2.5	165
2.7	69
2.16	149

Colossians
1.13	12
2.8–18	98

1 Thessalonians
1.10	12
2.13	59

1 Timothy
2.5	97

Titus
2.13	133

Hebrews
1.1	58
1.1,2	78, 101
1.5	140, 183
1.6	95
1.7–13	140
1.8	162
1.14—2.2	136
2.2	185
2.2,3	91, 99, 100, 102
2.3	53
2.5–18	158
2.6,7	163

2.9		166	9.23		174
2.12,13		140	9.24		66, 173
2.13		157	10.1		67, 174
2.16		136	10.5–7		140
3.1–6	13, 48–57, 59, 95, 114, 125, 163, 183		10.5		60
			10.38		135
3.1		166	11.7		77, 82
3.2		61	11.18,19		126
3.4		183	11.19		174–5
3.6		166	11.21		177
3.7		184	11.22		177
3.9		60	11.26		166
3.14		60	11.24–8		72–5, 168
3.15		60	12.18–28		163
3.17		60	12.18		80
4.1–9		58–65	12.19		77, 79
4.2		94, 168	12.22–7	61, 75–82, 84, 85, 99, 101, 120, 166, 169	
4.4		174			
4.7		184	12.24		97
4.8		166, 167	12.25		89, 185
4.10–13		58	12.26		60
4.13		58			
5.1		71	*James*		
5.5–10		65	1.1		129
5.5		71, 166	1.7		129
5.6,7		140	2.1		127, 129, 132–3
5.7		152	3.9		129
5.7,8		184	4.7,8		129
5.9		72	4.10		129
5.10		71,184	4.15		129
5.11		71	5.7–15		127–32, 133, 137
5.12		96	5.7,8		129
6.20		71	5.10		174
7		65–72	5.11		168
7.1–10		183			
7.2		79	*1 Peter*		
7.20		71	1.10–12		129, 133–6, 137
8.2		96	2.3		25
8.3–7		89	2.10		46
8.5	66, 77, 89, 96, 173, 174, 193		3.21		173
8.6		97	4.11		96
8.13		27			
9.2		182	*2 Peter*		
9.6		182	2.4		136–7
9.9		174–5	2.6		174
9.15		97			

1 John		5,6	136–8
4.9	113	6,7	169
4.12	112.113	9	137
4.20	112,113	14	137
Jude		Revelation	
5	168	19.7–9	43

Index of Patristic References

Didache
IV.11   193

Hermas
Vis. iv. 2.5   193
lv.11.4   194
Sim. i.9   194

Ignatius
Philadelphians 9   169
Magnesians 6   193
Trallians 3   193

Barnabas
7.3   80–1
12.4   46
12.8   62
12.9–10   194
14.1   53, 80
19.7   193

Justin
Dialogue 24.2   62
36.5–6   143
37—38   15
42.1   43
56.1   189
57.2   189
59   88
75.1–2   62
85.1   143
114.2   41
115.3–4   81

Apology I.40   43
I.51   143
I.62   88

II Clement
XIV.3   194

Melito
Homily on the Passion
40   174
84   15, 34, 81
87   85

Theophilus of Antioch
Ad Autolycum 22   81

Irenaeus
Adv. Haereses III.6.1   189
III.20.1   131
IV.3.1   117
IV.9.1–2   88
IV.10.2   125
IV.12.1   86
IV.34.9   34, 188
IV.36.3   189
IV.64.1   169
V.22.1   81
Proof of the Apostolic Preaching
44   189
46   15, 88
Fragment XIX   183

Hippolytus
Refutatio IX.33.10–11   81

Tertullian
Adv. Marcionem III.1.6   189
III.7.6   82
III.16,3–4   183
IV.10.3   132
IV.11.7   43
V.11.6   34

Origen
Homilies on Exodus XI.5 — 62

Eusebius
Eccl. Hist. I.ii.6–7 — 189
I.ii.9 — 88
I.iii — 183

Hilary
De Trinitate 4.25 — 189
4.27 — 125

Epiphanius
Adv. Haer. 67.6 — 184

Basil
De Spiritu Sancto 31 — 180

Chrysostom
Homiliae in Genesim XLVIII — 125
Comm. in Acta, Homi. XVI — 88
XVII.3 — 97
Homiliae in I Cor. XXIII — 20
Comm. in Ep. ad Gal. in 3.19 — 187

Jerome
Comm. in Gal. in 3.19 — 88

Augustine
De Trinitate II.2.10–12 — 189
II.16–17 — 188
III.11.4 — 185
III.11.26 — 117
Comm. in Johan. in 12.41 — 106

Index of Authors

Aalen, S., 56
Allen, E. L., 183
Allo, E.-B., 18, 141, 145

Bardy, G., 185
Barrett, C. K., 12, 23, 28, 96, 116, 118, 189
Bauer, K., 106, 109, 116, 118, 119, 125
Beare, F. W., 134
Beet, J. A., 2, 39
Bengel, J. A., 66
Bernard, J. H., 105, 116, 118
Bigg, C., 135, 137, 190
Blass-Debrunner, 181
Blunt, A. W. F., 182
Bonner, C., 180
Bonsirven, J., 18, 44, 56, 67, 93, 193
Bousset, W., 22, 132, 137, 141, 145, 152
Boylan, F., 66
Bruce, A. P., 63
Bruce, F. F., 85, 92
Bultmann, R., 3, 5, 9, 18, 56, 99, 106, 112, 118

Cadbury, H. J., 89
Camelot, T., 185
Charles, R. H., 186
Colson, F. H., 189
Cranfield, C. E. B., 135
Cullmann, O., 19

Daniélou, J., 4-5, 18, 61, 126
Daube, D., 129
Davey, F. N., 105, 116, 125
Davies, W. D., 34
De Romestin, H., 193

Dibelius, M., 133
Dodd, C. H., 38, 39, 105, 106, 111, 117, 118, 153, 189

Edwards, T. C., 19, 141
Ellis, E. E., 19, 45, 156, 179, 186, 189
Estius, G., 77

Foakes-Jackson, F. J., 87, 89, 94, 95, 96
Funk, R. W., 181

Glasson, T. F., 22, 110, 111, 119, 121, 122
Goodspeed, E. J., 180
Goudge, H. L., 13, 141, 145, 152
Grant, R. M., 190
Gunkel, H., 134

Hanson, R. P. C., 4-5, 13, 21, 28, 32, 39, 81, 89, 102, 145, 167, 181, 183
Harvey, W. W., 181
Headlam, A., 36, 37, 154, 156
Heitmuller, W., 118, 189
Héring, J., 14, 17, 18, 68, 73, 141, 191
Hodge, C., 22, 31, 141, 152
Hollmann, G., 55, 67, 73, 132, 137
Holzammer, J., 185
Hort, F. J. A., 1, 25, 133
Hoskyns, E. C., 105, 116, 125

Jeremias, J., 33
Johnston, C. F. H., 180
Jülicher, A., 39, 153

Kaufmann, D., 175
Kittell, R., 110, 191

INDEX OF AUTHORS

Kirk, K. E., 38, 156
Klöpper, A., 152
Knight, G. A. F., 24
Knopf, R., 136, 137, 190
Knowling, R. J., 128, 129
Knox, W. L., 15, 50, 71, 93, 94
Kroymann, A., 181
Kühl, R., 134, 135, 137

Lake, K., 87, 94, 95, 96, 180, 183
Lake, S., 180
Lampe, G. W., L., 67, 80, 102
Lee, E. K., 173
Lietzmann, H., 13, 24, 32, 38, 98, 141, 145, 151
Lightfoot, J. B., 1, 194
Lightfoot, R. H., 118, 189
Lindars, B., 5, 125, 156, 175

McFadyen, J. E., 17, 141, 151
Macgregor, G. H. C., 112, 116, 125
Maier, J.-L., 187, 189
Mallet, M., 185
Manson, W., 67, 73, 76
Mayor, J. B., 128, 133
Michaelis, W., 185
Michel, O., 53, 64, 67, 68, 70, 73, 100, 185
Migne, J. P., 180, 184, 186, 187, 189
Milligan, G., 182
Moffatt, J., 61, 73, 76, 141
Moule, C. F. D., 158
Moulton, J. H., 182
Munck, J., 33

Nairne, A., 66, 67, 68, 69, 73
Nygren, A., 37

Peake, A. S., 52, 61
Pirot, J., 180
Plummer, A., 14, 17, 25, 28, 141, 151
Preuschen, E., 85, 91

Quell, G., 110

Rackham, R. B., 102
Rashdall, H., 3
Rendall, H., 92
Rissi, M., 71
Robertson, A., 14, 17, 25, 141
Robinson, J. A. T., 171, 188
Robinson, T., 55, 76
Ropes, J. M., 132

Sanday, W. C., 36, 37, 154, 156
Schlier, H., 98, 99
Schmidt, K. L., 99
Selwyn, E. G., 134
Sender, J., 185
Simon, M., 68
Smith, J., 180
Spicq, C., 55, 56, 64, 67, 68, 73, 78
Stauffer, E., 190
Stieren, A., 183
Strachan, R. H., 28, 34, 145
Strack-Billerbeck, 22, 23, 30, 31, 68, 87, 92, 93, 94, 118, 187
Strathmann, H., 113, 119
Synge, F. C., 56, 183, 185

Temple, W., 105, 118

Van der Ploeg, J., 67, 70, 73, 192
Venard, L., 17, 37, 67

Wendland, P., 184
Wendt, H. H., 85, 87, 91
Werner, M., 88, 98, 193
Wesley, C., 164
Westcott, B. F., 1, 51, 66, 73, 76
Whitaker, G. H., 189
Whittaker, M., 194
Wickham, E. C., 66
Williams, C. S. C., 85, 96, 102
Windisch, H., 31, 51, 52, 55, 63, 68, 69, 70, 73, 76, 80, 100, 145, 152
Woolcombe, K. J., 19, 67, 102, 193

Zernov, N., 189